Saint Anthony Mary Claret

AUTOBIOGRAPHY

*The cover drawing
shows Sallent,
northwest of Barcelona,
where Antonio Claret
was born in 1807.*

SAINT ANTHONY MARY CLARET

Autobiography

Edited by

JOSÉ MARIA VIÑAS, C.M.F.
Director
Studium Claretianum,
Rome

Foreword by

ALFRED ESPOSITO, C.M.F.

Claretian Publications
Chicago, 1976

This is a translation by Joseph Daries, CMF
of *San Antonio María Claret, Autobiografía,* Barcelona, 1975,
ISBN. 84-7263-101-X

The drawings reproduced in this book are portions
of scenes sketched by Franklin McMahon for "The Spain
of Anthony Claret" in *US Catholic,* August 1971.

The type ornaments used in this edition are reproductions
of "flowers" in Spanish typographic specimen books
of the late eighteenth century.

CONTENTS

Contents

 Part Three

ARCHBISHOP

Contents

Part Four

CONTINUATION OF THE AUTOBIOGRAPHY

Contents

Part Five

SUPPLEMENTARY READINGS

FOREWORD

The General Prefecture for Religious Life has for some time wanted to bring out a pocket edition of the *Autobiography* of St. Anthony Mary Claret to enable all Claretians to enjoy the benefit of personal contact with the most authentic source of our charism and spirit.

Without discounting the value of consulting other editions, it was felt there was a real need to make this basic text fully available to all Claretians. The need seemed all the more pressing in view of the assessment of the General Chapter of 1973: "Although, on the one hand, the essential elements and rationale of our charism are sufficiently explicit and well defined in the declarations 'On the Charism of our Founder' and 'On the Spiritual Heritage of the Congregation' (1967), on the other hand, they do not seem to have been sufficiently assimilated personally or communitarily, or fully integrated into our life" (cf. RL, 7, a and b).

Our Claretian family's inner need to become vitally aware of its own charism is a matter that concerns the whole Church. Pope Paul's *motu proprio* "Ecclesiae Sanctae" prescribes that "for the betterment of the Church itself, religious institutes should strive to achieve an authentic understanding of their original spirit, so that adhering to it faithfully in their decisions for adaptation, religious life may be purified of elements that are foreign to it and freed from whatever is outdated" (II, 16, 3). This norm reflects the teaching of Vatican II: "It is to the Church's advantage that religious institutes have their own distinctive character and function. Hence they should know and faithfully maintain the spirit and goal of their founders, as well as their own sound traditions—all of which go to make up the heritage of each institute" (PC, 2, b).

Paul VI recalls these norms and commends them to every religious family: "The Council rightly insists on the obligation of men and women religious to be faithful to their founders' spirit, evangelic goals, and exemplary holiness, making this one of the principles for the renewal now in progress and one of the surest criteria for any course of action an institute should undertake" (ET, 11).

In particular, during the Audience that followed the General Chapter of 1973, Pope Paul offered the Claretian family the following recommendations: "Appreciate this spiritual heritage of yours; spare no effort in tending these roots if you wish to be a tree that is always young and flourishing—a tree that is able to adapt to the environment and to the changing needs of the times, so that it may continue to provide ripe fruit for the Church, as it has done in the past and still does through its outstanding sons" (cf. Chapter Documents, 1973, pp. 6 f.). And then he added familiarly, in Italian, "Fidelity to your traditions! Bè Claretians!" (p. 7). These words of the Holy Father touched upon an area that had deeply preoccupied the recently concluded General Chapter. In its "Open Letter" the Chapter remarks that, among other things, it has witnessed the Congregation undergoing "a crisis of Claretian identity and of the sense of belonging to the Congregation, at a time when secularism is obscuring the meaningful outlines of the Word" (OL, 11).

From yet another point of view, the Claretian Community has a constant vital need, through prayer and study, to further develop "the Congregation's original prophetic charism in the Church" (*Constitutions*, 1974, par. 18). Without this vital growth, the Congregation can neither respond to its vocation today, nor "engage in the ceaseless and dynamic search for new ways to accommodate its pastoral structures to the current needs of time and place" (ibid.).

In compliance with the guidelines of the General Chapter of 1973, and acknowledging gratefully the indispensable help of the Claretian Secretariat, the General Prefecture for Religious Life offers this work as a service to all Claretians on the one hundred twenty-fifth anniversary of St. Anthony Mary Claret's great foundation and on the eve of the twenty-fifth year of his canonization. We hope that in this Holy Year it will be a call to genuine conversion and renewal for the entire Claretian family.

Rome, Feast of St. Anthony Mary Claret
October 24, 1974
Alfredo M. Espósito, C.M.F.
General Prefect for Religious Life

*Pulpit
in Church of the Holy Rosary
at La Granja*

INTRODUCTION

St. Anthony Claret wrote his *Autobiography* at the command of Father Joseph Xifré, his spiritual director and then Superior General of the Congregation of Missionaries. He began it in 1861 (probably in October or November) and finished it toward the end of May, 1862. Later he wrote a *Continuation* that was completed in 1865, sometime before October 25, the date of his departure for Rome.

The *Autobiography* is a product of the Saint's mature years. He was 63 years old when he died, 54 when he began the work, and 58 when he finished it. He had already been back in Madrid for five years when he completed the first volume, which included the three fundamental stages in his apostolate: apostolic missionary, Archbishop of Cuba, and Confessor to the Queen. The *Continuation* of 1865 rounds out the picture with an insight into certain aspects of his spirituality and apostolate. It was a period of fullness in his spiritual life; during this time he had already received his major mystical graces. All of these circumstances put him in a position to present an authentic interpretation of the major events in his life.

It may be remarked in passing that the tremendous activity of these years forced him to write very rapidly. Certain repetitions and mistakes can only be explained by his great haste. Without taking time to reread what he had written, he passed it on to his confessor and confidant, Father Carmelo Sala, for correction. He asked his Missionaries at Vich to do the same for him when he entrusted the manuscript to them. It should be noted, however, that what the work loses in precision because of this haste, it gains in spontaneity and freshness. Its anecdotes and spiritual asides are never marred by that unintentional sort of insincerity that tends to creep into overly conscious writing. It is this spontaneous quality that puts one of the main features of the *Autobiography* in high relief—a faithfully accurate revelation of an apostolic soul—and this, precisely, is what makes the *Autobiography* a masterpiece.

The Manuscript of the Autobiography

The two volumes of the manuscript were completed and given to the Community of Missionaries at Vich in 1862 and 1865 respectively. There they remained, carefully rebound, in the local archives until the revolution of September, 1868, when the Missionaries were expelled and took the papers with them to France. When they returned to Spain, they brought back the manuscript of the *Autobiography* with them. Here it became part of the Claretian Archives that were set up in Vich after the death of the Founder in preparation for the introduction of his cause for beatification.

The archives were severely damaged during the Spanish civil war of 1936. Only a fraction of the original collection survived the fire. Providentially, the *Autobiography* was saved through the zeal of the curator, Father Pedro Bertrans, and the astuteness of Mrs. Dolores Lletjós, who hid it carefully in her house.

When the community was reorganized after the war, the *Autobiography,* together with a number of other documents that had been saved, was returned to the Claretian Archives at Vich. There it remained until 1954 when, by order of Father Peter Schweiger, Superior General of the Missionary Sons of the Immaculate Heart of Mary, it was transferred to Rome. It is presently kept in the General Archives of the Congregation, along with the greater part of the most important Claretian documents. To assure its preservation, the manuscript has been chemically treated and rebound in a single volume, the first in the series of sixteen manuscript volumes by the Saint.

Introduction

The Present Edition

As was mentioned above, the purpose of this edition is to facilitate frequent personal contact with the most authentic source of information on the Claretian charism and spirit. A pocket edition best serves this purpose. It is less cumbersome than B.A.C.'s 1959 edition, but ampler, because of its notes and indices, than Coculsa's 1949 edition. In addition to the text of the *Autobiography,* the present edition contains an appendix of supplementary autobiographical documents. Moreover, to provide a notion of the Saint's life between 1865 and his death in 1870, a selection from his *Correspondence* and the *Resolutions* that he made during the last years of his life has been included. An account of the Saint's death has been drawn from a text by an eyewitness, Father Jaime Clotet, who was very close in spirit to the Founder.

How to Read the Autobiography

(1) Try to cut through the surface of the work.

The *Autobiography* was written over a century ago, and feelings and attitudes have changed profoundly as the world has passed out of the romantic era into an age of existentialism and technology.

Moreover, it has already been noted that the Saint himself regarded the manuscript as no more than a rough draft that needed to be corrected and retouched before it could be published. A large number of repetitions and mistakes can be attributed to his haste in writing. Add to this the difficulty he experienced in Castilian, since for many years he had spoken, preached, and written in Catalan. Nevertheless this rapid, careless style, free of all artifice, affords a very high degree of authentic personal contact with the author.

(2) Try to grasp the author's point of view.

When St. Anthony wrote his *Autobiography,* he was writing precisely in his role as *founder* for the Missionaries of his Congregation. The work was written, then, with an expressly *formative* end in view. He uses the witness of his own life to initiate his readers into a glimpse of the Holy Spirit's action in the process of forming a missionary, from the beginning of his call to its fulfillment. Because of his charism as a founder, this action of the Holy Spirit manifested itself with the special intensity required of one who was to become the leader and model for all those men who were to identify themselves with him and his work.

In writing of his *vocation,* he shows us how nature and grace predisposed him to follow the path that led him from the explicit opening call of *"siempre, siempre,"* when he was a boy five years old, to the day of his ordination to the diaconate.

He also gives us a description of his *process of formation* for the priesthood in general and for the ministry of the Word in particular. This he does in the account of his voyage to Rome and his stay there, as well as in the report of his initial experiences as a missionary up to the year 1840 when he left the stability of the parish to begin his ceaseless missionary journeys.

At the outset of his career as an itinerant missionary in Catalonia and the Canary Islands, the Holy See granted St. Anthony Mary Claret the title of "Apostolic Missionary." The Saint came to look on this title as his own essential definition, which was enriched, as time passed, with the characteristic elements of his own charism. As a missionary his life was dedicated to evangelization and the prophetic ministry of the Word; hence, he did his utmost to avoid other functions of the ministerial priesthood such as administering the sacraments from a fixed base and on an established timetable. In itself, the designation "apostolic" simply referred to the Holy See, which had bestowed it on him, but Claret applied it to himself in the deeper sense of a distinct way of life: an apostolic life in the manner of the Apostles—a life of the strictest evangelical poverty shared in brotherhood with those God-given companions who were moved by the same Spirit.

These two essential traits, "apostolic" and "missionary," are a description of his very life, lived according to the special nuances of his own charism. This meant for him living the mystery of Christ, the Son who was sent as Master and Redeemer, the head and model of all missionaries. His only preoccupation was to follow and imitate Jesus Christ in prayer, work, and suffering and to seek always and only the glory of God and the salvation of men. It meant, furthermore, living the mystery of Mary, the Woman through whom the Son became man when He was sent to us (Gal. 4:4): Mary, the Mother of Christ, the Missionary, and mother of all missionaries in Christ; Mary, who became a mother through love, through her heart. Claret felt that it was in the furnace of this love that he was shaped into a being of charity that lights and kindles wherever it goes.

In addition to these essential charismatic elements in the *Autobiography,* Claret enumerates the various virtues he practiced and the methods he employed in order to live apostolically and fulfill his mission. He lists the motives for his zeal and the stimulus he received from considering the lives of Christ, the Apostles, the prophets, and all those men and women saints in whom he saw traits of his own vocation.

St. Anthony Mary Claret also describes the way in which his mission was fulfilled throughout the course of his life—first in Catalonia and the Canary Islands, then in Cuba, and later in Madrid. When he was forced to accept first the episcopate, and then the appointment as Confessor to the Queen, he lived up to his missionary vocation in the midst of these situations by taking advantage of every opportunity for evangelization and by following a way of life characterized by a spirit of poverty and fraternity. While he was in Cuba, he did his best to disentangle himself from all bureaucratic red tape so as to be free for the ministry of preaching. In Madrid he turned trips with the royal family into missions. He thought of the Escorial not just as a seminary and college but as a strategically placed mission house for spiritual exercises on an international level.

The *Autobiography* ends in 1865, and the rest of the Saint's life can be reconstructed from his *Correspondence* and *Resolutions.* As an exile in Paris and as a Council Father at Vatican I in Rome, he continued his life as an apostolic missionary in his poverty, in his exercise of the apostolate, and in his desire to return to Latin America, "the tender vine." Since he was unable to return to Latin America, he used to console himself with visits to the Colegio Pio Latino.

The many "silences" in the *Autobiography* can be explained by the author's aim of writing it mainly for the formation of his Missionaries. Thus he passes over a number of historically important events and lavishes a great deal of attention on apparently minor events that were meaningful to him in the context of his mission and spirit. For this reason the *Autobiography* needs to be supplemented by readings from other sources concerning other events in his life if one wishes to see him in his proper historical perspective. His humility, of course, was responsible for a number of those silences. His confessor, Father Carmelo Sala, remarks, "Whoever knew the Servant of God as I knew him can easily see, upon reading these notes of his, that he leaves unsaid far more than he reports. The reason for this is doubtless that in writing as he did he could fulfill the precept imposed on him by obedience and yet not jeopardize his deep humility" (C.M.F. Historical Archives, vol. 1, p. 364).

Another silence in the *Autobiography* relates to the absence of any structured plan for living his vocation and mission. For this one must turn to the *Constitutions* of 1857 through 1870. And for a grasp of his personal development, the *Correspondence* is indispensable. The *Autobiography* contains only the purest essence of his charism: his life and message, all that attracted his first disciples to him and continues to attract all whom the Lord has made partakers in the same grace.

A charismatic reading of the *Autobiography* in our day and age must of necessity be a sort of rereading, owing to the great historical and cultural differences between our milieu and that of the Saint. This is the conclusion drawn by the Claretian General Chapter of 1967 in its declaration "On our Spiritual Heritage": "There are elements in the personality of our Father Founder that belong to his charism and to his spirit as a founder: to these we must always look as a source of inspiration. But alongside these traits we find others that belong to his own personal psychology or to his environment that cannot be transmitted to the Congregation" (par. 11).

(3) Try to appreciate the spirit that moved the author.

The *Autobiography* was written in a climate of prayer, the kind of prayer that discovers the manifestation of God's love in the happenings of life. St. Anthony Mary Claret examined facts in the light of the Word of God, and especially in the light of these texts in which the Holy Spirit showed him the demands of his vocation. If the *Autobiography* is going to enlighten and move the reader, it has to be read in the same climate of prayer, which sees things happening in accordance with God's Providence. When read in this fashion certain passages in which the Saint talks about zeal have a certain holy contagion all their own.

(4) Try to read in personal communion with the author.

A canonized founder is a model whose authenticity has been attested to by the Church and by his fidelity to his charism and mission. But above all, he is a living model with whom we share the same vocational gift. What the Council says of our relationship with the saints as our brothers, friends, and benefactors (*Lumen Gentium* 49, 50) applies with all the greater force to our relationship with our own founder, with whom we are united in the same real family and whom God chose and filled with his Spirit precisely to be our father in Christ.

TRANSLATOR'S NOTE

Since the previous English translation of St. Anthony Claret's *Autobiography* had been long out of print, I gladly accepted the invitation of my Provincial to undertake a new and somewhat plainer translation. I have no doubt that the result is far from perfect, but I felt that, in a time of renewal and return to origins, so valuable a document should be made immediately available to English-speaking Claretians. Moreover, the edition I used incorporates footnotes and supplementary readings, as well as an introduction, an index, and a system of enumeration, which make it far more usable than the text on which the earlier translation was based.

I should like to express my gratitude to all those who encouraged me in this work. But above all I am thankful for the privilege of having been able to live so closely in thought with a saint who deserves to be better known than he is. I am sure that he would overlook my having said so hastily what needed to be said so urgently.

Joseph Daries, C.M.F.
Prescott, Arizona
Christmas Day, 1975

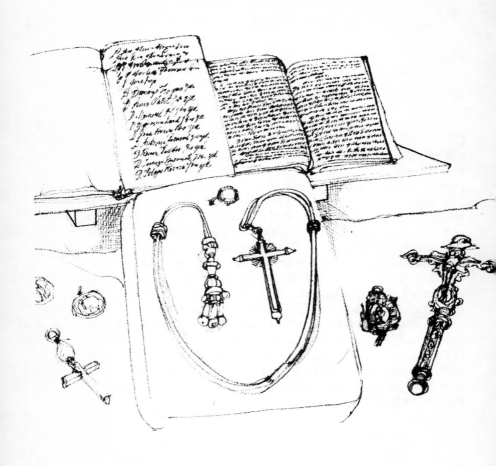

PRAYER BEFORE READING
THE *AUTOBIOGRAPHY*

Lord,
renew in our Congregation
the spirit that moved
our Father,
St. Anthony Mary Claret,
so that filled and strengthened by it
we may come to love what he loved
and put into practice
what he taught us.
We ask this
through Jesus Christ,
our Lord.
Amen.

El Escorial,
near Madrid,
entrusted by Isabella II
to Archbishop Claret,
who successfully
restored it.

BIOGRAPHY

OF

ARCHBISHOP ANTHONY MARY CLARET

JMJ

AUTHOR'S NOTE

1 Although Father Joseph Xifré, Superior of the Missionary Sons of the Heart of Mary, has frequently spoken and written to request that I write a biography of my insignificant self, I have heretofore always excused myself. I would not have agreed to do so even now had I not been ordered to.[1] Thus I am doing this only out of obedience, and out of obedience I am going to reveal several things that I would rather have left unknown. At any rate, may it all be for the greater glory of God and my sweet mother Mary and for the embarrassment of this poor sinner.[2]

I Shall Divide This Biography into Three Parts

2 The first part will include the principal events of my life from my birth until my departure for Rome (1807–39).

The second part will contain events pertaining to the missions (1840–50).

The third part will deal with the most notable events that occurred after my consecration as archbishop (1850–62).

Barcelona,
Church of Santa Maria del Mar

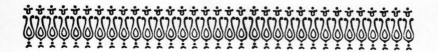

PART ONE

Early Life

Chapter I

MY BIRTH AND BAPTISM

3 **I** was born[1] in the village of Sallent, deanery of Manresa, diocese of Vich, province of Barcelona.[2] My parents, whose names were John Claret and Josephine Clará,[3] were married, upright, and God-fearing people, very devoted to the Blessed Sacrament and Mary Most Holy.

4 I was baptized in St. Mary's Parish, Sallent, on December 25, Christmas Day, 1807, although the parish books say 1808. The reason for this is that they counted the year as beginning on December 25, and so it is that mine is the first entry in the books for the year 1808.

5 I was christened Anthony Adjutor John. My mother's brother, Anthony Clará, was my godfather, and he wanted me to be named after him. My father's sister, Mary Claret, was my godmother. She was married to Adjutor Canudas, so they gave me her husband's Christian name. My third name, John, was my father's name. Later, out of devotion to Mary Most Holy, I added the sweet name of Mary, my mother, my patroness, my mistress, my directress and my all, after Jesus. Thus my name is Anthony Mary Adjutor John Claret y Clará.[1]

6 I was one of eleven children, whom I shall list in order, giving the year of their birth:

(1) My sister Rose, born in 1800. Formerly married, she is now a widow. She has always been hard-working, upright, and pious. She is the one who has loved me the most.[1]

(2) My sister Marian was born in 1802 and died when she was two years old.

(3) My brother John (1804) was heir to all our goods.[2]

(4) My brother Bartholomew (1806) died when he was two years old.

(5) Myself (1807 or 1808).

(6) One sister (1809) died shortly after birth.

4

(7) My brother Joseph (1810) married and had two daughters who became Sisters of Charity or Tertiaries.[3]

(8) My brother Peter (1813) died when he was four years old.

(9) My sister Mary (1815) became a Tertiary Sister.[4]

(10) My sister Frances (1820) died when she was three years old.

(11) My brother Manuel (1823) died when he was thirteen years old, after studying humanities in Vich.

Chapter II

EARLY CHILDHOOD

7 Divine Providence has always watched over me in a special way, as will be seen in this and other instances I shall relate. My mother always breast-fed her children, but in my case she could not do so because of ill health. She sent me to stay day and night with a wet nurse who lived in our town.[1] The owner of the house of which the wet nurse was mistress had made a fairly deep excavation beneath it in order to enlarge the cellar. One night when I happened not to be there, the foundations, weakened by the digging, gave way. The walls buckled and the house collapsed, killing my wet nurse and burying her and her four children under the rubble. If I had been in the house that night, I would surely have suffered the same fate as the rest. Blessed be God's Providence! I owe so many thanks to Mary Most Holy, who preserved me from death in my childhood and has freed me since then from so many predicaments. How ungrateful I am!

8 The first ideas I can remember date back to when I was five years old. When I went to bed, instead of sleeping—I never have been much of a sleeper—I used to think about eternity. I would think "forever, forever, forever." I would try to imagine enormous distances and pile still more distances on these and realize that they would never come to an end. Then I would shudder and ask myself if those who were so unhappy as to go to an eternity of pain would ever see an end to their suffering. Would they have to go on suf-

fering? Yes, forever and forever they will have to bear their pain!

9 This troubled me deeply, for I am by nature very compassionate. The idea of an eternity of torment made such a deep impression on me, either because of the tenderness it evoked in me or because of the many times I thought about it, that it is surely the thing that to this day I remember best. The power of this idea has made me work in the past, still makes me work, and will make me work as long as I live, in converting sinners, in preaching, in hearing confessions, in writing books, in distributing holy cards and pamphlets, and in having familiar conversations.[1]

10 The reason is that, as I have said, I am so soft-hearted and compassionate that I can't bear seeing misfortune or misery without doing something to help. I would take the bread out of my own mouth to give it to the poor. In fact, I would abstain from putting it into my mouth in order to have something to give to those who are asking for it. I am even scrupulous about spending anything at all on myself when I think of the needs I can remedy. Well, then, if these momentary physical misfortunes affect me so much, it is understandable what I feel in my heart at the thought of the everlasting pains of hell—not for me, but for all those who willingly live in mortal sin.

11 I often say to myself: It is of faith that there is a heaven for the good and a hell for the wicked. It is of faith, too, that the pains of hell are eternal. It is also of faith that a single mortal sin is enough to damn a soul because of the infinite malice of mortal sin, which is an offense against an infinite God. Since these principles are all so certain, the thought of the ease with which people sin—as if it were like taking a glass of water, as if it were something funny or amusing—the thought of the crowds that stay continuously in mortal sin and are thus on the road to death and hell—this thought robs me of rest, and I feel like running and crying out. And I tell myself:

12 If I saw someone about to fall into a pit or a fire, I would surely run and cry out a warning to save him from falling.

Why shouldn't I do the same to save someone from falling into the pit and fire of hell?

1 3 I simply can't understand how other priests who believe the same truths that I do, and as we all should, do not preach and exhort people to save themselves from falling into hell.[1]

1 4 I wonder too how the laity, men and women who have the faith, can help crying out. What if a fire broke out in a house in the middle of the night and the people in the house and in the neighborhood were asleep and unaware of the danger? Wouldn't the first person who noticed the fire run through the streets shouting "fire, fire in such and such a house!" Well, why not shout "hellfire!" to awaken those who are asleep in their sins, lest they awake to find themselves burning in everlasting fire?

1 5 This idea of a lost eternity that began to move me so vividly at the tender age of five[1] and that has stayed with me ever since and that, God willing, I will never forget is the mainspring and goad of my zeal for the salvation of souls.

1 6 In time I felt a further stimulus for zeal of which I shall speak later, namely, the thought that sin not only condemns my neighbor but is an offense against God, my Father.[1] This idea breaks my heart with pain and makes me want to run like. . . . And I tell myself, "If a sin is infinitely malicious, then preventing a sin is preventing an infinite offense against my God, against my good Father."

1 7 If a son had a very kind father and saw that he was being maltreated for no reason at all, wouldn't the son defend the father? If the son saw that this good father was being led to execution, wouldn't he do all that he could to set him free? Well, then, what should I be doing for the honor of my Father, who is offended with such indifference and who, though innocent, is being led to Calvary to be, as St. Paul says, crucified anew by sin? Wouldn't it be a crime to remain silent? What would be the sense of not doing everything we could? My God, my Father! Help me to prevent all sins, or at least one sin, even if I should be cut to pieces in the attempt.

Chapter III

FIRST INCLINATIONS

18 For my greater embarrassment I should like to quote the words of the author of the Book of Wisdom (8:19): "I was a boy of happy disposition. I had received a good soul as my lot." That is, I received a good nature or disposition from God, out of his sheer goodness.[1]

19 I remember that during the war of independence, which lasted from 1808 to 1814, the people of Sallent were so frightened of the French—and with good reason, since the French had burned the city of Manresa and the town of Calders, near Sallent[1]—that everyone fled when they heard the news that the French army was on its way. During the first evacuation I recollect being carried on someone's shoulders; but during the last evacuation, when I was four or five, I went on foot and gave grandfather Clará, my mother's father, a helping hand.[2] It was at night, and his eyesight was failing, and I guided him through the obstacles with such patience and kindness that the poor old man was very glad to see that I hadn't run off to join my brothers and cousins who had abandoned the two of us. I always showed him a great deal of affection until he died, and not only him but also all those who were elderly and disabled.

20 I couldn't stand for anyone to make fun of them, as young boys are often wont to do, despite the exemplary punishment meted out to the boys who made fun of Elisha.[1]
    Moreover I remember that when I was seated in church and an old man would come in, I would stand up gladly and give him a seat. I would always greet old people on the street, and if I had the pleasure of talking with one of them, I enjoyed it immensely. God grant that I have known how to use the advice of these elderly gentlemen to advantage.[2]

21 My God, how good you are! How rich in mercy you have been to me! If you had given others the graces you have given me, they would have cooperated with them so much more.

Mercy, Lord: I'll begin to be good from now on, with the help of your grace. .

Chapter IV

EARLY EDUCATION

2 2 I was barely six when my parents sent me to school. My first schoolmaster was a very active and religious man, Mr. Anthony Pascual.[1] He never punished or upbraided me, but I was careful not to give him any cause for doing so. I was always punctual, always attended classes, and always prepared my lessons carefully.

2 3 I learned the catechism so well that whenever I was asked to I could recite it from beginning to end without a mistake. Three of the other boys learned it as well as I had, and the teacher presented us to the pastor, Dr. Joseph Amigó. This good man had the four of us recite the whole catechism on two consecutive Sunday nights. We did it without a single mistake before all the people in the church. As a reward he gave each of us a holy card, which we have treasured ever since.

2 4 When I had mastered the catechism, I was given Pintón's *Compendium of Sacred History*[1] to read, and between my reading and the teacher's explanations, the work was so deeply fixed in my memory that I could repeat it and discuss it with ease and without getting confused or flustered.

2 5 Besides having a very good elementary teacher, which, as I have said, is no small gift from heaven, I also had good parents who cooperated with my teacher in molding my understanding in truth and nurturing my heart in the practice of religion and all the virtues. Every day after lunch, which we ate at a quarter past twelve, my father had me read a spiritual book, and at night we would sit for a while around the table, where he would always tell us something edifying and instructive until it was time for us to retire.

26 Whatever my parents or teacher told me or explained to me, I would grasp it perfectly, notwithstanding the fact that I was a very small boy. I didn't really comprehend the wording of the catechism although, as I have said, I could parrot it extremely well. Nevertheless, I can see now the advantage of knowing it by heart, because in time, without quite knowing how or adverting to it, those great truths that I had rattled off without understanding them would come back to me so forcibly that I would say, "Ah! That's what that meant! How stupid you were not to understand that!" Rosebuds open in time, but if there were no buds there would be no blossoms. The same holds for religious truths: if there are no catechism lessons, then there is complete ignorance of religious matters, even among those who otherwise pass for intelligent persons. How useful my catechism lessons and the advice of my parents have been to me!

27 Later on, when I was living alone in the city of Barcelona and witnessed so much evil, I would imagine those good people speaking to me: That is evil, you should avoid it. You had better rely on God, your parents, and teacher than on these unhappy people who don't know what they're doing or saying.

28 My parents and teacher not only instructed me in the truths I had to believe but also in the virtues I needed to practice. With regard to my neighbor, they told me never to take or covet what belongs to others and that, if I ever found something, I should return it to its owner. It just so happened that one day after school, as I was walking along the street toward home, I saw a quarter[1] lying on the ground. I picked it up and wondered to whom I should return it. Since I couldn't see anyone on the street, I decided that it must have fallen from the window of the nearest house. So I went up to the house, asked for the head of the house, and gave him the quarter.

29 I was trained so well in obedience and resignation that I was always content with whatever was done, decided, or given to me by way of food or clothing. I never remember saying "I don't like this" or "I want that." I was so used to thinking

like this that even later, when I was a priest, my mother, who was always very fond of me, used to say, "Anthony, would you like this?" I would always answer, "I always like what you like." "But," she would say, "there are always some things we like better than others." And then I'd say, "Whatever you give me is what I like best of all." And so she died without finding out what material things I liked the best.[1]

Chapter V

AT WORK IN THE FACTORY

30 When I was still a small boy in elementary school, a distinguished visitor to the school asked me what I wanted to be when I grew up. I answered that I wanted to be a priest.[1] Accordingly, when I had successfully completed my elementary school, I was enrolled in the Latin class taught by a very holy and learned priest, Dr. John Riera. From him I learned and memorized nouns, verbs, genders, and a bit more, but as the class was discontinued I could no longer study and had to give it up.[2]

31 Since my father manufactured thread and cloth, he set me to work in his factory.[1] I obeyed without a word, a long face, or any sign of displeasure. I set to work as hard as I could and never spent an idle, half-hearted day. I did everything to the best of my ability so as not to displease my dear parents in the slightest, because I loved them very much and they loved me.

32 What used to hurt me the most was to hear that my parents would have to scold a worker for not doing his job properly. I am sure that I suffered more than the one who was being corrected because I am so tender-hearted that when I see someone hurt I feel it more than he does.

33 My father set me to work on every job available in his well-equipped little thread and textile factory. For a long time I and another young man were in charge of putting the finishing touches on the work of everyone else in the shop.

Whenever we had to correct anyone, it upset me a great deal; yet I did my duty. I always tried to find something good to say about the piece of finished work. I would praise its good points, saying that this or that about it was very good but that it had such and such a defect and if these little defects were corrected, it would really be a perfect job.

34 I didn't know why I did things this way, but in time I came to see that it was the result of a special grace of kindness that the Lord had granted me. This is why the workers always took correction from me and mended their ways. My friend, however, who was a better worker than I but lacked this gift of kindness, always got upset when he had to correct anybody. He would scold the workers harshly and they would get angry, and often they wouldn't know what it was they were supposed to correct. I learned from this that everyone, even the rudest people, should be treated kindly and affably and that much more may be gained by kindness than by harshness and irritability.

35 My God, you have been so good to me! I have been very late in understanding the many great graces you have given me.[1] I have been a useless servant and have not properly invested the talent you have entrusted to me. But Lord, I give you my word that I will work. Be a little patient with me. Don't take my talent away; I'll invest it wisely now. Give me your holy grace and your divine love and I give you my word that I will work.

Chapter VI

FIRST DEVOTIONS

36 Ever since I was a small boy I have been attracted to piety and religion. I used to attend Mass on all feasts and holy days and on other days, too, when I possibly could. On feast days I usually attended two Masses, a Low Mass and a High Mass, always together with my father. I cannot remember ever playing, looking around, or talking in church. On the contrary, I was always so recollected, modest, and devout that when I

compare those early years with the present I am ashamed because, to my great embarrassment, I must admit that even now I lack the fixed attention and heartfelt fervor that I had then.

37 I attended all the functions of our holy religion with great faith. The services I liked best were those connected with the Blessed Sacrament, and I attended these with great devotion and joy. Besides the constant good example of my father, who had great devotion to the Blessed Sacrament,[1] I had the good fortune of discovering a book entitled *Courtesies of Jesus in the Blessed Sacrament.* How I loved that book! I liked it so much that I learned it by heart.[2]

38 When I was ten years old, I was allowed to make my First Communion. Words cannot tell what I felt on that day when I had the unequaled joy of receiving my good Jesus into my heart for the first time. From then on I always frequented the sacraments of Penance and Communion, but how fervently and with what devotion and love: more than now—yes, more than now, I must say to my embarrassment and shame. Now that I know so much more than I did then, now that the many benefits I have received since then have accumulated continually, in gratitude I should have become a seraph of love, whereas God knows what I am. When I compare my early years with the present, I grow sad and tearfully confess that I am a monster of ingratitude.

39 Besides assisting at Holy Mass, frequent Communion, and Benediction of the Blessed Sacrament, which I did with great fervor because of God's goodness and mercy, I also attended the pastor's catechism class and explanation of the Gospel that took place every Sunday and feast day. These sessions always closed in the afternoon with recitation of the Holy Rosary.

40 In addition to attending these morning and afternoon services, I used to enter the church at nightfall, when hardly anyone was there, and talk alone with our Lord. With great faith, trust, and love, I would speak to God, my good Father. A thousand times over I would offer myself to his service. I

wanted to become a priest so that I could dedicate myself to his service day and night. I remember telling Him, "Humanly speaking, I see no hope, but you have the power to make it happen, if you will." Then, with total confidence, I would leave it all in God's hands, trusting Him to do whatever had to be done: which He did, as I shall say later.[1]

41 At this time I chanced upon another book called *A Good Day and a Good Night,*[1] which I read with great pleasure and profit. After reading from it awhile, I would close it, press it to my heart, look up to heaven with tears in my eyes, and say, "Lord, how many good things I was ignorant of. My God, my Love, who could ever help loving you?"

42 The realization of how much good I have derived through reading good and pious books has prompted me to distribute them generously, in the hope that they will bring my neighbors, whom I love, the same happy results they brought to me. May all men know how good and lovable and loving God is. My God, make all creatures come to know, love, and serve you with full faith and fervor. All you creatures, love your God, for He is good and his mercy is endless.[1]

Chapter VII

EARLY DEVOTION TO MARY

43 During these same years of my childhood and youth, I had a very warm devotion toward the Blessed Virgin Mary. I only wish that I had the same devotion now. To use Rodriguez's comparison,[1] I am like those old servants in great houses who hardly do anything and, like old pots and pans, are kept in the household more out of pity and charity than for any great usefulness. That is how I am in the service of the Queen of heaven and earth: she puts up with me out of pure charity. To show that this is the plain truth, without the least exaggeration, I am going to relate what I used to do in honor of Mary Most Holy.

44 When I was a little boy I was given a pair of rosary beads,

and I was more pleased with them than with the greatest treasure. I used them after school when my classmates and I marched in double file to the nearby church where our teacher led us in reciting a part of the rosary.[1]

45 At about this time I discovered in our house a book called *El Roser,* the rose-tree, which contained pictures and explanations of the mysteries of the rosary. I learned from it how to recite the rosary, litanies, and other prayers. When my teacher heard of this, he was very pleased and had me kneel by his side in church so that I could lead the rosary. When the older boys saw how this had put me in the teacher's good graces, they learned it too. From then on we alternated in leading every other week, so that all came to learn and practice this holy devotion that, after Holy Mass, is the most profitable.

46 After that time, I recited the rosary not only in church but at home every night, as was the custom of my parents. After I had finished grammar school and had begun to work regularly in the factory, as I mentioned in chapter 5, I recited the three parts daily along with my fellow workers, who kept on working as I led them. We said the first part before eight o'clock breakfast, the second before lunch at noon, and the third before nine in the evening when they went home to dinner.

47 Besides the entire rosary that we said every working day, we also recited a Hail Mary on the hour and the Angelus at its due times. On feast days I spent more time at church than at home, as I rarely played with other children. I used to entertain myself at home, and even in the midst of these innocent diversions I seemed to hear the voice of the Virgin calling me to church. I would say "I'm coming," and off I went.

48 I never tired of being in church before the image of Our Lady of the Rosary, and I talked and prayed so trustingly that I was quite sure the Blessed Virgin heard me.[1] I used to imagine a sort of wire running from the image in front of me to its heavenly original. Although I had not yet seen a telegraph line at that time, I had imagined how it would be to have a telegraph line to heaven. I can't explain how attentive,

15

fervent, and devout I was at prayer then, but I was more so then than I am now.

49 As a small child I and my sister Rose, who was very devout, made frequent visits to the shrine of the Virgin called Fussimanya, a league away from my home. I cannot describe the devotion I felt at this shrine. Even before I got there, as soon as I could see the outline of the chapel, I felt so emotional that tears of tenderness welled up in my eyes. We started saying the rosary and kept praying all the way to the chapel. I have visited the shrine at Fussimanya whenever I could, not only as a child but as student, priest, and even as archbishop before I left for my diocese.

50 All my joy was to work, pray, read, and think about Jesus and Mary. I enjoyed keeping silence and spoke very little because I liked being alone so as not to be disturbed in my thoughts.[1] I was always content, happy, and at peace with everyone. I never had a quarrel or fight, great or small, with anyone.

51 While I was engaged in these holy thoughts that so delighted my heart, I suddenly had the most terrible and blasphemous temptation against the Blessed Virgin Mary. This is the greatest pain I have felt in my whole life. I would have preferred to be in hell to be free of it. I couldn't eat, sleep, or look at her image. What suffering! I went to confession, but because I was too young to know how to express myself very well, the confessor made light of what I was saying, and I was in the same predicament as before. What bitterness! This temptation lasted until the Lord Himself chose to come to my aid.

52 Later I had another temptation against my own good mother, who loved me very much and whom I loved in return. I conceived a great hatred and aversion for her, and, to overcome the temptation, I forced myself to treat her with much tenderness and humility. I recollect that when I went to confession and told my director about my temptation and the means I had used to overcome it, he asked me, "Who told you to do these things?" I answered, "No one, Father." Then

he told me, "It is God who has been teaching you, son; keep on as you have been doing and be faithful to his grace."

53 No one dared use foul language or hold bad conversations in my presence. Once I happened to be present at a gathering of young men—ordinarily I didn't join in because I was well aware of the kind of talk that went on in such gatherings—and one of the better young men told me, "You'd better leave, Anthony. We're going to talk about bad things." I thanked him for the advice and left, never to join them again.

54 My God, how good you have been to me and how poorly I have responded to your favors! If you had given such graces to any other son of Adam, he would surely have done better than I. I am so embarrassed and ashamed. How shall I answer you on judgment day when you say, "Render an account of your stewardship"? (Luke 16:2.)

55 Mother Mary, how good you have been to me and how ungrateful I have been to you! My Mother, I wish to love you from now on with all my heart, and not only to love you myself, but to bring everyone else to know, love, serve, and praise you and to pray the holy rosary, a devotion that is so pleasing to you. Mother, help me in my weakness and laziness so that I may be able to live up to my resolutions.

Chapter VIII

IN 1825, AROUND MY EIGHTEENTH BIRTHDAY, I MOVE TO BARCELONA

56 Because I wanted to improve my knowledge of manufacturing techniques, I asked my father to send me to Barcelona. He agreed and took me there. But, like St. Paul, I had to earn what I needed for food, clothing, books, teachers, etc., with my own two hands. My first move was to submit a petition to the Board of Trade for admission to classes in design. My request was granted and I used it to some advantage.[1] Who would have guessed that God would one day use in the interests of religion the studies in design that I undertook for

17

business reasons? And, in fact, these skills have been most useful to me in designing prints for catechisms and works on mysticism.

5 7 Besides design I studied Castilian and, later, French grammar, but always with an eye to their usefulness in business and manufacturing.

5 8 Of all the things I have studied or worked at during my life, I have understood none better than manufacturing. Apropos of this, in the firm I worked for, there were catalogs of patterns shown at the yearly displays in Paris and London, and they were kept up-to-date to be in step with the latest fashions.[1] God gave me such a ready wit in this that all I had to do was analyze any pattern and in short order a copy would emerge from the loom exact to the last detail, or even with improvements if my employer so desired.

5 9 I found copying patterns difficult at first, but by applying myself day and night, both on workdays and holidays, to study, writing, and designing, I came to be successful at it. I only wish that I had applied myself as busily to virtue, so that I might have become better than I am. When, after much thought, I had managed to take a design apart and put it back together, I felt such a sensation of joy and satisfaction that I would walk back home quite beside myself with contentment. I learned all this without a teacher. In fact, far from teaching me how to understand patterns and imitate them perfectly, my instructors in the art actually tried to conceal it from me.

6 0 One day I told the shop superintendent that the pattern we both had in hand could be worked out in such and such a manner. He took a pencil and drew a plan of the way the loom should be set up for the job. I made no comment but told him that if he didn't object, I would study it. I took the pattern and his sketch for the loom-setting home with me. In a few days I brought him a sketch of the setup needed to produce the pattern and showed him how the one he had sketched would not have produced the pattern in question but a different one, which I also showed him. The superinten-

dent was amazed at my sketches as well as at my reasoning and explanations.

61 From that day forward he held me in high esteem, and on holidays he used to take me with him on outings with his sons. His friendship, advice, and sound principles were very beneficial to me because he was not only a well-educated man but also a faithful husband to his wife and a good father to his children, a good Christian, and a realist both in principle and practice. To tell the truth, some of this man's advice was very useful for someone like me who had been brought up in a small town like Sallent, for at that time the very air we breathed was filled with constitutional ideas.

62 With regard to manufacturing, I had become adept not only in design but also in presetting looms. A number of workers asked me to do them the favor of setting up their looms because they were not skilled at it. I helped them and they respected and liked me for it.

63 News of the technical ability the Lord had given me spread through Barcelona. This moved some gentlemen to call on my father to ask him what he thought of our forming a company and starting our own factory. My father found the idea very attractive, as it would mean growth for his own factory. He talked with me about it, pointing out the advantages and possible fortune it might bring me.

64 But God's ways are unsearchable, for although I really enjoyed manufacturing and had made considerable progress in it, I couldn't make up my mind. I felt an inner repugnance for settling down and also for causing my father to contract any further liabilities on my behalf. I told him that I thought the time was not ripe, that I was still very young, and that because I was so short of stature, the workers wouldn't take orders from me. He told me not to be concerned about that because someone else could handle the workers and I would only be involved in the directorship of the business. I continued to decline, however, saying that we would consider the matter later but that just now I didn't wish to accept. My decision proved to be truly providential. This was the first time

I had ever opposed my father's plans. The reason, of course, was that God willed something else for me: He wanted me to be a priest, not a businessman, although at the time such ideas never entered my head.[1]

65 My life at this time was an embodiment of what the Gospel says about the thorns choking the good grain.[1] My ceaseless preoccupation with machines, looms, and creations had so obsessed me that I could think of nothing else. My God, how patient you were with me! Oh Virgin Mary, there were even times when I forgot you! Mercy, my Mother!

Chapter IX

WHY I GAVE UP MANUFACTURING

66 During those first three years in Barcelona, the fervor that I had had at home began to cool.[1] True, I received the sacraments frequently during the year. I attended Mass on all feasts and holy days of obligation and daily prayed the rosary to Mary and kept up my other devotions, but with none of my former fervor. My only goal and all my anxieties were about manufacturing. I can't overstate it—my obsession approached delirium. Who can say? Perhaps the very intensity of my inclination was the means God used to take away my love for manufacturing.

67 Toward the end of my third year in Barcelona, obsessed as I was, whenever I was at Mass on holy days, I experienced the greatest difficulty in overcoming the thoughts that came to me. It is true that I loved to think and dwell on my projects, but during the Mass and my other devotions I did not want to and I tried to put them out of my mind. I told myself that I'd think about them later but that for the present I only wanted to think on what I was doing and pray. My efforts seemed useless, like trying to bring a swiftly rotating wheel to a sudden stop. I was tormented during Mass with new ideas, discoveries, etc. There seemed to be more machines in my head than saints on the altar.[1]

68 In the midst of this whirligig of ideas, while I was at Mass one day, I remembered reading as a small boy those words of the Gospel: "What does it profit a man if he gain the whole world and suffer the loss of his soul?" This phrase impressed me deeply and went like an arrow to my heart. I tried to think and reason what to do, but to no avail.

69 I was like Saul on the road to Damascus, but I was in need of an Ananias to tell me what to do. I went to the house of the Fathers of St. Philip Neri, walked through the cloisters, saw an open door, knocked and entered. There I met a Brother Paul, who was very fervent and devout, and I told him simply about my resolves. The good brother patiently and charitably heard me out, and then he told me in all humility, "Sir, I'm only a poor lay brother; I'm not the one to counsel you. I'll take you to a very wise and virtuous priest who will tell you what you should do." He took me to Father Amigó, who listened to me, approved of my decision, and counseled me to study Latin.[1] I obeyed him.

70 The warmth of piety and devotion reawakened in me. I opened my eyes and recognized the dangers to soul and body that I had been passing through.[1] I shall briefly relate some of them.

71 That last summer, the Blessed Virgin saved me from drowning in the sea. Because I had been working so hard, I didn't feel very well during the summer. I began to lose all appetite, and the only relief I could find was to go down to the sea, wade in it, and drink a few drops of the salt water. One day as I was walking along the beach on my way to the "old sea" on the other side of La Barceloneta, a huge wave suddenly engulfed me and carried me out to sea. I saw in a moment that I was far from shore, and I was amazed to see that I was floating on the surface, although I didn't know how to swim. I called out to the Blessed Virgin and found myself on shore without having swallowed even a drop of water. While I was in the water, I had felt exceedingly calm, but afterwards, on shore, I was horrified at the thought of the danger I had escaped through the help of the Blessed Virgin.

72 Mary also saved me from a worse danger, not unlike that of the chaste patriarch, Joseph. While I was in Barcelona, I used to visit a fellow townsman of mine from time to time. I never spoke with anyone else in the house except him. When I arrived there, I would go straight to his room and talk only with him, but the others in the house always saw me coming and going. I was fairly young then, and although it's true that I had to buy my own clothes, I liked to dress—I won't say luxuriously—but with a certain elegance, perhaps too much. Who knows? Maybe the Lord will take me to task for this on judgment day. One day I went to the house and asked after my friend. The lady of the house, a young woman, asked me to wait for him, as he was coming back soon. I had waited a little while when I realized that her intentions were passionate, as her words and gestures made clear. I called out to the Blessed Virgin and ran out of that house, never to return. I didn't tell anyone about what had happened, for fear of ruining the lady's reputation.

73 God dealt me all these blows to wake me up and help me escape from the dangers of the world. But it took an even harder blow, which came to me as follows. A young man of my own age suggested that we pool our interests, and I agreed. We began by entering a lottery and were quite lucky at it. As I was always very busy with my job, about the only thing I could do was act as trustee. He bought the tickets and I took care of them. On the day of the drawing I gave him the tickets and he would tell me how much we had won. Since we bought a large number of tickets, we won in every drawing, sometimes quite a lot. We subtracted what we needed to buy more tickets and invested the rest with brokers at 6 percent. I kept the receipts and that was all. My companion did all the rest.

74 I already had a large number of receipts that added up to a pretty sum when one day, lo and behold, he came and told me that one of our tickets had won 24,000 duros but that when he went to collect the money he found that he'd lost the ticket. And he was telling the truth, all right, because he had gambled it all away and lost. But that wasn't all. He went to my room while I was away, picked the lock of my trunk,

and took all the receipts of our partnership. He even took my personal money and pawned my books and clothes for a loan, which he lost at gambling. Finally, in an attempt to recoup his losses, and finding that he had nothing more to gamble with, he broke into the house of an acquaintance, stole the jewels of the lady of the house, and sold them. He gambled the money and lost again.

75 Meanwhile the lady discovered that her jewels were missing and surmised that this person had taken them. She reported him to the authorities, who captured the thief. He confessed his crime, was prosecuted and sentenced to two years in prison. I simply can't describe how great a blow this was to me—and not just because of my financial loss, although that was great enough, but because of my loss of honor. I thought to myself, "What will people say? They'll think you were this fellow's accomplice in gambling and burglary. Just think—a friend of yours in jail, in the penitentiary!" I was so embarrassed and ashamed that I hardly dared show my face on the street. I thought that everyone was looking at me, talking about me, focusing on me.

76 My God, how good and wonderful you have been to me! You surely used strange means to uproot me from the world and an odd kind of aloes to wean me from Babylon. And you, my Mother: what proper thanks can I show you for saving me from death in the sea? If I had drowned, as by all rights I should have in that condition, where would I be now? You know quite well, my Mother. I would be in the lower depths of hell because of my ingratitude. With David I should say: *Misericordia tua magna est super me, et eruisti animam meam ex inferno inferiori.* [1]

Chapter X

MY RESOLVE TO BECOME A CARTHUSIAN MONK AT MONTE-ALEGRE

77 Disenchanted, weary, and bored with the world, I considered leaving it for the solitary life of a Carthusian and pursued

my studies with this end in view.[1] I felt that I would be failing in my duty if I didn't tell my father of this decision, and the first chance I had, I did so, during one of his many business trips to Barcelona. He was deeply moved when I told him that I wanted to give up manufacturing. He told me of all the fond hopes he had for me and his business and for the partnership we might have entered. When I mentioned that I wanted to become a Carthusian, his sorrow reached its peak.

78 But since he was a good Christian, he told me, "I don't want to thwart your vocation, God forbid. Think it over carefully, commend it to God, and consult with your spiritual director. If he says that this is God's will, then I respect and worship it, however it may pain me. Even so, I'd rather see you become a secular priest than a monk. Whatever happens, may God's will be done."

79 I dedicated myself to the study of Latin grammar with the greatest concentration. My first teacher was a certain Father Thomas, whose Latin was very good and who taught me for two and a half months. Then he had a stroke, lost his speech, and died within a few hours. What a setback! After this I studied with Don Francisco Más y Artigas,[1] and continued to do so until I left Barcelona to begin courses in philosophy, as I shall relate next.

80 My older brother John married Mary Casajuana, the daughter of Maurice Casajuana, whom the bishop of Vich had placed in charge of collecting the rents of certain properties and seigniories in Sallent. This man was very highly esteemed by the bishop and frequently went to see him. On one of these visits he spoke of my insignificant self. Who knows what it was he said, but it caused the bishop to want to meet me.

81 I was told I should go to Vich, but I didn't want to because I was afraid that he might upset my plans for becoming a Carthusian. I told my teacher this and he answered, "I'll go with you to see a Father of the Oratory, Father Cantí, a man of wisdom, prudence, and experience who will tell you what you should do." We presented ourselves to the good father,

and after hearing all my reasons for not going to Vich, he told me, "Go, and if the Lord Bishop knows that it is God's will that you enter the Carthusians, far from opposing you, he will be your protector."

82 I held my peace and obeyed. I left Barcelona after living there four years. During that time my fervor had cooled and I had been filled with the winds of vanity, praise, and applause, particularly during the first three years. How bitterly I regret and lament it all now! But the Lord took care to humiliate and embarrass me. Blessed be God for all the goodness and mercy he has shown me.

Chapter XI

THE MOVE FROM BARCELONA TO VICH

83 At the beginning of September, 1829, I left Barcelona and because my parents wanted me to go to Sallent, I did so to please them. I stayed with them until September 29, Michaelmas, when we left after hearing Mass. It was a poor trip because of the rain that accompanied us all the way. We reached Vich that night, completely soaked.[1]

84 On the following day we went to see the bishop, Paul of Jesus Corcuera, who received us kindly.[1] So that I might have more time for study and my particular devotions, I was stationed with the Steward of the Bishop's Palace, Msgr. Fortián Bres, a very good priest who showed me a great deal of affection.[2] I lived with him throughout my stay in Vich, and later whenever I visited Vich I was a guest in his house. This good man was my sponsor when I was consecrated Archbishop of Cuba in the cathedral at Vich.

85 In the early days of my stay in Vich, I asked whether anyone could recommend a good priest to hear my general confession. I was advised to go to a priest of the Oratory of St. Philip Neri, Father Peter Bach.[1] I made a general confession of my whole life to him and afterward always made my weekly confessions with this very good director. It is worth

noting that God has used three Fathers of the Oratory of St.
Philip Neri to counsel and direct me at the most crucial mo-
ments in my spiritual life: Brother Paul and Fathers Anthony
Amigó, Cantí, and Peter Bach.

86 After arriving in Vich, I confessed and received Commu-
nion every week, but after a while the director had me con-
fess twice a week and receive Communion four times a week.
I served Mass daily for Father Bres. Every day I made a half-
hour of mental prayer, visited the Blessed Sacrament during
Forty Hours' Devotion, and also visited the shrine of Our
Lady of the Rosary in the Dominican Church, rain or shine.
And even though the streets were filled with snow, I never
omitted my visits to the Blessed Sacrament and the Blessed
Virgin Mary.[1]

87 Every day at table we read the life of the saint of the day.
Furthermore, with the director's approval, on three days,
Monday, Wednesday, and Friday, I took the discipline and on
Tuesday, Thursday, and Saturday I wore the cilice.[1] Through
all these devotional practices I returned to my first fervor,
without slacking off in my studies to which I applied myself
to the utmost of my ability, always with the purest and most
upright intention possible.[2]

88 During my first year of philosophy, in the midst of all
my studies and devotions, I never lost sight of my longed-for
Charterhouse.[1] I had a large picture of St. Bruno on my desk.
Nearly every time I went to confession I spoke to my director
of my desire to enter the Carthusians, and so he came to believe that God was calling me there. Thus he wrote to the
Father Prior,[2] and both agreed I should go at the end of that
year's course. He also gave me two letters, one for the Father
Prior, the other for a religious he knew there.

89 Quite content, I undertook the journey to Barcelona,
Badalona, and Monte-Alegre. Shortly before my arrival at
Barcelona, a hurricane came up, so dreadful that I was terrified. I had studied so much that year that I was a little weak
in the chest, and as we ran for cover from the great sheets of
rain, the strain of running and the clouds of dust that rose

from the parched earth began to suffocate me severely. I thought, "Perhaps God doesn't want you to join the Carthusians." This thought alarmed me greatly. What is certain is that I didn't have the will to go on, and so I returned to Vich. When I told my director he fell silent, without telling me that it was good, bad, or indifferent. And so the matter stayed.[1]

90 I had told no one but my director about my desire to become a Carthusian; hence all the rest knew nothing about it. In those days a vacant benefice in Sallent was being claimed by a priest who lived in the town though he was not born there. Unfortunately, the man was not all that one would have liked. The vicar general, who had sized up the problem, talked to the bishop and made him see that the priest in question should not have the benefice. To prevent his entering the community, they had me claim the benefice since I, as a native, should have preference. I obtained the position, and on February 2, 1831[1] the bishop gave me tonsure, the vicar general gave me my stipend, and on the following day I went to Sallent to take possession of the benefice. From that day on, I always wore the cassock and had to recite the Divine Office.

91 During Christmas, Holy Week, and vacations I resided in Sallent, by reason of the benefice; the rest of the year I resided in Vich because of my studies. I have already mentioned some of my personal devotions. Besides these, every month all of the students had to assist at a general communion called the Academy of St. Thomas. The bishop had also installed the Congregation of the Immaculate Conception and of St. Aloysius Gonzaga in the seminary chapel. All tonsured resident and non-resident seminarians were members of this Congregation. If anyone without tonsure wished to attend, he had to submit a petition to the bishop. The members received Communion in a body every third Sunday of the month. The bishop himself came to say Mass in the seminary chapel, during which he gave us Holy Communion and, on the evening of the same day, delivered a sermon.

92 Every year in the chapel, during Lent, we made an eight-day retreat, from Sunday to Sunday. The bishop attended all the morning and evening exercises. I recall that during a ser-

mon one day he said, "Perhaps someone will ask why the
bishop is spending so much time with the students. I would
tell him that I know what I'm doing. If I can have good students now, I'll have good priests and good pastors later. Think
how much more rest I'll have then! . . . It is very important
for students to be continually nourished spiritually during
their studies; otherwise they will grow up to be proud, and
pride is the source of all sin. I would rather have them know
a little less and be pious, than to know a great deal with little
or no piety and be puffed up with the wind of vanity."

93 After that first year of philosophy I no longer thought
about becoming a Carthusian and realized that that vocation
had only been temporary. The Lord had been calling me away
so that I would come to detest the things of the world and,
once detached from them, might remain in the clerical state,
as the Lord has given me to understand since.

94 While I was in studies, I joined the congregation of *Laus
perennis* of the Sacred Heart of Jesus. The hour of prayer assigned me is from four to five p.m. on St. Anthony's Day in
June. I was enrolled by Father Ildefonso Valiente, rector of
the College of Manresa, who came to my house.[1] In the same
town I am enrolled in the Perpetual Rosary, and my assigned
hour of prayer is from one to two p.m. on June 29, the feast
of St. Peter. In Vich I was also enrolled in the Confraternity
of the Rosary and that of Our Lady of Mt. Carmel, as well as
in the Congregation of Our Lady of Sorrows.[2]

95 I had the following experience while I was in my second
year of philosophy at Vich. That winter I had caught a bad
cold and was ordered to bed; so I obeyed. One day as I lay
there at about ten-thirty in the morning, I felt a terrible
temptation. I turned to Mary, called on my guardian angel,
and prayed to all my name-saints as well as to those to whom
I have a special devotion. I fixed my attention on indifferent
objects so as to distract myself and forget about the temptation. I made the sign of the cross on my forehead so that the
Lord would free me from evil thoughts, but everything I did
was in vain.

96 Finally I turned over on my other side, to see if the temptation would go away, when suddenly I saw the Blessed Virgin Mary, very beautiful and gracious. Her dress was crimson, her mantle blue, and in her arms I saw a huge garland of the most beautiful roses. I had seen lovely artificial and real roses in Barcelona but none as lovely as these. How beautiful it all was! As I lay face up in bed, I saw myself as a beautiful white child kneeling with hands joined. I never lost sight of the Blessed Virgin, on whom I kept my eyes fixed. I remember distinctly thinking to myself, "She is a woman and yet she doesn't give you any evil thoughts; on the contrary, she has taken them all away from you." The Blessed Virgin spoke to me and said, "Anthony, this crown is yours if you overcome." Next I saw the Blessed Virgin place on my head the crown of roses that she held in her right hand (besides the garland, which she held between her arm and her right side). I saw myself crowned with roses in the person of that little child, and I was speechless.

97 I also saw a band of saints standing at her right hand, in an attitude of prayer. I didn't recognize them, except that one seemed to be St. Stephen. I believed then, as I do now, that those were my patron saints praying and interceding for me so that I wouldn't fall into the temptation. Then, on my left, I saw a great crowd of demons in battle array, like soldiers who fall back and close ranks again after a battle. I said to myself, "What a host of them there is—and so fearful!" During all of this I remained as if caught by surprise, without quite realizing what was happening to me. As soon as it had passed, I felt free of the temptation and filled with a joy so deep that I couldn't grasp what had been going on within me.

98 I am quite sure that I was neither asleep nor suffering from dizziness or anything else that could have caused a state of illusion. What made me believe that what had happened was real, and a special grace from Mary, was the fact that from that moment on I was free from temptation and for many years stayed free of any temptation against chastity. If later there have been any such temptations, they have been so insignificant that they hardly deserve to be called temptations. Glory to Mary! Victory through Mary![1]

Chapter XII

ORDINATIONS

99 The bishop would not ordain anyone who was enrolled in the complete course of studies until he was well-advanced in the course. He followed a regular procedure. After four years of theology, he conferred the four minor orders, preceded by a ten-day retreat. After the fifth year, he conferred the subdiaconate, preceded by a twenty-day retreat. After the sixth year, he conferred the diaconate, preceded by a thirty-day retreat. Finally, after the seventh year, he conferred the priesthood, preceded by a forty-day retreat.

100 Although this was his constant procedure, he altered it in my case, wanting to see me ordained sooner.[1] Whether it was because I already had to say the Office or because of my age, he chose to ordain me in the following manner. After my first year of theology, when I had already begun my second, he gave me minor orders during the Ember Days of St. Thomas, 1833.[2] During Trinity Ember Days, 1834, he ordained me to the subdiaconate. At that ceremony Jaime Balmes received the diaconate. He was first among the deacons and I was first among the subdeacons. He sang the Gospel and I the Epistle. The two of us accompanied the priest who presided over and closed the procession on ordination day.[3]

101 During the Ember Days of St. Thomas in that same year of 1834, I received the diaconate. At the ordination the bishop read those words of St. Paul in the Pontifical: "For it is not against human enemies that we have to struggle, but against the Sovereignties and the Powers who originate the darkness in this world. . . ." At that moment the Lord made me understand clearly the meaning of the demons I saw during the temptation I described in the preceding chapter.[1]

102 On the thirteenth of June, 1835, I was ordained to the priesthood, not by the bishop of Vich, who had an illness of which he was to die on July 5, but by the bishop of Solsona.[1] Before my priestly ordination I made a forty-day retreat. I

have never made a retreat so full of sufferings and trials but neither, perhaps, so replete with great graces. I realized this on the day I said my First Mass, June 21, the feast of St. Aloysius Gonzaga, a patron of the Congregation, as well as on my ordination day, the feast of St. Anthony, my own patron saint.

103 I sang my First Mass in my home town, to the great satisfaction of my relatives and the whole town. Since I had been studying moral theology during all my vacations and holidays, I knew it as well as my catechism. Thus, on St. James's Day, I passed my examinations and received faculties for preaching and for hearing confessions. On August 2, Feast of the Portiuncula, I began to hear confessions. I was in the confessional for six straight hours, from five until eleven in the morning. I gave my first sermon in September of that year, a panegyric for the feast day of the patron saint of the town. The next day I gave another sermon, on the faithful departed of the town, which won the admiration of all my fellow citizens.

104 After I had performed these functions in my home town, I returned to my studies in Vich, but because of the civil war[1] the students were unable to gather in the seminary and had to pursue their studies in private conferences. At this time, as the Ecclesiastical Governor and Vicar Capitular[2] had no one to fill the post of assistant pastor in my parish, he wanted me by all means to go there and study in conference, as I was doing in Vich, for the remainder of my training. I did so out of obedience and finished my studies, as the certificate I received from the Seminary of Vich attests:

105 "I, the undersigned, Secretary of the Conciliar Seminary of the City of Vich, certify that Father Anthony Claret, a native of Sallent in this diocese, has studied and satisfactorily completed three years of philosophy, during which he studied: first, logic, ontology, and the elements of mathematics for the school year of 1829 to 1830; second, general and special physics, for that of 1830 to 1831; third, a private course in metaphysics and ethics, for that of 1831 to 1832. Likewise he has studied and passed four years of theological studies during the school years 1832 to 1836. Finally, in the afore-

said seminary, he has successfully completed three years of moral theology, from 1836 to 1839. This may be seen in the records of matriculation and qualification, kept in my office, by anyone who applies through me.

"In witness of which I grant this certificate to the petitioner and sign and seal it with the seal of this Secretariat. Given at Vich this twenty-seventh day of August, in the year eighteen hundred thirty-nine. Augustine Alier, Secretary." (Seal).[1]

Chapter XIII

ASSISTANT PASTOR
AND ADMINISTRATOR

106 Once I had settled in the parish of St. Mary in Sallent, I was occupied both with daily studies and matters of the ministry. The pastor and I divided the work of preaching between us, alternating on the Sundays of Advent and Lent, and on Corpus Christi and other major feasts, when we preached from the pulpit at the principal High Mass. On other feast days we preached in the evening after we had finished teaching the catechism class.

After two years as assistant, my superior made me administrator since the pastor had left for political reasons and I was left alone in administering the parish.

107 I followed a regular plan of life. Every year I made a ten-day retreat, a practice I have followed ever since I joined the seminary. Every eight days I received the sacrament of reconciliation. I fasted on Thursdays and Saturdays, took the discipline on Monday, Wednesday, and Friday, and wore the cilice on Tuesday, Thursday, and Saturday.

108 Every day before leaving the house I made my mental prayer alone, since I rose so early. In the evening I was joined at meditation by my sister Mary, who is now a Tertiary,[1] and by an elderly servant, since there were just the three of us in the house. After meditation, we said the rosary together.

109 I preached on all Sundays and feast days, as the Council of Trent requires.[1] On the Sundays of Advent and Lent and on the principal feast days I preached at Mass, whereas on the remaining Sundays I preached in the evening after the catechism class, which I held every Sunday of the year without a single exception.

Besides the Sunday catechism class I also had a daily Lenten class in the church from two to three in the afternoon for girls, and one in the rectory from seven to eight at night for boys.

110 Every day I celebrated Mass very early and went to the confessional, where I stayed as long as there were penitents. Every evening I walked through the main streets of the town, especially those where there were sick people. I visited them every day to bring them the Viaticum, until they either died or got better.[1]

111 I never made any personal social calls, not even to my relatives, although there were a number of them in town. I loved and served everyone equally, rich or poor, relatives or strangers, townsmen or outsiders—and there were many of the latter because of the civil war. Day or night, winter or summer, I was quick to serve them all. I frequently visited the many houses in the outlying countryside. I worked as hard as I could and the people cooperated, made progress, and loved me for it.[1] They always showed me signs of their affection, particularly when I tried to leave for the foreign missions, as in fact I did when I went to Rome to enter the Congregation for the Propagation of the Faith, as I shall relate in Part Two.

112 And you, my God, how good you have been to me, guiding me gently along the paths that you have traced for me! As the parish was not my final goal, I felt a deep desire to leave it and go to the missions in order to save souls, even if it meant undergoing a thousand labors and even death.[1]

NOTES TO PART ONE

Author's Note

1.1 Father Joseph Xifré (1817–99) was a cofounder of the Congregation of Missionary Sons of the Immaculate Heart of Mary and its third Superior General (1858–99). He was also the Saint's spiritual director, and in virtue of both positions of authority he first requested and later (1861) commanded him to write the *Autobiography*.

1.2 Some of the Saint's expressions might seem to contradict this note of humility. During the informative process for beatification, his confessor, Fr. Carmelo Sala, remarked, "Whoever knew the Servant of God as I knew him could easily see, upon reading these notes of his (the *Autobiography*), that he leaves unsaid far more than he reports. The reason for this is doubtless that in writing as he did he could fulfill the precept imposed on him by obedience and yet not jeopardize his deep humility" (*Informative Process,* Tarragona, session 8, a, 134).

Chapter I

3.1 The interpretation of a phrase in the Saint's birth record has given rise to a controversy as to whether he was born on December 23 or 24, 1807. The commoner and more probable opinion holds for December 23. (Cf. *Autob.,* par. 3, note 1, B.A.C. edition, hereafter referred to as *Writings.*)

3.2 Sallent is located about 51 kilometers from Barcelona. During the Saint's childhood it had a population of about 2,000. There were many family-operated textile works in the vicinity. Water power from the river Llobregat, which flows through the town, coupled with the drive of the hard-working inhabitants has made Sallent an expanding industrial center. Claret's episcopal coat of arms includes a souvenir of his birthplace:

"The bridge, the river and the waterfall indicate my birthplace, Sallent. My father is from one side of the river, my mother from the other, and that is the symbolism of the sun, Claret, and the moon, Clará" (*Correspondence*, Letter 145).

3.3 John Claret Xambó (December 22, 1774–April 11, 1854) was, like his ancestors, a weaver. Josephine Clará Rodoreda (September 10, 1771–October 25, 1842) came from a working-class family.

5.1 He added the name Mary to Anthony at the time of his episcopal consecration (October 6, 1850) and included her device on his shield: "The name 'Mary' indicates my spiritual origin, for she is my mother and the patroness of the Church I was baptized in. Mary saved me from the waves of the sea when I was a little boy, etc." (*Correspondence*, Letter 145).

6.1 Rose (1800–74) married Joseph Muntañola and had four children by him. She used to accompany Anthony to the shrine of Fussimanya. (Cf. par. 49.)

6.2 John. Cf. par. 80.

6.3 Joseph (1810–70), who married Manuela Solá, had a factory in Olost where his brother was an occasional guest. (Cf. par. 121.) Joseph's two daughters, Dolores and Mary, became Carmelites of Charity.

6.4 Mary (1815–94) accompanied Anthony when he was made Administrator of the parish of Sallent. When he embarked on his fully apostolic career, she entered the Carmelites of Charity, where she became Mistress of Novices. She was a witness in Vich at the Informative Process for her brother's beatification and revealed many details of the psychology and virtues of Claret as a seminarian and priest.

Chapter II

7.1 "Humanly speaking, it is interesting to note how long the child lived among strangers, for this must have had an influence on his character. That impressive humility of his, that marked sense of obedience and respect may well be the consequence of this period of displacement and lack of understanding, and of the many hours when he must have felt smaller than anyone else" (J. L. Acevedo de Blixen: *Alto camino* [Montevideo, 1955], p. 10).

9.1 St. Anthony Mary Claret underlined a passage in his personal copy of the *Life of St. Teresa* of Avila where she, at the same age, used to repeat *"por siempre, por siempre."* Nevertheless the effect on her was personal, whereas the effect on Anthony was apostolic—for others. His first biographer was quite right in saying that Claret "was an apostle before he was a man" (F. Aguilar, *Life,* p. 15).

13.1 The reason is, of course, their lack of faith. To live a life like Claret's, consumed by zeal, requires a special movement of the Holy Spirit.

15.1 "I used to think frequently on eternity and it made an even greater impression on me then than it does now" (Claret, *Résumé, Collected Writings,* vol. 7, p. 446).

16.1 In the mature years of his apostolic life, Claret reveals the motives for his zeal according to a more objective scheme, in which the glory of God and love for the Father take precedence over the desire for his neighbor's happiness. (Cf. pars. 203 ff.)

Chapter III

18.1 "God gave Anthony Mary Claret the nature that best suited his apostolic mission: practical intelligence dominating the speculative; extraordinary willpower; optimism and faith in his own initiatives; ease in adapting to circumstances; balance and dynamism" (J. Puigdesens, *The Spirit . . .,* pp. 405, 145).

19.1 Manresa was three hours from Sallent by railroad; Calders, six. Manresa was taken and burnt by the French in 1810 and 1811. In 1812 they returned, and the Saint, who was a little more than four years old at the time, refers to this attack.

19.2 John Clará Reguant (1738–1814) was, at this time, seventy-four years old.

20.1 2 Sam. 2:23–24.

20.2 In the *Constitutions* of 1857, Claret counseled his younger Missionaries to go on walks with the elderly. In his *Rule for Clerics Living in Community* he says, "The young lack prudence, and the old lack drive; put them both together and each will have the advantages of the other."

Chapter IV

22.1 Pascual received his bachelor's degree from the University of Cervera and was Anthony's teacher throughout his elementary schooling. (Cf. par. 45.)

24.1 Toward the end of his life the Saint was still recommending this work to the Spanish bishops assembled in Rome for Vatican I as a suitable text for minor seminarians. (Cf. *Writings,* p. 504.)

28.1 A quarter was worth three céntimos.

29.1 The Saint's mother died in 1842, when he was 35 years old.

Chapter V

30.1 The distinguished visitor was probably the Archbishop of Palmyra and Abbé of la Granja, Bishop Félix Amat, who had retired in Sallent, together with his sister, the mother of His Excellency, Torres Amat. Bishop Félix conferred the sacrament of Confirmation on Anthony on December 12, 1814.

30.2 Anthony attended only one course, and perhaps not a complete one, because his teacher died and the Latin school closed in 1819. (Cf. Solá, *History of Sallent,* pp. 323-24.)

31.1 His first job in the little family factory was tending the spinning jenny, loading the bobbins that had to be fed into the shuttles of the looms. (*Apostolic Process,* Vich, session 69.)

35.1 This spirit of kindness "that the Lord had granted me" (par. 34) stood him in good stead throughout his apostolate. He remarks later, "Meekness is a sign of vocation to the ministry of the apostolic missionary" (Cf. par. 374).

Chapter VI

37.1 Devotion to the Eucharist was a characteristic of his spirituality throughout his life. It is included in the symbolism of his episcopal coat of arms: "The Host that is pictured in Mary's heart signifies both her being the Mother of God and the faith and devotion I wish to have towards the Blessed Sacrament" (*Correspondence,* Letter 145).

37.2 *The Courtesy of Jesus in the Blessed Sacrament toward Men, and Their Ingratitude toward Jesus in the Blessed Sacrament.* Written in Tuscan and Portuguese by Fr. John Joseph of St. Teresa, Discalced Carmelite. Translated into Castilian by Iñigo Rosende, Priest, Barcelona,

1766. The book is divided into two parts. The first treats of fourteen "courtesies" of Jesus in the Blessed Sacrament. The second treats of ten "ingratitudes" of men. It ends with four colloquies, for before and after communion. Its style is affective: "The author has provided sustenance for the heart alone and not for curiosity" (Prologue).

40.1 Although the Saint's desire to be a priest dates back to when he was seven years old (par. 30), he must have experienced a special call at this time: "1820, 12 years old. God called me. I offered myself to his holy will" (*Résumé, Writings,* p. 446). At the same time, Anthony found it impossible to follow his vocation because of the closing of the Latin school.

41.1 A devotional book, with a rule of life, Christian prayers, meditations, sacraments, aspirations, and a résumé of the spiritual life in the form of a dialogue between confessor and penitent. The entire book is pervaded by the spirit of St. Alphonsus Mary Liguori.

42.1 Ps. 106:1.

Chapter VII

43.1 Alphonsus Rodríguez, S.J., *Practice of Perfection* (Barcelona, 1861), vol. 1, tr. 1, chap. 12, p. 47. The Saint's personal copy.

44.1 "My parents, who are now in heaven, inspired in me a devotion to the Holy Rosary when I was still very young. They bought me a pair of beads and had me enrolled in the Confraternity of the Rosary in our parish" (*Writings,* p. 450). "Before I had reached the age of reason I knelt daily to say a part of the rosary. I took part in the "Rosary Schedule" and fulfilled it perfectly, confessing and receiving Communion and all else required by the schedule" (*Writings,* p. 429). The principal obligation of the schedule was the yearly recitation, on a predetermined day and hour, of the entire rosary. The Saint's assigned day was June 29 (par. 94).

48.1 "He prayed to the Virgin as warmly and trustingly as one can on earth, because he was thoroughly persuaded that Mary, who is body and soul in heaven, heard him from the image he prayed before" (*Writings,* p. 429).

50.1 "I was nearly always in the presence of God and my desires were to serve and love Him. I had more of an interior life then than now" (*Writings,* p. 446).

Chapter VIII

56.1 When *The Catechism Explained* was being printed, he wrote to the printer, Caixal, to settle some of the engraver's difficulties: "Allow me to say frankly but without boasting that when I was a layman in Barcelona, I dedicated myself, among other things, to the study of design, and on three occasions I received an award from the Board of Trade" (*Correspondence,* Letter 63).

58.1 Claret worked for a manufacturer of cotton textiles, "dels Vigatans," at 10 Carmen Street. More than 100 workers managed the 76 looms. The owner was Ignacio Prat, a native of Vich.

64.1 In Barcelona, Claret's *natural* vocation was manifested: manufacturing. He had exceptional ability, a strong natural bent, persistence, and success. But this was not God's final plan for him, and although He took him away from the looms, the spirit of *work* remained as a basic psychological trait for the rest of his life. He preferred to look on his apostolic mission as a *work,* not as a conquest. Furthermore, as he had begun working for his father, his attitude toward work was tinged with a filial feeling, which was only supernaturalized and intensified when he began working in the interests of his heavenly Father.

65.1 Matt. 13:7.

Chapter IX

66.1 This was not just a simple case of lukewarmness. In Sallent, his soul had known only one objective: that of his apostolic calling. In Barcelona, however, his natural calling to manufacturing asserted itself and divided his soul. The development of this natural vocation would have meant the smothering of his apostolic vocation.

67.1 He refers to the baroque or plateresque altarpieces (such as that of St. Mary of the Pine), of which some were burnt and others removed when the Romantic movement was rediscovering the values of the Gothic.

69.1 Fr. Francis of Paula Amigó (1793–1865) was superior of the Oratory at Barcelona.

70.1 These dangers, interpreted in the light of a lively faith, became insights into the relativity of human values—love, property, freedom, life itself—and into the dangers of a world dominated by the forces of evil.

76.1 Ps. 86:13: "Your love for me has been so great, you have rescued me from the depths of Sheol."

Chapter X

77.1 Just as Anthony had looked for the best environment when he went to Barcelona to study manufacturing, so now, when he wanted to flee the world, he looked to the environment of the Charterhouse. He has spoken elsewhere of his love of solitude. Even at the height of his apostolic activity he safeguarded the solitude of his "inner cell" and to some extent kept a certain exterior isolation. He had little contact with people outside the exercise of his ministry.

79.1 Don Francisco was commonly referred to as "the blind" because of his physical condition, but he had a great clarity of soul. A number of students from the best families attended his classes. He was a counselor as well as a teacher, and Anthony had recourse to him for some more decisive advice (par. 81). Don Francisco lived to see Anthony become a missionary and an archbishop, and he dedicated his Latin-Spanish Dictionary to him. The Saint continued to seek his advice both in writing his own books and in running the Religious Library. (*Correspondence*, Letter 62.)

Chapter XI

83.1 The trip from Sallent to Vich took about ten hours. (D.F.C., *Itinerary of Catalonia* [Barcelona, 1823], p. 52.) Vich was to become Anthony's spiritual homeland, an episcopal city with a seminary, numerous clergy, many religious houses. Bishop Corcuera had initiated a sort of spiritual golden age distinguished by martyrs, saints, and founders such as Blessed Almató, O.P., St. Joaquina de Vedruna, Fr. Coll, O.P., Fr. Bach of the Oratory, etc.

84.1 His Excellency, Bishop Paul of Jesus Corcuera (1776–1835), a native of Cadiz, canon of Sigüenza, and rector of the seminary, was elected Bishop of Vich December 21, 1824, was consecrated in Madrid April 17, 1825, and took possession of his diocese on August 15 of that year. St. Anthony Mary Claret always held him in great esteem and veneration as a model of episcopal initiative, particularly in the formation of seminarians.

84.2 Don Fortián Bres had already been the Steward of Bishops Veyán and Strauch. He received Anthony as a *famulus,* but soon ascertaining his true worth, he became his friend. Claret repaid his benefactor and friend, even to the extent of performing a miracle for him during an illness. (Cf. C. Fernández, *The Blessed,* vol. 1, pp. 174 ff.)

85.1 Father Peter Bach (1796–1866) entered the Oratory of St. Philip Neri in Vich in 1824. He was expelled in 1835 and took refuge in France and Rome. He returned to Spain to restore the Oratory at Vich, where he was superior for thirteen years. He founded an order of nuns called "dels Saits," an asylum for sick priests, and St. Joseph's College for poor seminarians. (Cf. Oratorian Fathers, *Biographical Souvenir of Fr. Peter Bach* [Vich, 1915].)

86.1 The Constitutions of the Seminary prescribed a fortnightly confession. To help them meditate, Bishop Corcuera regularly gave the seminarians copies of *The Art of Commending Oneself to God* by P. Bellati, S.J. One of Claret's favorite themes as a seminarian was the Passion, especially that moment "when after the scourging He fell to the ground, bathed in his own blood. During this meditation he always felt the most fervent emotions" (Claretian Archives, Vich, par. 627). Faithfulness in visiting the Blessed Sacrament and the Blessed Virgin required a special effort, given the rigorous climate of Vich.

87.1 Through the indiscreet spying of one of Don Fortián's maids, we know that he took the discipline at night in the attic and that he put on a crown of thorns as well. While he was scourging himself he would repeat, "Lord, you on the Cross and I in a cozy bed!" He fasted every Saturday and on the vigil of Feasts of the Blessed Virgin. (*Informative Process,* Vich, session 37.)

87.2 "This cleric (Claret, writing of himself in the third person in *The Well-Instructed Seminarian*) remembers what the Apostle said: 'In God we live and move and have our being' (Acts 8:28), and so he considers himself like a fish in the water or a bird in the air. Thus he is always in the presence of God, whom he fears as a Lord who sees him, whom he loves as a Father who gives him all good things, whom he invokes continually and whom he praises and serves without ceasing, directing everything to his greater honor and glory" (I, p. 1, sec. 1, chap. 8). As a reminder of the presence of God, Claret used to put small pebbles in his shoes. (*Informative Process,* Vich, session 37.)

88.1 The Charterhouse of Monte-Alegre was founded in 1270 near Mataró and moved to Conrería in 1415. Burnt in 1835, it has been inhabited since 1901, with the sole exception of the Spanish civil war period.

88.2 Don Ildefonso Falgás, a Carthusian in 1804, prior (1825–32), definitor (1832), Vicar General of the Spanish congregation (1833 until its dispersal in 1835).

89.1 The suffocation made him realize the extent of the illness in his chest and that he lacked sufficient health to be a Carthusian. Antonio Camps, a fellow townsman and seminarian, affirmed that Claret had repeated hemorrhages and that some vestiges of them remained until 1837. Doctors have formed several hypotheses as to the tubercular condition of Claret, the seminarian. ("El Padre Claret enfermo," in *El Correo Catalán,* May 7, 1950.)

90.1 Fr. Clotet corrected the date in the manuscript: "It was in 1832, according to the letter of the secretary of the bishop of Vich. J. Clotet, 18 November 1872." The parish archives note that Anthony began to work at Sallent in July, 1832.

94.1 Fr. Ildefonso Valiente (1802–70), Jesuit (1817).

94.2 "I believe it was in 1819 that, by the grace of God, I was admitted into the Congregation of the Perpetual Rosary. On November 11 I joined *Laus perennis.* On June 9, 1833 I professed in the Congregation of Our Lady of Sorrows. On October 6, 1833 I was enrolled as a confrere of the Holy Rosary. In 1831 I was admitted to the Congregation of St. Aloysius in the seminary at Vich. On June 4, 1834, to that of the Sacred Heart of Jesus" (*Writings,* p. 438). On November 11, 1831, Fr. Valiente, at the same time he enrolled Claret in the Confraternity of the Sacred Heart of Jesus, also enrolled him in that of the Heart of Mary, established at the Jesuit College in Manresa, an offshoot of the Primaries of St. Mary ad Pienam and of St. Eustace of Rome. (Ramos, *An Apostle of Mary,* p. 25.)

98.1 In other documents the Saint tells of the same vision in the third person: *Method for Giving Missions* (Cuba, 1857), p. 63; *Origin of the Trisagion* (Barcelona, 1856), pp. 22 ff. On various occasions he preached about it, again in the third person, but his emotional tone gave him away. (F. Aguilar, *Life,* p. 24; various witnesses at the *Informative Process,* Tarragona, session 14; *Apostolic Process,* Madrid, session 50, Vich, session 22.)

    This vision and the consequent grace of chastity were of transcendent importance in the life of the Saint. It came at a time when he was discovering in Scripture the roots of his vocation to the apostolate. He himself understood the far-reaching apostolic implications of this vision at the time of his ordination to the diaconate (par. 101), for St. Stephen was transformed from a local patron to a principle of vocational identity. (Cf. "A Student Devoted to Mary," *Writings,* p. 433.) Further-more, he experienced in his own person God's strategy of conquering the Serpent through the Woman, a strategy he was to expound doctri-nally in his "Pastoral Letter on the Immaculate Conception," and in "Egoism Overcome." From yet another standpoint, virginity in the ser-vice of the Kingdom of God is a guarantee of zeal, witness, and spiritual fruitfulness.

Chapter XII

100.1 The bishop told Dr. Bres the real reason: "Don Fortián, I want to ordain Anthony now because there is something extraordinary about him." The bishop of Tortosa, who revealed this statement in 1870, add-ed that Bishop Corcuera's discernment in the case of young seminarians was a supernatural gift. (F. Aguilar, *Life,* p. 414.)

100.2 It was the twenty-first. The ceremony took place in the Church of St. Philip Neri. Balmes was ordained subdeacon at this ceremony. (Aguilar, op. cit., p. 405.)

100.3 It was May 17, in title of his benefice, and took place in the Church of St. Justus, which was that of the seminary.

101.1 It was on the twentieth day of the month in the Church of the Presentation. Fr. Valier, a confidant of the Saint, says that Claret had a vision of the deacons, Sts. Stephen and Vincent. Fr. Blanch says, "We are inclined to believe that during his ordination to the diaconate he already received some notion that he would have to fight effectively against the demons and the forces of evil. In fact, in the prayer he said at the beginning of every mission, which contains the essence of his spirit, he alludes to this text of St. Paul (Eph. 6:12), which he trans-lates thus in *The Well-Instructed Seminarian* (vol. 2, chap. 25): 'Our struggle is not against flesh and blood or merely against men, but against....'"

102.1 Fr. John Joseph Tejada Saenz (1768–1838), a Mercedarian in 1785, professor of theology (1795), definitor general (1824), general of the order (1827), and Bishop of Solsona (1832). He worked hard for the restoration of his order after the war of independence, and for that of his diocese after the war of 1835. The ordination took place in the episcopal palace.

104.1 Upon the death of Ferdinand VII (1833), civil war broke out again between the Carlists and the Liberals and was characterized by religious persecution. Sallent enjoyed a relative calm since it was a bastion of the Liberals.

104.2 The Vicar Capitular, Don Luciano Casadevall (1785–1852), was an eminent figure of his time. Pope Gregory XVI esteemed him very highly. (M. Genis y Aguilar, *Bishop Casadevall* [Vich, 1896].)

105.1 In the declaration he made on entering the Company of Jesus, Claret gives further details of his studies: "For three years I studied philosophy from the text of Andrew Guevara. . . . For three years (and one year outside the seminary, with due permission) I studied the theology of St. Thomas. We covered the following treatises: God and His Attributes, the Angels, Human Acts, Laws, the Incarnation, and the State of the Soul After Death. I studied Moral Theology for three years privately, by the advice and with the approval of His Excellency the Vicar General and the superiors of the seminary, following the text of Fr. Larraga and the *Compendium* of St. Alphonsus Liguori" (*Writings*, p. 440).

Chapter XIII

108.1 He means a Carmelite of Charity. The old servant's name was Jaime and he was sixty years old. The house was big enough to accommodate seven, and Claret opened the available rooms for children's catechism classes. His sister Mary has informed us that the Saint slept for only two hours, although obedience required him to spend six hours in bed. His bed's only furnishing was a straw mattress. (*Informative Process*, Vich, session 38.)

109.1 *Council of Trent*, session 24, chaps. 4 and 7, *De ref.*

110.1 On entering the Jesuits, the Saint declared, "I really enjoy visiting the sick, hearing confessions, and exhorting the people, both because it never tires me and because I myself have benefited by it these last years" (*Writings*, p. 441).

111.1 He revealed the secret of winning hearts in this advice to a pastor: "You should be particularly careful in all that you say and do, to look to the good of your flock, showing them how desirous you are for their spiritual and temporal well-being, and how much you regret their trials, while trying to alleviate them. Thus you will win their esteem as a beloved father and a watchful pastor, and you will become so dear to their hearts as to merit their complete confidence. If you act otherwise, the contrary will be the case. Believe me: I know by experience" (*Advice to a Priest*, app., par. 12). General Pavía, who knew Claret at this time, declared, "His conduct was such that, young though he was, his preaching, advice, and example kept the people closely united" (C. Fernández, *The Blessed,* vol. 1, p. 102).

112.1 In the "Explanation of the Parable of the Talents" (*Advice to a Priest,* app.), he shows the difference between a missionary and a parish priest. While both have received the talent of the priesthood, the parish priest has received only the single additional talent of the parish, whereas the missionary has received the four talents of the whole world. In a letter to a missionary candidate who was being tempted to become a canon, he wrote, "Consider that being a missionary is greater than being a pastor or a canon. The dangers in these last two states are greater, and the fruits lesser, than in the missionary state" (*Correspondence,* Letter 886).

Roadway at La Granja

PART TWO

Missions

Chapter I

GOD'S CALL TO PREACH MISSIONS

113 Ever since I lost the desire to become a Carthusian—
which God had used to uproot me from worldliness—I not
only thought about becoming holy myself, but I was continuously trying to imagine what I could do to save the souls of
my neighbors. Hence I prayed continuously to Jesus and
Mary, offering myself to them for this purpose. The lives of
the saints, which we read daily at table, and my own spiritual
reading all contributed to this. But what moved and stimulat-
ed me most was reading the Holy Bible, to which I have always been very strongly attracted.[1]

114 There were passages that impressed me so deeply that
I seemed to hear a voice telling me the message I was reading.[1] There were many such passages, but the following stand
out: "You whom I brought out from the confines of the
earth and called from the ends of the world." By these words
I understood how the Lord had called me without any merit
on the part of my birthplace, my parents, or myself. "You to
whom I said, 'You are my servant, I have chosen you, not rejected you'" (Isa. 41:9).

115 "Do not be afraid, for I am with you; stop being anx-
ious and watchful, for I am your God. I give you strength, I
bring you help, I uphold you with my victorious right hand"
(ibid., 10). Here I understood how the Lord had drawn me
safely out of the narrow escapes to which I have referred in
Part One, and of the means He used to do so.

116 I understood what great enemies I would have to face
and the awful and terrifying persecutions that would arise
against me, but the Lord told me, "All those who raged
against you shall be put to shame and confusion; they who
fought against you shall be destroyed and perish.... For I,
Yahweh, your God, I am holding you by the right hand; I

tell you, 'Do not be afraid, I will help you'" (ibid., 11 and 13).[1]

117 "See, I turn you into a threshing sled, new, with doubled teeth; you shall thresh and crush the mountains and turn the hills to chaff" (ibid., 15). Through these words the Lord made me understand the effect that my preaching and the mission He had entrusted to me were to have. The "mountains" are the proud, the rationalists, and others of that sort, and the "hills" are the lustful, both of which loom above the place where all sinners pass. I shall argue with them and convince them of their sin, and hence the Lord tells me, "You shall winnow them and the wind will blow them away, the gale will scatter them. But you yourself will rejoice in Yahweh, and glory in the Holy One of Israel" (ibid., 16).

118 The Lord made me understand that I would not only have to preach to sinners but that I would also have to preach to and catechize simple farmers and villagers. Hence He said to me, "The poor and needy ask for water, and there is none, their tongue is parched with thirst. I, Yahweh, will answer them. I, the God of Israel, will not abandon them (ibid., 17). I will make rivers well up on barren heights, and fountains in the midst of valleys; turn the wilderness into a lake, and dry ground into a waterspring" (ibid., 18).[1]

119 I had the same experience on reading the prophet Ezekiel, especially chapter 3, at these words: "Son of man, I have appointed you as sentry to the House of Israel. Whenever you hear a word from me, warn them in my Name. If I say to a wicked man: You are to die, and you do not warn him; if you do not speak and warn him to renounce his evil ways and so live, then he shall die for his sin. But I will hold you responsible for his death. If, however, you do warn a wicked man and he does not renounce his wickedness and his evil ways, then he shall die for his sins, but you yourself will have saved your life" (Ezek. 3:18–19).[1]

120 In many passages of the Bible I felt the voice of God calling me to go forth and preach. The same thing happened to me while I was at prayer. Thus it was that I determined to

leave the parish[1] and go to Rome, to present myself to the Congregation for the Propagation of the Faith so that they could send me anywhere in the world.[2]

Chapter II

DEPARTURE FROM SPAIN

1 2 1 Before I could leave the parish I had to contend with a great many difficulties both on the part of church superiors and the townspeople, but with God's help I managed it. I set out for Barcelona with the intention of obtaining a visa and embarking for Rome, but in Barcelona they wouldn't grant me one and I had to turn back. I went to Olost, where a brother of mine, Joseph, had a factory. From there I traveled to la Tría de Perafita, where I met an Oratorian, Father Matavera, a man of great experience, learning, and virtue, whom I told of my voyage and the reasons for which I was undertaking it, as well as the difficulties I had encountered. The good father listened to me with great patience and charity and encouraged me to continue in my purpose. I listened to him as if he were an oracle and presently resumed my travels. Having obtained a passport for the Spanish interior, I headed for Castellar de Nuch, Tosas, Font del Picasó, and Osseja—this last town being already across the border in France.[1]

1 2 2 My itinerary took me through Castellar de Nuch, Tosas, Puerto, Font del Picasó, Osseja, Olette, Prades, Perpignan, Narbonne, Montpellier, Nimes, and Marseilles, where I sailed on the steamer *Tancrede*. I landed at Civitavecchia and finally I arrived in Rome.[1]

1 2 3 I shall now relate the principal events of my trip. I left Olost very early and made my way to the parish of Castellar de Nuch to spend the night. The pastor gave me a kind reception, God reward him.[1] I said my prayers and went to rest, which I really needed since I had been traveling on foot all day long through fairly deserted places. Very early next day I celebrated Mass and pushed on to Tosas. Here I learned that there was a band of robbers around Puerto, so I stayed on

until I heard that they had left. I began the climb toward Puerto, and just before I cleared the hilltop of Font del Picasó, a man emerged and pointing his rifle at me shouted "Halt!" He came up and told me I'd have to accompany him to his chief, the leader of a group of ten armed brigands. The chief asked me a number of questions, which I answered in detail. He asked me if I had a pass. I said I did, handed it over to him, and he returned it to me. He asked me why I hadn't gone through Puigcerdá. I told him it didn't really matter to me whether I went through Puigcerdá or any other way, since a person with the right papers can go any way he pleases. I could see that I was embarrassing them.

1 24 I had noticed that off to one side a large group of people were being held prisoner, and at a signal all started marching, while the armed men were still talking with me. Finally the chief told me that they'd have to take me with them to Puigcerdá to show me to the governor. I told them that I had nothing to fear from the governor, but that they might, for arresting someone with the proper legal papers. They formed ranks and started marching toward Puigcerdá. They were walking briskly, and I began to slow down gradually. Seeing that this didn't seem to bother them, I began to think, "If they'd wanted to take you prisoner, they'd have put you at the head or in the middle of the column, but they've let you stay to the rear. This means you'd better go quickly." So, without a word, I turned around and started heading for France. After I had gone several paces, the same man who had taken me prisoner turned around and caught sight of me leaving. He shouted after me and came running. When he caught up with me, he said in a low voice, "Don't tell anyone about this." I told him, "God go with all of you!"

1 25 How many thanks I owe the Lord for freeing me and those people who had been taken prisoner! I must also add, for the glory of God, that a few days earlier a young ordinand and I had agreed on traveling to Rome together. The day we had agreed on for our departure came, and he didn't show up. He sent me a message not to wait for him because he couldn't go with me. When I heard this, I walked on by myself and met with the adventure I have just related. My friend left a

few days later, and passing through the same place was taken by that same band of thieves. They stole all his money and, to search him the better, made him strip and even took the shirt off his back, as he told me when we met at the port of Marseilles. Yes, how many thanks I owe God. My Father, may you be blessed for the great providence and care you have always shown me wherever I have been.

Chapter III

EVENTS OF MY JOURNEY THROUGH FRANCE

126 On the evening of that same Saturday when our Lord and the Blessed Virgin had freed me from the thieves, I entered the first city inside France, Osseja, where I had a warm welcome. As I was carrying a pass for the interior of Spain, they took it and gave me a refugee's pass. With this pass in hand I resumed my trip through the town of Olette. The people there insisted that I stay, but my mind was set on going to Rome. From Olette I passed on to Prades and there again I met people who received me with all charity. Next I went to Perpignan, where they exchanged my pass for one to Rome. I was also welcomed there by people I had never seen or known before. I passed through Montpellier, Nimes, and other towns, and just on the merits of my pass, without any further recommendation, I met unknown people everywhere who seemed to be waiting just for me! Blessed be God's Providence for all his creatures and especially for me!

127 As I was nearing Marseilles a person joined me on the road. He took me to a house where I was very well lodged for the five days I had to wait for my boat in Marseilles. The next day as I was leaving the house to go to the Spanish Consulate —I was legally obliged to go there to get my passport stamped —I asked the first person I met on the street to tell me where the consul lived. This same gentleman not only told me the name of the street but was kind enough to accompany me there. He acted as spokesman for me and I was well taken care of. Afterwards he accompanied me to my lodgings. Dur-

ing the whole five days, in the morning and the evening, he came to my apartment and took me on a guided tour of the churches, the cemetery, and all of the most beautiful religious sites in that town. Never once did he so much as mention worldly places or things to me.

128   Finally the hour for my sailing arrived. It was one o'clock in the afternoon. Shortly before this, the gentleman came to my room, took my little bundle of things, and steadfastly insisted on carrying it. And so we went, the two of us, to the port and said our farewells at shipside. All five days he had been so courteous, attentive, friendly, and preoccupied with my welfare that it seemed to me some great lord had sent him to look after me with all care. He seemed more like an angel than a man—modest, happy, and at the same time, serious. He was so religious and devout, always taking me to churches, which pleased me greatly. He never suggested entering a café or anything of that sort, nor did I ever see him eat or drink because at mealtime he would leave me and come back later.[1]

Chapter IV

EVENTS ABOARD SHIP

129   At one in the afternoon we sailed. I had said vespers and compline earlier, so as not to be praying distractedly during all those maneuvers that have to be done during the first few hours at sea, and also just in case I might get seasick and not be able to pray. On reaching the boat, where people of all nationalities were gathered for that passage, I heard a group speaking Castilian. This cheered me up and I asked, "Are you Spaniards?" They answered yes, that they were Benedictine monks who had left Navarre because of the action of General Maroto[1] and were on their way to Rome. They told me of the sufferings and trials they had undergone and of their present miserable predicament. They also mentioned that there was another Spaniard on board, a Catalan, who was in very bad shape, having been robbed while crossing the harbor. Sure enough, it was the same man who was to have accompanied me and had not kept his word. When I saw him, he really

was reduced to misery and I did what I could to console him. We spent the afternoon and evening in these conversations.

130 Since my voyage to Rome was not intended as a pleasure trip but one in which to work and suffer for Jesus Christ, I felt that I ought to look for the humblest and poorest place aboard so as to have a better chance of suffering. With this in mind, I bought a ticket for standing-room on the deck near the bow, which was the poorest and cheapest passage. After I had gone off by myself to say my rosary and other devotions, I looked for a place where I could rest a bit and could find nothing more suitable than a pile of coiled rope, which I sat on, resting my head on an artillery piece in the battery on one side of the ship.

131 In this position, I meditated on how Jesus might have rested when he set out in the boat with his disciples. It turned out to be an ideal meditation, for the Lord even chose to add something of a tempest to it. I was just about to doze off when such a storm arose that we were shipping water. I sat motionless on my pile of rope and pulled my cloak over my head. I had a little bundle of provisions and my hat in my lap, and I pressed them close to my body, leaning my head forward a bit so that the water from the waves that were crashing over the boat could run off. When I heard a wave striking I would bow my head, brace my back to it, and the water would come rushing over me.

132 Thus I passed the whole night until the dawn came and with it a rain that stilled the tempest. First I had been drenched with seawater and now I was being drenched with sweet rainwater. My entire luggage consisted of a shirt, a pair of socks, a handkerchief, a folding razor, a comb, my breviary, and a very small edition of the Bible. Since deck passengers were given nothing to eat, they had to carry their own provisions for the trip. Knowing this before I left Marseilles, I had bought my provisions, which consisted of a pound-loaf of bread and a piece of cheese. These were all my provisions for the five days from Marseilles to Civitavecchia—stops, storms, and all. The storm had been so strong that a great deal of water had washed over me. My cloak was drenched, and the

bread and cheese were soggy, but I had to eat them as they were. Although they were quite salty I was so hungry that they tasted very good to me.

133 On our second day out, after the storm had calmed and the rain stopped, I took out my breviary and said Matins and the little hours. When I had finished my prayers, an English gentleman walked over. He said that he was a Catholic and liked priests. After we had chatted awhile he went to his cabin, and in a short time I saw him coming toward me with some silver coins on a tray. When I saw him, I thought, "What are you going to do? Will you accept the money or not?" I said to myself, "You don't need it, but those poor Spaniards do; so take it and give it to them." And that is just what I did. I accepted it, thanked the man, and went to divide it among those poor people, who went at once to the kitchen or refreshment counter to buy whatever food they needed.

134 Other passengers did the same. They gave me money and I distributed it to the others, not keeping so much as a penny for myself although it had been intended for me. I didn't take a mouthful of the food they had bought; I was content with my water-soaked bread. The Englishman was very edified when he saw how poor and detached I was and how the others were eating food that they had bought with the money I'd given them, while I ate none of it. He told me that he was getting off at Leghorn and traveling overland to Rome. He gave me a card on which he had written his name and the address of the palazzo in which he would be staying and told me to come and see him and he would give me whatever I needed.

135 This whole adventure confirmed what I had already believed: that the best and most effective means to edify and move people is good example, poverty, detachment, fasting, mortification, and self-denial. Since this English gentleman was traveling in Oriental luxury, with his coach, servants, birds, and dogs aboard, one might imagine that my appearance would move him to contempt. But the sight of a priest who was poor, detached, and mortified moved him so deeply that he couldn't do enough for me. And not only he but all

the passengers showed me great respect and veneration. Perhaps if they had seen me rubbing elbows with them at table, and ordering rich and elegant dishes, they would have criticized and looked down on me as I often saw them do with others. Virtue, it would seem, is so necessary for a priest that even the wicked want us to be good.

136 After five days at sea we landed at Civitavecchia and headed for Rome, where we arrived without incident, through God's goodness and mercy.[1] How good you are, my Father. Let me serve you always with fidelity and love. Give me your constant grace to know what pleases you and the will power to put it into effect. My Lord and Father, I want nothing more than to know your holy will, so that I may do it; nothing more than to love you with all my heart and serve you with all fidelity. My Mother—Mother of Fair Love—help me!

Chapter V

ARRIVAL IN ROME AND ENTERING THE JESUIT NOVITIATE

137 It must have been about ten in the morning when we arrived in Rome. The religious went to a house of their order and we parted company. I and the Catalan ordinand went to the nearest house to ask where any Catalan seminarians might be staying. We approached the entrance of the Carmelite priory, the Transpontina,[1] and asked the brother porter whether there was a Spanish religious in the house. He told us that indeed the head priest, Father Comas, was a Catalan.[2] We went to his cell and were welcomed. We asked him whether he knew of a place where there were any Catalan ordinands. He told us that there were some at San Basilio, and he was charitable and kind enough to accompany us there despite the fact that the Transpontina is about an hour's distance from San Basilio.[3]

138 The Catalan ordinands received us kindly although they had never seen or heard of us before. I began immediately to apply myself to the task for which I had made my journey.

The only letter of recommendation I had was addressed to His Excellency, Bishop Vilardell, a Catalan, who had recently been consecrated bishop of Lebanon and had just left for his new post when I arrived in Rome.[1] I then applied to the Cardinal Prefect of the *Propaganda Fide,*[2] but he had just left for a stay in the country and they told me that he would be gone for the whole month of October. I believed that this was providential since it gave me time to make the retreat I had always made since my student days but had been unable to make this year because of my trip.

139 With this in mind, I went to visit one of the fathers of the professed house of the Company of Jesus.[1] He praised my idea of making the exercises and gave me a copy of St. Ignatius' Book of Exercises, which I was to follow in making them. After some advice that he thought I needed, I began the Exercises. On the days he appointed, I gave him an account of my spirit, and during the closing days he remarked, "Since God our Lord is calling you to the foreign missions, it would be better for you to join the Company of Jesus because it would be the means whereby you could both be sent and accompanied by others. For it is a very dangerous business going it alone." I answered, "As for me, I know well enough that it would be better, but what could I do that the Company would admit me?"

140 I had formed such a high and overblown opinion of the Company that I would never have dreamed of their admitting me. I thought of all those fathers as giants of virtue and learning and of myself as a pigmy in both—and so I told the priest who was directing me. But he encouraged me and told me that he would write a memorandum to the Father General, who lived in that same professed house.[1]

141 He did as he said, and on the day after he had received the request, the General asked to see me. I went, and as I arrived at his door, the Father Provincial was leaving.[1] The General spoke to me for some time and then said, "That father who was leaving as you entered was the Father Provincial, and he lives at Sant' Andrea de Monte Cavallo. Go there and tell him that I'm sending you, and that whatever he may do

for you I will consider a favor. I went there directly, was very well received, and on November 2 was already living in the novitiate, so that I found myself a Jesuit overnight.[2] When I contemplated myself dressed in the holy habit of the Company, I could hardly believe my eyes; it all seemed a dream, an enchantment.

142 As I had just finished making the Exercises, I was full of fervor. With all eagerness I was bent on aspiring to perfection. And since I saw so many good things in the novitiate, everything attracted my attention. I liked everything and it was engraved on my heart. I had something to learn from everyone, and in truth I learned it, with the help of God's grace. I was deeply embarrassed at seeing everyone else so advanced in virtue and myself so backward. I was most embarrassed and ashamed on the Vigil of the Immaculate Conception, during the reading of the list of good works performed in preparation for the feast, as a homage to the Blessed Virgin Mary.

143 Whenever a feast of our Lord, the Blessed Virgin, or a special saint was drawing near, the novitiate followed this custom: Each of the novices, with the permission of his spiritual director, proposed to practice a virtue which he was inclined toward or needed. Each would perform acts of the virtue in question and note down carefully what he did and how he did it. This continued until the eve of the feast, when the list was closed and the virtues practiced were written in the form of a letter and posted in the box on the rector's door.[1] Then one of the rector's assistants collected the lists and made a master list of them, like a litany, and this was read at night when all were gathered in chapel.

144 This list began as follows: Virtues which the fathers and brothers of this house have practiced in honor of the Blessed Virgin Mary, in preparation for the feast of her Immaculate Conception. Someone has performed so many acts of such a virtue, in such a manner—and thus it went through the whole catalog. Of all the practices I observed in that holy house, this seemed to me to be one of the best and the one that pleased and profited me the most. As the name of the one who practiced the virtue was not revealed, there was no danger of any-

one becoming vain; and we all benefited from learning how a virtue had been practiced so that we could do something similar on another occasion. How often I used to tell myself, "How well this virtue would suit you! You must put it into practice." And I would, with the help of God's grace.

145 The Jesuit rule calls for no mandatory mortifications, but there is perhaps no other order in which they are more practiced. Some mortifications are seen, others are not, but they must all be done with the permission of the director. On Fridays everyone fasted, and the same almost held true for Saturdays, because that evening when each was served an egg with his salad, nobody took it. Most left their dessert untouched, or else took very little. They also left a great part of the other dishes untouched, and always the ones they liked best. I observed that they all ate very little any day, and that the stoutest fathers were always the ones who ate the least.

146 There was a priest there called the spiritual father of the house,[1] who nearly every day, except Sunday, took nothing but bread and water, and did that on his knees, at a low table in the middle of the refectory. He stayed in this posture throughout the Community's dinner or supper. Anyone who saw that venerable man on his knees in front of the little table set with bread and water felt terribly ashamed to be sitting comfortably and enjoying a meal.

147 There was also a father called the collector or corporal.[1] On Wednesdays, Fridays, Saturdays, and the vigils of important feasts, he would pass around a little blank notebook in which each person would briefly jot down the thing he wanted to do: e.g., Father or Brother So-and-so would like to eat off the floor, say grace before and after meals with arms outstretched in the form of a cross, serve at tables, wash dishes, etc.

All of this was done without breaking silence, in the following manner. When the time came, the collector would make his rounds, knock at each door, open it, and wait outside. The father inside would come to the door, take the notebook back to his table, write on a single line what he wanted to do, and return the notebook to the collector. Thus it was passed around to everyone. Then it was brought to the rector, who would say, "X and Y, yes; the rest, no." The collector would make the rounds again, knocking at and opening the door, and letting each one know, by a movement of his head, whether the answer was yes or no.

148 Besides these external and public mortifications, there were others of a more private character, such as wearing the cilice, small arm-chains, hairshirts; taking the discipline, etc.; cleaning chamberpots, lavatories, sooty lamps, etc. But to do any of these things, permission was always required.

149 Some of the mortifications assigned were unasked for and hardly looked like mortifications. I will mention a few that I experienced. I have never liked playing games, and for that reason they made me play every Thursday when we went to a park. I begged the rector, in all simplicity, to be good enough to let me study or pray instead. He answered me roundly that I should play and play well. I applied myself so thoroughly to playing that I won all the games.

150 Once I noticed that one of the priests of the house had to celebrate Mass very late on feast days, and I realized that having to wait that long fasting must have been very inconvenient for him, although he never complained about it. Out of compassion for him I went to the Superior and told him that, if it was his good will and pleasure, I would say a late Mass because a late breakfast didn't bother me. Thus, the other priest could say Mass earlier at my assigned time, which was much easier. The Superior said he would see, and the result was that from then on I was scheduled to say Mass even earlier.

151 I have already mentioned that when I left for Rome the only books I brought with me were a one-volume breviary and a small-print edition of the Bible, which I could read every day, since I have always been a great reader of the Scriptures. When I got to the novitiate, they assigned me a room supplied with all the books I would need except the Bible, which I was so attached to. When they came to get my regular clothing they also took the Bible I had brought. I asked for it and was told, "Very well." But the fact is that

I never saw it again until the day I had to leave because of sickness; only then was it returned to me.[1]

152 The Lord did me a great favor in bringing me to Rome and introducing me for however short a time to those virtuous fathers and brothers. I only wish that I had profited more by it. But if I haven't, my neighbor has. It was there that I learned how to give the Spiritual Exercises of St. Ignatius, and methods for preaching, catechizing, hearing confessions usefully and effectively, as well as many other things that have stood me in good stead.[1] Blessed be you, my God, for being so good and merciful to me. Make me love and serve you with all fervor; make all creatures love and serve you. All you creatures, love and serve your God. Taste and see by experience how sweet it is to love and serve your God. My God, my only good!

Chapter VI

PRAYERS I WROTE DURING THE NOVITIATE

153 Since during our recreations we talked of nothing but virtues, devotion to Mary, and means for winning souls for heaven, the flame of zeal for the greater glory of God and the salvation of souls took fire in my heart and totally consumed me.

I offered my all to God without reserve. I was continuously thinking and planning what I could do for the good of my neighbor, and since the time had not yet come for me to set out on my work, I busied myself with prayer. Among others, I composed the following two prayers:[1]

154 *First Prayer.* "O Mary most holy, conceived without original sin, Virgin Mother of the Son of the Living God, Queen and Empress of heaven and earth: Since you are the Mother of pity and mercy, deign to turn your eyes toward an unhappy exile in this vale of tears, anguish, and misery who, though unworthy, has the great happiness of being your son. O Mother mine, how much I love and esteem you, and

firmly trust that you will grant me perseverance in your holy service and grace until death.

155 "I beseech and beg you, my Mother, to destroy at the proper time the heresies that devour the flock of your most holy Son. Remember, O most gracious Virgin, that you have the power to end them all. Do so out of charity for that great love you bear toward Jesus Christ your Son. Look upon the souls redeemed through the infinite price of Jesus' Blood, who are falling once more under the power of the demon, and neglecting your Son and you.

156 "What is lacking then, my Mother? Would you perhaps avail yourself of some instrument with which to remedy so great an evil? Here is one who however vile and contemptible he knows himself to be, is yet assured that he will serve the better for this end, since your power will shine forth all the brighter, and all will see that it is you who are at work, not I. Come now, loving Mother, let us lose no time. Here I am: dispose of me as you will, for you know that I am wholly yours. I trust that you will do this out of your great kindness, pity, and mercy, and I ask you this through the love you bear for the Father, Son, and Holy Spirit. Amen."

157 *Second Prayer.* "O Immaculate Virgin and Mother of God, Queen and Mistress of grace: Deign out of charity to cast your glance upon this lost world. Consider how all have abandoned the way that your most holy Son deigned to teach them. His holy laws have been forgotten and so much has been perverted that one might well say: *non est qui faciat bonum, non est usque ad unum.*[1] The virtue of faith has been extinguished in them, so that it can scarcely be found upon the earth. Ah, once this godly light goes out, all is dark and shadowy, and men cannot see where they are falling. And yet they rush with headlong strides along the path that leads them to eternal loss.

158 "And would you, my Mother, have me, who am a brother of these luckless ones, look on indifferently at their utter ruin? Ah, no! Neither the love that I bear God, nor that I bear my neighbor, could stand it. For how can I say that I

love God if, seeing my neighbor in this plight, I do not come to his rescue? How can I have charity if, knowing that thieves and murderers are set to rob and kill all those who pass along a road, I do not warn all those who are heading there? How can I have charity if, knowing that ravenous wolves are devouring my Master's flock, I hold my peace? How can I have charity if I am silent at the theft of those most precious jewels that cost the lifeblood of a God, or at the sight of people setting fire to the house and heritage of my most loving Father?

159 "Ah, my Mother, I cannot still my voice on such occasions. No, I shall not be silent, even if I knew it meant that I should be cut to pieces. I shall shout, cry out, lift up my voice to heaven and earth to remedy so great an evil. I shall not be silent, and when my voice is hoarse or mute from all my crying I shall lift up my hands to heaven, make my hair stand on end, and stamp my feet upon the ground to make up for my lack of speech.

160 "Therefore, my Mother, I shall start this moment to speak and cry out. I come to you, yes, to you, Mother of Mercy. Deign to offer me your aid in my great need. Never tell me that you cannot, for I know that in the order of God's grace you are all-powerful. Grant all men, I beseech you, the grace of conversion, for without it we can do nothing; then send me and you shall see how they will be converted. I know that you will give this grace to all who truly seek it. Yet even if they do not seek it it is only because they fail to see how much they need it, and because, being so near death, they cannot tell what remedy is best for them. It is this, above all, that moves me to even deeper compassion.

161 "Hence I, the first and foremost sinner, plead for all the rest, and offer myself as an instrument for their conversion. Although I am bereft of every natural talent for this end, it matters not, *mitte me*: thus it will be all the better seen that *gratia Dei sum id quod sum,* by God's grace I am what I am. Perhaps you will say that they, sick madmen that they are, will not listen to the one who wishes to heal them and would rather despise me and persecute me to the death. It matters not. *Mitte me,* send me, because *cupio esse anathema pro*

fratribus meis, I would desire to be anathema for my brothers. Or perhaps you will say that I will not be able to support the many hazards of cold, heat, rain, nakedness, hunger, thirst, and all the rest. Doubtless, of my own I can bear nothing, but I trust in you and say: *omnia possum in ea quae me confortat,* I can do all things in her who strengthens me.

162 "O Mary, my Mother and my hope, consolation of my soul and object of my love, consider all the graces for which I have asked you in the past, all of which you have granted me. Shall I find that this ever-flowing stream has only now gone dry? No, no, it has never yet been heard, nor shall it ever be, that anyone who turns devotedly to you has ever yet been turned away. My Lady, you can see that all these things I ask you are for the greater glory of God and you, and for the good of souls. Hence I hope to obtain them and I know I shall obtain them. That you may grant this all the sooner, I do not offer you my merits, for I have none to offer. Rather I shall say that, since you are the Daughter of the Eternal Father, Mother of the Son of God, and Spouse of the Holy Spirit, it is most becoming that you be filled with zeal for the honor of the Blessed Trinity, whose loving image man's soul is—an image, furthermore, that has been washed in the blood of God made man.

163 "Since both Jesus and you have done so much to enrich this image, will you now abandon it? True, it has deserved to be abandoned, but I ask you out of love not to forsake it. I beg you by all that is most holy in heaven and on earth; I beg you by Him who, despite my unworthiness is a daily Guest beneath my roof, to whom I speak as to a friend, who obeys my voice and comes down from heaven at my word. This is that same God who preserved you from original sin, who became incarnate in your womb, who crowned you with glory in heaven and made you Advocate of sinners. And this same Being, although He is God, listens to me and obeys me every day. Listen to me then, at least this once, and deign to grant me the grace I ask of you. I am confident that you will do this, because you are my Mother, my relief, my consolation, my strength and my all, after Jesus. Long live Jesus and Mary! Amen."

164 *Aspiration.* "O Jesus and Mary, the love I bear you makes me long to be joined with you forever in heaven; but this same love is so intense that it causes me to ask for a long life, in which to win souls for heaven. O Love, O Love, O Love!"

These two prayers, as I have said, I wrote while I was in the novitiate in Rome. The Father Minister read them and was pleased with them.[1] May it all be for the glory of God and the salvation of souls.

Chapter VII

DEPARTURE FROM ROME AND ARRIVAL IN SPAIN

165 I was very happy in the novitiate where I was always occupied with our classes in catechizing, preaching, and hearing confessions. Moreover, on Fridays we always went to the hospital of San Giacomo[1] to hear the confessions of the sick, and on Saturdays to preach in the prison. I entered the novitiate on November 2, 1839, All Souls' Day, and four months later, on February 2, 1840, Feast of the Purification of Mary, we began the Spiritual Exercises of St. Ignatius, which lasted for a month. I began them with great joy and with a firm desire to derive much profit from them.

166 I was making great progress when suddenly one day I felt such a stabbing pain in my right leg that I couldn't walk. I had to go to the infirmary. Appropriate remedies relieved the pain somewhat but not totally, and it was feared that I might be permanently lame.[1] When the rector saw my condition, he said, "What is happening to you is not natural. You have always been so content, happy, and healthy, and just now, during these days especially, this has happened. It makes me think that the Lord wants you for something else." He added, "If it's all right with you, the General should be consulted because he is so good and has so much godly knowledge. We shall consult him." I replied that the plan seemed a good one, and so I went to see the General. He listened to me attentively, and after he had heard my account of the whole

matter he told me, without faltering for an instant, "It is God's will that you go quickly, quickly to Spain. Have no fear. Courage!"

167 In the face of this forthright decision, I had no choice other than to return to Spain. In time I came to see that the Father General had been inspired when he spoke to me. In a letter that he wrote me later, he said, "God brought you to the Company not that you should remain in it, but that you might learn in it how to win souls for heaven."[1] In mid-March I left Rome for Catalonia.[2] The fathers of the Company wanted me to settle in the city of Manresa, while the Rev. Father Fermin de Alcaraz wanted me to go to Berga, where missions were being held.[3] Nevertheless, in view of my condition, I was given complete freedom to decide. I placed myself under observation in Olost. From Olost I went to Vich, where my superior told me to go to neither of the places that had been suggested but to Viladrau, and to this end I was named regent of the parish and left for Viladrau on May 13. Here I successfully recovered from my illness.

168 In the parish of Viladrau there was an elderly and disabled pastor and an assistant pastor from the town itself. The assistant[1] was in charge of all the temporalities (from which he gave me enough for my bare subsistence), while I cared for the spiritual needs of the people. Nevertheless, since he was an assistant pastor, he was responsible for their spiritual needs as well, in my absence. This was very convenient because it allowed me to start out on missions from there.

169 How admirable God's Providence is! He freed me from going to Berga, where my mere presence would have put me in danger because the royalists were in power there. Blessed be God, who made everything work together for his greater glory and the salvation of souls.

Chapter VIII

BEGINNING OF THE MISSIONS
AND HEALING THE SICK

170 After I had settled in the parish of Viladrau as regent, I did my best to care for the spiritual welfare of the people. On Sundays and feast days I explained the Gospel in the morning at the main Mass, and in the evening I taught catechism to children and adults of both sexes. I visited the sick daily. As Viladrau was not a fortified town, the opposing political factions seized control of it from time to time. Because doctors are usually public figures of some note, they were so harassed by both factions that they were eventually forced to move, and so the town was left without a single doctor.

171 Thus I had to become not only the spiritual but also the bodily physician of the people, on the basis of my general knowledge and consultation of the medical books I procured.[1] When some doubtful case arose, I would look it up in my books, and the Lord so blessed my remedies that none of those I visited died. And so the word got around that I was healing people, and the sick came in from various places around.

172 I started giving missions in the parish of Viladrau on August 15, 1840, while I was conducting a novena in honor of the Assumption of the Blessed Virgin Mary. Next I gave another in the parish of Espinelvas, an hour away from Viladrau. Then I went to the parish of Seva. The mission here was more sensational than the others. A large number of people underwent conversion and made general confessions. This was the start of my fame as a missionary.

173 During November I held an All Souls' novena in Igualada and Santa Colona de Queralt, and it was enthusiastically received. Thus I remained in Viladrau for eight months, going out on missions and returning. But I couldn't continue in this way any longer. As I have said, when I was in town, I visited the sick daily and they all got better. The only time any sick

person died was while I was away. When I returned from a mission, the relatives of the deceased would come up to me saying, as Martha and Mary did to our Savior, *"Domine, si fuisses hic, frater meus non fuisset mortuus,"*[1] and because, unlike Jesus, I couldn't raise them from the dead, they stayed dead. I was terribly upset at seeing the tears of the people and listening to all the reasons they gave why I shouldn't leave the parish to go preaching.

174 This forced me to ask my superior to relieve me of my duty as regent and free me from any parish obligations. I asked him to let me know his decision soon so that I could go and preach missions wherever he chose. This he did, and I left Viladrau with deep feelings on the part of the people for the cures our Lord had worked through me, which I know were more than merely natural. I didn't offer to heal people for money or any other kind of gain, for I never accepted anything for what I did; I did it only because of the people's need, out of charity.

175 During the summer several children became sick, and after I had given them only one application of a certain remedy they all got well. At one o'clock one morning, I visited a young man twenty-five years old who was unconscious and on the point of dying. I applied a simple remedy, and he recovered his senses and in two days was completely cured.

176 . . . . [1]

177 A young boy of eighteen was also cured. He was completely paralyzed, beyond remedy, and any effort on his behalf was considered useless. One day as I was walking along the street I saw him at the door of his house. I asked his mother what was wrong with him and how long he had been that way. After she had explained the case to me, I told her what to do, and in a few days I saw the boy, cured, in church, attending Mass.

178 . . . .

179 The town of Viladrau had been reduced to a state of ex-

haustion by the civil war. It had been sacked at least thirteen
times, subjected to surprise attacks from both factions, and
had suffered so many fires and deaths that, as a result of all
the horror, sadness and disgust had taken possession of many
of the people, especially the women, who were showing
symptoms of hysteria. When they came to talk with me
about it, I had them take some plain olive oil and boil some
herbs in it. They made a kind of ointment out of this and
applied it to themselves, and all of them were cured.

180 During my stay in Viladrau all the sick of the town, as
well as those who were brought there from other places, were
cured. As word of this spread, in whatever town I went to,
people would bring me a large number of sick persons suffering from all kinds of illness. There were so many sick and so
many different illnesses, and I was so busy hearing confessions, that I didn't have time for prescribing physical remedies. I told the people, instead, that I would commend them
to God, and in the meantime I would make the sign of the
Cross over them, saying, *"Super aegros manus imponent et
bene habebunt."*[1] After I did this, they said that they were
cured.

181 I am of the opinion that these people were cured through
the faith and trust with which they came, and that our Lord
rewarded their faith with both bodily and spiritual health, for
I would also exhort them to make a good confession of all
their sins, and they did. Furthermore, I believe that the Lord
did all this not because of any merits of mine—I don't have
any—but to show the importance of the Word of God that I
was preaching. Because these people had been so long accustomed to hearing nothing but evils, blasphemies, and heresies,
our Lord God was calling their attention to His Word by
means of these bodily healings. And indeed people came in
droves, listened fervently to the Word of God, and made general confessions in their own towns, or even in others, because
often it was impossible to hear the confessions of the many
who wanted to confess.

182 My God, how good you are! You use the very weakness-
es of the body to cure those of the soul. You make use of

this miserable sinner to heal both bodies and souls. What the prophet said could clearly be seen: *Domini est salus.*[1] Yes, Lord, health was yours and you were giving it.

Chapter IX

ON HEALING THE POSSESSED, AND ON THE MANY FICTITIOUS CASES OF POSSESSION

183 Another kind of infirmity that caused me even greater trouble and took a lot of my time was the cure of those who were possessed or obsessed by the devil. When I began preaching missions, I saw a large number of people who claimed to be possessed. Their relatives would ask me to exorcise them and, since I was duly authorized, I did so. Only one in a thousand could be called a genuine case of possession. There were other causes, physical or moral, that I won't go into here.

184 Seeing that so many people had no such demons and that, besides this, they made me lose a lot of time I needed for hearing the confessions of those who had been converted through my preaching, I said to myself, "It is far more necessary for you to be casting the devil out of souls in mortal sin than it is from bodies, even when there really are demons there." I thought that even this might be a snare of the devil, so I resolved to give up exorcisms and try another approach, which was as follows.

185 Whenever people came to me claiming to be possessed, I asked them whether they really wanted to be cured and whether they believed that, by doing what I said, they would be cured. If they assured me that they did, I demanded three things of them: First, that they bear all things patiently and never lose their temper. For I had noticed that some people become hysterical as a result of their bad dispositions and temper tantrums and that patience tends to calm them down.

186 Secondly, I forbade them to drink wine or any other liquor, and I told them that this was indispensable in casting

out their sort of demon. For I had also noticed that a number of people who drank too much tried to put the blame for their condition on the devil.

187 Thirdly, I made them say seven Our Fathers and Hail Marys every day to the Blessed Virgin in honor of her Seven Sorrows. Moreover, I insisted that they make a good general confession of their whole life and receive Communion with great devotion. Whatever their trouble, they would come back after a few days to thank me and tell me that they were free and cured. I'm not saying that there are no possessed persons. There are, indeed, and I have encountered some—but very few.

188 In the course of missions I have met people, converted by the sermons, who have frankly admitted to me that they had never been possessed or even physically ill but had fabricated the whole thing for various reasons, such as to attract attention or to be coddled, pitied, helped, or a thousand other things.

189 One woman of this sort told me that everything she had done had been done with full knowledge and willful malice, but that some of the things she did were so striking and bizarre that she began to wonder about them herself. Doubtless the devil was at work with her. Not through diabolical possession, but through the malice in her heart, for she knew that in the natural course of things she couldn't do some of the things she did.

190 Another lady, who lived in a large city, told me that she was so adept at faking possession that she had been having exorcisms performed over a long period of time, during which she had deceived twenty of the wisest, most virtuous, and most zealous priests in that city.

191 These cases, and other cases of truly repentant sinners who were moved by grace to humbly confess their trickeries and diabolical fictions, taught me to move very cautiously in such matters. This is why I finally came to adopt the approach I have outlined above. My God, how many thanks I owe you for helping me understand the tricks of the devil

and of deceivers. This understanding is a gift from your divine hand. Lord, enlighten me so that I may never err in giving spiritual direction. I am well aware, Lord, that if anyone needs wisdom, all he has to do is ask you for it and you will give it to him abundantly, and you will grant it without reminding him of his unworthiness. But sometimes out of pride or laziness we neglect to ask for wisdom and so we lose it, and this happens even to those who pass for wise and eminent theologians.

Chapter X

192 **THE CARE I TOOK TO SEE THAT THE SUPERIOR SENT ME TO PREACH, SINCE I WAS WELL CONVINCED THAT TO BE EFFECTIVE, A MISSIONARY MUST BE SENT**[1]

193 In mid-January of 1841, after eight months as regent in Viladrau, where I had been ministering to the parish, leaving it from time to time to preach in various other towns to which my bishop sent me, I finally left it for good, so as to be permanently free to preach wherever he might send me, without any fixed residence.[1] My address, during the few days I stayed there, was at Vich. From this city I would set out with a list of the towns I had to preach in.

194 Other bishops often asked my own bishop to let me preach missions in their dioceses. As long as he granted their requests I would go, for it was my inflexible rule never to preach in any church or diocese except at the express command of my bishop, and this, for two weighty reasons. First, because it meant that I would be acting out of holy obedience, a virtue that is so pleasing to God that He rewards it instantly. In acting thus I was assured of doing God's will and of being sent by Him, not by my whim. Besides, I could see God's blessing in the results that were forthcoming. The second reason was one of convenience. Because there were so many demands for my services from far and near, I could satisfy them all by saying, "I'll be very happy to go if my bishop

sends me." Thus they would leave me in peace and arrange things through him, so that it was up to him to send me.

195 I had come to realize that a missionary must never thrust himself into an assignment. He should offer his services to the bishop, saying, "Here I am, send me." But he should not go until his bishop sends him, because when he is sent, it will be by God's sending. All the Old Testament prophets were sent by God. Jesus Christ himself was sent from God, and Jesus in turn sent his Apostles.

196 In the two miraculous draughts of fish—which were symbolic of the missionary apostolate—we can see the need for a mission both as to the time and to the place we should preach, if we are to catch souls.

The first catch, narrated by St. Luke (chap. 5), shows us that a mission is so necessary that without it nothing can be accomplished. The evangelist tells us that Jesus ordered his Apostles, "Lower your nets for a catch." Simon answered, "Master, we have toiled all night long and have caught nothing; but if you say so, I will lower the nets." Upon doing this they caught such a great number of fish that their nets were at the breaking point. They signaled to their mates in the other boat to come and help them. St. Peter was amazed and Jesus told him, "Do not be afraid. From now on you will be catching men." Here we can see that the catch was a symbol not only of the Apostles' mission but also of their need to be sent and of the right moment for them to preach.

197 The second miraculous catch took place after the Resurrection of Jesus, as St. John narrates in chapter 21 of his Gospel. The Apostles had been fishing but had caught nothing. Jesus appeared to them without their recognizing Him. When He asked them whether they had anything to eat they answered, "Not a thing." Then Jesus told them, "Cast your net off to the starboard side, and you will find something." So they made a cast and took so many fish they could not haul the net in. They counted the fish, and there were a hundred fifty-three large ones. In this second catch we can see not only the need to be sent but also the need to preach at the right time, in the right place, and with the right intention if

the souls of big sinners are to be caught—and not just a hundred fifty-three but vast numbers—since 100, 50, and 3 are mystical numbers.

198 This need for being sent to a particular place by a bishop was something that God himself helped me understand from the very beginning. Thus, no matter how evil and demoralized the towns I was sent to, great fruits were always obtained, because it was God who sent me to them and prepared them and predisposed them for me. Missionaries may rest assured, then, that they should go to no town, however good, unless they go under obedience; but that under obedience they should not hesitate to go to any town, however bad. As far as any possible difficulties or persecutions are concerned, let them have no fear: God has sent them through obedience and He will take care of them.[1]

Chapter XI

THE GOAL I HAD IN MIND WHENEVER I WENT TO A TOWN TO WHICH MY SUPERIOR SENT ME

199 Whenever I went to a town, I did so without any worldly goal in mind; my only aim was to glorify God and save souls. I was often forced to remind people of this because I knew that it was the most convincing argument for good and bad alike. I would tell them:

200 You know that men nearly always do whatever it is they do for one or another of the following reasons: (1) for gain or money, (2) for pleasure, (3) for fame. I have not come to preach a mission in this town for any of these three reasons. Not for money, because I don't want a penny from anyone and I won't take one. Not for pleasure, for what pleasure could I get out of wearing myself out from early in the morning until night? If some of you have to wait your turn for three or four hours to go to confession, you get tired. But what about me? I must be there all morning and afternoon; and at night, instead of resting, I have to preach—and not for

just one day, but day after day, for weeks, months, and years. Just think about that, my brothers and sisters.

201 Maybe I do it for fame? Hardly. You must be well aware of the calumnies I'm exposed to. One person may praise me, but another makes all sorts of charges against me, as the Jews did against Jesus, speaking ill of his person, his words, and his actions until finally they seized Him, scourged Him, and put Him to death on a most painful gibbet of shame. But I tell you, with St. Paul, that I am not afraid of any of these things, nor do I esteem my life more than my soul; and I would gladly risk everything to fulfill the ministry of preaching the Gospel, which I have received from God our Lord.[1]

202 No, I repeat, I have no mere earthly aim but a far nobler one. My aim is to make God better known, loved, and served by everyone. If only I had all human hearts, with which to love God! My God, people do not know you! If they did, you would be loved far more than you are. If people only knew your wisdom, power, goodness, beauty, and all your divine attributes, they would all have become seraphim consumed with the fire of your divine love. This is my aim: to make God known, so that He may be loved and served by all.

203 Another of my aims is to prevent all the sins and offenses that are being committed against God—that same God who is loved by seraphim, served by angels, feared by powers, adored by principalities—that God who is offended by a vile earthworm, man. Be astonished at this, you heavens! If a noble knight saw an innocent damsel being outraged and in distress, he could not contain himself but would rush to her aid. How, then, can I do enough when I see God offended and outraged?

204 If you saw your father being beaten and stabbed, wouldn't you run to defend him? Wouldn't it be a crime for you to look on indifferently at your father in such a plight? Well then, wouldn't I be the greatest criminal in the world if I didn't try to prevent the outrages that men are perpetrating against God, who is my Father? My Father, I shall defend you, although it should cost me my life. I shall throw my

arms about you and with St. Augustine tell sinners: Enough of wounds; it is enough! Halt, you sinners, halt! Stop scourging my Father. You've already scourged Him enough and opened far too many wounds. If you must scourge someone, scourge me, for I deserve it; but don't mistreat and scourge my God, my Father, and my Love. O love of mine, my love!

205 I am also driven to preach without ceasing by the sight of the throngs of souls who are falling into hell—for it is of faith that all who die in mortal sin are damned. It is estimated that about eighty thousand die each day, and how many of them die in mortal sin and hence are damned? As the saying goes, *"talis vita, finis ita*—your death will be as your life has been."

206 And when I see the way people live—so many of them set in their ways and living in habitual mortal sin; not a day goes by that they don't add to the number of their sins. They sin as easily as they'd take a glass of water; they commit iniquities as if it were a joke, for a laugh. They are really tragic figures, marching on their own two feet toward hell. As Zephaniah says, "They shall walk like blind men, for they have sinned against Yahweh."[1]

207 If you saw a blind man about to fall into a pit or over a cliff, wouldn't you warn him? That's just what I'm doing and must do in conscience: warn sinners and make them see the precipice of hell that they are about to fall into. Woe is me if I don't, for they could hold me responsible for their damnation.[1]

208 Perhaps you may tell me that they are only going to insult me and that I should leave them alone and not bother about them. No, my good brethren. I can't abandon them: they are my own dear brothers and sisters. Tell me, if you had a very dear brother who was so sick that he was delirious and in his fever insulted you and said every foul thing in the world to you, would you abandon him? I'm sure you wouldn't. You'd feel all the more sorry for him and do everything you could for his recovery. Well, that's the way I feel about sinners. The poor creatures are just delirious. That makes them

all the more deserving of compassion. I can't abandon them. I have to work for their salvation and pray to God for them, saying with Jesus Christ, "Father, forgive them, for they don't know what they're doing or saying."[1]

209 When you see a condemned man on his way to the gallows, it moves you to pity. If you could do something to free him, you'd do it. Well, brothers and sisters, when I see a person in mortal sin, I see someone drawing nearer with every step to the gallows of hell. And seeing him in this unhappy state, I happen to know the way to free him: that he be converted to God, ask God's pardon, and make a good confession. Woe betide me if he doesn't.

210 Maybe you'll say that a sinner isn't interested in hell, or doesn't even believe in it. All the worse. Do you think that this will stop him from being damned? Indeed no; rather it's an even clearer sign of his fatal condemnation, as the Gospel says: "He who does not believe will be condemned."[1] Bossuet remarks[2] that this truth does not depend upon whether a person believes in it; even though he doesn't believe in hell, he'll go there if he has the misfortune of dying in mortal sin, no matter what his opinion on the subject.

211 I tell you quite frankly that whenever I see sinners, I grow restless, I cannot quiet down, I cannot be consoled, my heart goes out to them. To give you an idea of how I feel, I'll draw a comparison. If a loving mother saw her child in danger of falling from a high window or into an open fireplace, wouldn't she run and shout, "Look out, baby, you're going to fall!" Wouldn't she run up behind the child and take hold of him and pull him back if she could? My brothers and sisters, you should know that grace is stronger and braver than nature. Well then, if the natural love a mother feels for her child can make her run to him, shout at him, take hold of him, and pull him back from the brink of ruin, that is just what grace does in me.

212 Charity urges and impels me; it makes me run from town to town shouting, "Sinner, my son, look where you're heading; you're about to fall into hell. Stop! Don't take

another step!" I often ask God, as St. Catherine of Siena did: "Lord, let me stand at the gates of hell and stop anyone from entering, by telling each of them, 'Where are you going, poor fool? Turn back! Make a good confession and save your soul. Don't come here, to be lost for all eternity!'"[1]

213 Another force that drives me to preach and hear confessions is my desire to make my neighbor happy. If there is so much joy in healing the sick, freeing the prisoner, consoling the afflicted, and cheering the sad, then there is far greater joy in bringing one's neighbor to the glory of heaven. It means saving him from every evil and bringing him to the enjoyment of every good—and for all eternity. Mortals cannot understand this just now, but when they are in glory they will know the great good that was offered them and that they will have, happily, attained. Then they will sing the everlasting mercies of the Lord and bless those who have been merciful to them.

Chapter XII

HOW I WAS MOVED TO PREACH MISSIONS BY THE EXAMPLE OF THE PROPHETS, OF JESUS CHRIST, OF THE APOSTLES, FATHERS, AND OTHER SAINTS

214 Besides my unfailing love for poor sinners, another force that has driven me to work for their salvation is the example of the prophets, of Christ himself, of the Apostles, and of the many men and women saints whose lives and histories I have read, noting down some of the more salient passages for my use and profit and as a stimulus to work harder. A few of these fragments follow.[1]

215 *Isaiah,* son of Amos, of the royal house of David, was a prophet and preacher. His main object was to confront the inhabitants of Jerusalem and Israel with their infidelities and to announce the chastisement that God would visit upon them through the Assyrians and Chaldaeans, as He did, in-

deed. His brother-in-law, the impious King Manasseh, put him to death by having him sawn in half.

216 *Jeremiah* prophesied some 45 years. His main object was to exhort his people to repent, announcing to them the chastisements that the Lord would visit upon them. He was carried off to Egypt and met his death in the city of Tanis, where he was stoned to death by his fellow Jews. The principal trait of this great prophet was his tender-hearted love for his neighbor, a charity full of compassion for both their temporal and spiritual needs, a charity that never let him rest. Thus, even in the midst of the tumult of war, the confusion of a kingdom going to ruin, and the very death throes of his people in Jerusalem, he worked with constant dedication for the well-being of his fellow-citizens, thus meriting the fair name of "Lover of the brethren and of the people of Israel."

217 *Ezekiel* prophesied and preached some 20 years and had the glory of dying as a martyr for justice sake. He was killed near Babylon by the prince of his people, whom he had reproached for worshiping idols.

218 *Daniel* was endowed with incredible gifts, as one of the great prophets. Not only did he predict future events, as did the rest of the prophets, but he also specified the time when they were to occur. Out of envy he was thrown into the lions' den, but God freed him.

219 *Elijah,* the prophet, a man of fervent and powerful prayer and of great and extraordinary zeal, was persecuted to the point of death, but he was not allowed to die and was carried off in a fiery chariot.

220 Ecclesiasticus, speaking of the 12 prophets who are called *lesser* only because of the shortness of their writings, says that they gave new strength to Jacob and saved themselves through the virtue of faith.[1]

221 I am ever more deeply impressed at the thought of Jesus moving from town to town, preaching everywhere—not just in big cities, but in little villages and even to a single woman.

When he spoke to the Samaritan woman, he was tired and thirsty from traveling, and the moment was as inconvenient for him as it was for the woman.

222 From the very beginning I have been thrilled by the preaching style of Jesus, his likenesses and parables. And how He was persecuted! He was a sign of contradiction, persecuted for his teaching, his works, and his very person. Finally, they took his life amid affronts, torments, and insults, making Him suffer the most shameful and painful death imaginable.

223 I was also much encouraged by reading the Acts of the Apostles. St. Peter in his first sermon converted three thousand men, and in his second, five thousand.[1] With what great zeal and fervor he preached! And what shall I say of St. James, St. John, and the other Apostles? With great concern and zeal they rushed from one kingdom to another, preaching zealously and without fear of human respect, considering that God must be obeyed rather than men. This was their answer to the scribes and Pharisees when the latter forbade them to preach.[2] Scourging could not intimidate them into giving up their preaching; on the contrary, they counted themselves fortunate to be able to suffer something for the sake of Jesus Christ.

224 But the zeal of St. Paul has always awakened my deepest enthusiasm.[1] He went from place to place, a vessel of election, carrying the teaching of Jesus Christ. He preached, wrote, and taught in synagogues, prisons—everywhere. He worked and made others work, in season and out of season. He suffered scourgings, stonings, persecutions of all sorts, as well as the fiercest calumnies, but he was never daunted; on the contrary, he so rejoiced in tribulations that he could say that he did not wish to glory, save in the cross of Jesus Christ.[2]

225 I also took much heart from reading the lives and works of the Fathers of the Church: St. Ignatius Martyr, St. Clement of Alexandria, Tertullian, Origen, St. Cyprian Martyr, St. Eusebius, St. Athanasius, St. Hilary, St. Cyril, St. Ephraim,

St. Basil, St. Gregory Nazianzen, St. Gregory of Nyssa, St. Ambrose, St. Epiphanius, St. Jerome, St. Paulinus, St. John Chrysostom, St. Augustine, St. Cyril of Alexandria, St. Prosper, Theodoret, St. Leo the Great, St. Caesarius, St. Gregory the Great, St. John Damascene, St. Anselm, St. Bernard.

226 I frequently read the lives of those saints who were distinguished for their zeal in saving souls, and I felt the good effect of it, for I applied to myself those words of Augustine: "*Tu non eris sicut isti et istae?*"[1] Will you not be like these men and women and work as they did at saving souls? The lives of the saints that most moved me were those of St. Dominic, St. Francis of Assisi, St. Anthony of Padua, St. John Nepomucene, St. Vincent Ferrer, St. Bernardine of Siena, St. Thomas of Villanova, St. Ignatius Loyola, St. Philip Neri, St. Francis Xavier, St. Francis Borgia, St. Camillus de Lellis, St. Charles Borromeo, St. Francis Regis, St. Vincent de Paul, and St. Francis de Sales.[2]

227 In the course of meditating on the lives and works of these saints, I used to feel such a burning within me that I couldn't sit still. I had to get up and run from one place to another, preaching continually. I can't describe what I felt inside me. Nothing tired me; I wasn't terrified at the awful calumnies being leveled against me, or afraid of the greatest persecutions. Everything was sweet to me, as long as I could win souls for Jesus Christ and heaven and save them from hell.

228 Before ending this chapter, I would like to present two models of truly apostolic zeal who have always moved me deeply. The first is the Venerable José Diego of Cadiz; the second, the Venerable Master Avila. Of the former, we read in his Life: "The servant of God, moved by zeal to win souls for Jesus Christ, spent his whole life tirelessly in the apostolic ministry. He continually undertook long, tiresome journeys, always on foot, without regard for the inclemencies of the season as he went from place to place to announce God's Word and attain the results he longed for. He loaded himself with cilices, took the discipline twice a day, and observed a rigorous fast. After the hardship of his days, he took his nights' rest praying before the Blessed Sacrament, a devotion

that so pleased him that he gave it his most tender and fervent love."[1]

229 From the *Life of the Venerable Avila.*[1] His baggage train was a little burro. On it, he and his companions piled their cloaks and saddlebags. The latter contained a supply of hosts for celebrating Mass at hermitages, as well as cilices, rosaries, medals, holy cards, and some wire and pliers for making rosaries. He never carried food but trusted in God's providence. It was a rare day when he ate meat; most of the time he ate only bread and fruit.

230 His sermons usually lasted two hours and were so fluent and varied that they could hardly have been shorter. He spoke so clearly that all could understand him, and no one ever grew tired of listening to him. Day and night his only thought was how he might increase God's glory, reform morals, and convert sinners.

In preparing his sermons he avoided using many books or elaborate concepts, and his talks were relatively free of scriptural allusions, far-fetched examples, and other such finery. With a simple thought and a single cry, he could set the hearts of his listeners afire.

231 While Father Avila was preaching in Granada, another preacher, the most famous of his day, was also engaged in preaching there. People would leave this preacher's sermons crossing themselves in amazement at the many fine and profitable things that had been so beautifully said. But when they left Master Avila's sermons they all went out with bowed heads, not saying a word to one another, rapt and repentant from the sheer force of the truth, virtue, and excellence of the preacher.[1]

232 His preaching was directed mainly toward withdrawing sinners from their unhappy state by showing them the ugliness of sin, the wrath of God, the awful punishment that awaits the impenitent, and the reward that awaits the truly contrite and repentant. God gave his words such power that Luis of Granada says: "One day I heard him preach a sermon on the wickedness of those who for carnal pleasure do not

hesitate to offend God, basing his remarks on a text in Jeremiah, 'Be astonished, you heavens, at this.' In truth, he spoke with such great dread of spirit, that it seemed to me that the very walls of the church began to shake."[1]

233 O my God and my Father, may I know you and make you known; love you and make you loved; serve you and make you served; praise you and make all creatures praise you. Grant, my Father, that all sinners be converted, all the just persevere in grace, and all of us attain to eternal glory. Amen.

Chapter XIII

THE EXAMPLE AND ENCOURAGEMENT I RECEIVED FROM CERTAIN WOMEN SAINTS

234 If I was moved by the example of men saints, as I have said in the preceding chapter, I was moved still more by the example of women saints. How deeply they impressed me! I would ask myself, "If a woman has such feelings and desires and does so much to save souls, what ought I, a priest, however unworthy, be doing?" The reading of their lives affected me so much that I copied out excerpts of their words and works, some of which I wish to quote here.

235 From the *Life of St. Catherine of Siena.*[1] "She had a singular devotion and love toward those saints who spent their lives working for the salvation of souls, and since St. Dominic had founded his Order to spread the faith and save souls, she revered him so much that when she saw some of his friars passing by, she noted where they had set their feet and later, with all humility, would kiss their footprints."[2]

236 "Magdalen at Jesus' feet chose the better part, but not the best, says St. Augustine; for the best is to unite both parts, the active and contemplative, as St. Catherine of Siena did."[1]

"She regarded all as bathed in the precious Blood of

Jesus Christ and, considering the many upon whom the benefits of the Redemption are wasted, she wept tenderly. Especially during her ecstasies she was heard to pray for the conversion of the infidel, often repeating this prayer: O eternal God, like a Good Shepherd turn your merciful eyes upon the many sheep who, though separated from the fold of your Church, are yet yours, since you have bought them with your Blood."[2]

237 "One day the Lord let her glimpse the joys of heaven and told her: 'See how many joys are lost forever by those who break my law to do their pleasure. See the fierce chastisement by which my justice must exact satisfaction from sinners, who would not give it through their penance. Consider, too, the blindness of those mortals who gamble away a good that includes all other goods by living a life subjected to their passions. My providence has placed the saving of many souls into your hands. I shall give you words and instill in you a teaching that all your adversaries will be powerless to resist or contradict.'"[1]

238 "The ministry of preaching is the greatest that Jesus gave his Church. With this sword he armed his twelve captains, the Apostles. This sacred ministry of preaching is properly a duty of bishops alone, for they, as shepherds, must feed the flock from whose midst they may delegate others to aid them in their task. Gregory XI commanded Catherine to preach before him and the entire consistory of cardinals and other princes. She spoke so masterfully of heavenly things that they listened to her as motionless as statues, so struck were they with her admirable spirit. She preached before His Holiness and the cardinals on many other occasions and they always listened admiringly and profitably, venerating her as a new apostle, powerful both in words and works. She also preached to the laity, and as her own heart burned with the fire of holy zeal, her words broke out in flames, and so many sinners repented and changed their lives that she had to keep a number of confessors in her retinue, some of them with papal authority to absolve reserved cases."[1]

239 From the *Life of St. Rose of Lima*.[1] "She felt the deep-

est sympathy for those in mortal sin, because she knew by the light God gave her how miserable they were. She cried continually over their misery and asked God to convert all sinners. She even used to say that she would gladly suffer all the torments of hell herself alone, as long as she could do so without sinning, if by doing so no one would be damned. For this reason she had a great desire to see the Gospel preached to unbelievers and penance preached to sinners. One of her confessors had offered himself to go to the missions, but was afraid of the dangers of the voyage. He consulted the saint and she told him: 'Go, my dear father, and don't be afraid. Go, convert the infidel. Consider that the greatest service men can render God is the conversion of souls, and this is the proper work of the apostles. Can there be any joy greater than that of baptizing a single person, although it be the humblest little Indian, and have him enter heaven through the gates of baptism?'"

240 "She used to persuade all the friars of St. Dominic to busy themselves with this apostolic ministry, telling them that it was no less important to the spirit of their profession than the study of sacred theology—indeed, that this ministry was the goal of all their theological studies. She also used to say that if it were permitted her she would walk from one kingdom to another preaching the faith until all unbelievers were converted, and that she would go out into the streets, wearing a cilice, with a crucifix in her hand, and shout to sinners in order to awaken them and move them to repentance. She was determined to raise an orphan child, pay for his studies and have him ordained a priest, so that he could convert the infidel and be a preacher, since she could not do so herself."

241 "She was deeply troubled at the thought of preachers who did not seek the good of souls in their sermons. Once a Dominican friar of the monastery of the Rosary was preaching in Lima, to great applause because of his florid style. One day the saint told him with great modesty, but forcefully: 'My father, see how God has made you his preacher to convert souls, not to waste your talents idly on these useless flowers. You are a fisher of men: cast your net so as to catch

men, not the air and vanity of applause. And remember, God will hold you accountable for so exalted a ministry.'"

Even if she could not preach, she took every opportunity in conversation to use the eloquence God gave her to draw others to love virtue and hate vice.

Chapter XIV

ON THE SAME SUBJECT

242 From the *Life of St. Teresa*.[1] "I arranged that not only this man, but others as well, should practice prayer. As I saw that they were friends of prayer I told them to meditate, and helped them to do so by giving them books."[2]

243 "Who could look upon the Lord covered with wounds and afflicted by persecution and not embrace them, love them, and desire to share them with Him? Who could glimpse something of the glory He gives those who serve Him, without realizing that everything we might possibly do or suffer is as nothing in view of the reward that we await? Who could look upon the torments of the damned without counting our torments as delights in comparison, and without realizing how much we owe the Lord for having spared us so many times from going to that place?"[1]

244 "What an added glory and contentment it will be for the blessed to know that, however late they started, there was nothing that they might have done for God that they left undone! They held back nothing that they were able to give, in accordance with their ability and their state in life; the more they could do, the more they did. How rich they will be who have left all things for Christ. How honored they will be who sought not honor, but delighted in being humbled. How wise will they be who were thought to play the fool— for so men thought the Word incarnate—and how few wise fools there are nowadays, because of our sinfulness. Now, yes now it seems that we have seen the last of all those whom people scorned as madmen on seeing them perform the heroic works of true lovers of Christ. O world, world, how you

go on gaining in honor simply because there are so few who know you truly!"

245 "But do we really believe that God is better served because the world regards us as wise or discreet? Indeed this would seem to be the case, if judged by the current fashion in discretion. For it seems to us that there is little edification unless people, each according to his state, go about with an air of great composure and assurance. It seems to us, nowadays, though we be a friar, clerk, or nun, that to wear an old or mended habit would be a novelty and a scandal to the weak. And what would we say of being recollected and given to prayer? So goes the world, and so forgotten the quest for perfection and the great vehemence of the saints, that I think much harm is added to the misfortunes of our times by the fact that religious do not commit the scandal of putting into act, as they put into words, the truth that the world is of little account. From such a scandal the Lord could draw great advantage: for if it would falsely scandalize some, it would truly bring others to remorse. Would it hurt us to have a living picture of Christ and his Apostles in our midst? We need one more than ever before."[1]

246 "One day while I was praying I felt myself suddenly—who knows how?—plunged into hell. I knew that the Lord wanted me to see the place that the devils had been preparing for me, a place which I had merited by my sins. It all took place quite quickly, yet I doubt that I shall ever forget it however long I live. The entrance seemed to be a long, narrow alley, like some very low, dark, and confining furnace. The ground appeared to be covered with muddy, foul-smelling water, swimming with vermin. At the end of it there was a niche like a closet in which I saw myself closely confined. All that I saw was delightful in comparison with the awful things I felt: what I have said about it can hardly do it justice."

247 "It seems to me that what I felt could not begin to be explained or understood; but I felt a fire in my soul, the nature of which I cannot describe. My bodily pains were so unbearable that, though I have experienced the gravest pains and, as the doctors have said, the greatest pains in this world,

such as the contraction of my sinews when I was paralyzed—not to mention others, some of them caused, as I have said, by the devil—all of these were as nothing in comparison to what I felt then, especially in view of the fact that I saw that they would never end. But even this was as nothing in comparison with the soul's agony: a crushing sense of suffocation, an affliction so painful, together with such a sense of hopeless and cruel discontent that I cannot describe it. To say that the soul is constantly being torn away is not enough, for that would seem to imply that someone else is taking one's life; but here the soul itself is tearing itself asunder. The fact is that I simply cannot find words to describe the inner fire and despair I felt at such dreadful pains and torments. I could not see who was inflicting this torture on me, but I felt myself burning and being torn to pieces, so to speak, and I can only say that this inner fire and despair are the worst pain of all."

248 "While I was in that pestilent place, devoid of all comfort, I could neither sit nor lie down. I was lodged in a sort of hole in the wall; yet there was no room because those walls, so horrible to look at, pressed in upon me, stifling me. There was no light; all was thickest darkness. I cannot understand how, but everything that is painful to see could be seen. At that time the Lord did not wish me to see any more of hell. Since then I have had another vision of the dreadful punishments with which certain vices are chastised. They were dreadful to look at, but as I did not feel the pain, they did not frighten me as much as those in the other vision, in which the Lord wanted me truly to feel the torments and spiritual affliction, as if I were suffering them in my own body. I have no idea how the experience happened, but I know that it happened through the goodness of God, who wanted me to see with my own eyes the place from which he had freed me out of mercy. For just to hear about hell is nothing. Neither were any of my occasional thoughts about it (although these were few, since fear has always had small influence on my soul); nor even what I had read, such as stories of demons tormenting souls with pincers. No, all of this was mere nothing in comparison with that pain. In short, a picture is one thing, reality another. And all the burning in the world is but a trifle in comparison with the fire in that place."

249 "I was terrified then and I still am as I write, although it all happened some six years ago. Fear seems to make my blood run cold even now, and of all the labors and sorrows that have come my way I can remember none that does not fade into nothingness in comparison, and I think that our complaints are largely without foundation. Again I say that this was one of God's greatest mercies toward me. I have benefited greatly from it, both by losing the fear of this life's trials and contradictions, and by gaining the strength to bear them and thank the Lord who freed me, as I now see it, from such endless and terrible evils."

250 "Since then, as I have said, everything here seems easy in comparison with just a moment of suffering there. I am shocked to think how many books I read on the pains of hell and did not fear them or grasp what they meant. Where was I? How could I have taken delight in things that were leading me to such an evil place? May you be blessed forever, my God, for now I see that you loved me more than I loved myself. How often, Lord, you have freed me from that fearful prison, and how often I have turned back to enter it against your will!"

251 "But I also received the greatest pain of my life from that vision: the thought of the many souls that are being lost (especially the Lutherans, who were already members of the Church through Baptism), as well as a great longing for the salvation of souls. For it seems to me that I would surely undergo many deaths gladly, for a single soul. I have observed that in this world, if we see a person whom we particularly like in some trouble or sorrow, our very nature leads us to sympathize with him, and if the sorrow is great it touches us as if it were our own. Well then, at the sight of a soul forever in the greatest of all troubles, who would be able to bear it?

"No heart could bear the thought of it without great suffering. In this life, we know that pain will end at least in death, yet we are moved to compassion. In the next life, there is no end to pain, and so I cannot understand how we can be at peace, seeing the number of souls that the demon carries off every day."

252 "This makes me feel that in a matter of such great consequence we should content ourselves with nothing less than
the utmost possible effort. May we spare no effort, and may
it please the Lord to grant us the grace we need to this end."[1]

253 "One day the Lord let her see many of the joys of heavenly glory and said: 'See, my daughter, what those who oppose me lose; do not fail to tell them of it.'"[1]

254 "Once, when I was in prayer, I felt so great a joy that,
since I was so unworthy of such a good, I began thinking how
much more I deserved to be in the place I had seen as my lot
in hell (the manner of which, as I have said, I shall never forget). At this thought my soul began to burn all the more and
such a rapture of the spirit fell upon me that I cannot describe it. It seemed to me that I was immersed in and filled
with that Majesty that I have known on other occasions.
Within this Majesty I was given to understand a truth that
is the fulfillment of all truths: I cannot say how, for I saw
nothing. I was told—I could not see by whom—although I
knew that it was Truth itself: 'It is no small thing that I am
doing for you; it is a thing for which you are in my debt. All
the ills of this world befall it from not clearly understanding
the truths of Scripture, and not a jot of it will pass away.' It
seemed to me that I had always believed this, as all the faithful do. 'Alas, daughter,' he told me, 'Few are they that truly
love me, for if they did, I would reveal all my secrets to them.
Do you know what truly loving me means? It means understanding that everything that displeases me is a lie. What you
do not understand now, you shall see clearly, in the good it
does your soul.'"[1]

255 "At this time I learned of the misfortunes in France and
the havoc wrought by the Lutherans, as well as of the growth
of this misguided sect. I was much aggrieved and, as though I
could do anything or were a person of any consequence, I
cried to the Lord and implored Him to remedy this great evil.
It seemed to me that I would have laid down a thousand lives
for the rescue of just one of the many souls that were being
lost there. And seeing that I was but a puny woman, unable
to serve God as I would (and all my care, then as now, has

been to see to it that God, who has so many enemies and so few friends, should at least have good friends), I determined to do the little that was in my power, namely, to observe the evangelical counsels as perfectly as I could and see to it that the few nuns who live with me should do likewise, trusting in the great mercy of God, who unfailingly comes to the aid of all those who have determined to leave everything for his sake. I hoped that my sisters, since they were all that I might desire, would have virtue enough to resist the bad example of my faults and thus help me offer the Lord some solace, and that busying ourselves with prayers for the success of the preachers and scholars who defend the Church, we might do what we could to help this Lord of mine, who is so oppressed by those whom He has favored that it seems as if they wish to nail Him to the cross again and deprive Him of a place on which to rest his head."

256 "O my Redeemer, my heart cannot dwell on this without becoming deeply troubled. What is it with these Christians nowadays? Must those who owe you the most be the very ones to grieve you? Must it always be those for whom you have worked the greatest wonders, those whom you have chosen as your friends, those in whose midst you have walked and to whom you have given yourself in the sacraments? Are they not content with the torments you have already endured for them?"

257 "Surely, my Lord, those who abandon the world lose nothing. For if the world treated you so lawlessly, what should we expect? Are we, perhaps, better deserving of its esteem? Have we done it greater favors than you have to merit its friendship? What am I saying! How can we hope for more, since through the mercy of God we are not in that pesthole where the devil's minions already are? They have earned just punishment at his hands and have reaped eternal fire with their pleasures. There they must remain, although it breaks my heart to see the many souls that are lost. Were their evil not so immense, I could not stand to see more of them lost each day."

258 "O my sisters in Christ, help me to pray to the Lord for

this, because this is why we have come together in this place. This is your calling and these must be your occupations, your desires, your tears, and your prayers."[1]

Chapter XV

ON THE SAME SUBJECT

259 From the *Life of St. Mary Magdalen of Pazzi.*[1] "It would be hard to find any apostolic man with a more burning zeal for the salvation of souls. She had a lively and most tender concern for their welfare, and it seemed to her that she had no love at all for the Lord unless everyone else loved Him, too. On learning of the great strides that the faith was making in the Indies in her day, she would say that if her vocation allowed, she would travel throughout the world to save souls and would envy the birds their wings that she might fly about everywhere to accomplish the task. 'If only it were possible for someone to take me to the Indies,' she used to say, 'so that I could take those little Indian children and instruct them in our holy faith, so that Jesus might be the Master of their souls and that they might possess Jesus!'"

260 Then, speaking of infidels in general, she would say, "If I could, I would gather them all together and bring them to the bosom of the Church, that She might purify them of all their infidelities and regenerate them as her children, drawing them to her breast and nourishing them with the milk of the sacraments. How well she would feed and nurse them at her breasts! Ah, if I could bring them to her, how gladly would I do it!"

261 Considering the harm done to souls by widespread heresies, she used to say, "Our souls should be weeping turtledoves, always lamenting the blindness of heretics." And on learning that the faith of Catholics had grown so lukewarm, she would say, "Pour forth, O Word of God, pour forth a living, burning faith in the hearts of your faithful. Rewarmed and enkindled in your heart with infinite charity, may their faith be matched by their works and their works by their

faith." On other occasions, when praying for the conversion of sinners, she would say in accents of fire that the Lord should not listen to her, but to the sighing of his own precious Blood.

262 She wanted to instill this ardent zeal for the salvation of souls in everyone. Thus she continually told the nuns entrusted to her care to pray to God for souls. "Let us ask for as many souls as the steps we take around the convent, and as many as the words we say in singing the Divine Office." She brought all the warmth of her feelings to bear on the works permitted her as a nun, so that her biographer was able to fill 14 chapters with examples in proof of her zeal for saving souls. Of all the things that she could do—disciplines, fasts, vigils, prolonged prayer, exhortations, corrections, etc.—she omitted not the slightest act. She would give herself to whole months of the strictest penance for the reparation of any sin commended to her prayers.

263 We know that many souls were saved through the prayers of St. Teresa of Jesus and St. Mary Magdalen of Pazzi, and that many are now being saved through the prayers of good and fervent nuns. For this reason I have always been ready to preach retreats and sermons to nuns (although my time has been too restricted to allow me to be their confessor), namely, that they might commend me to God in their prayers. Sometimes I would tell nuns that they must play the part of Moses on the mountain, while I played Joshua's in the field of battle—they praying and I wielding the sword of God's Word. Thus, just as Joshua claimed victory through the prayers of Moses, so I would expect to claim it through the prayers of the nuns. And to urge them on to greater heights of prayer, I would tell them that we would share the merits of the victory.

Chapter XVI

MEANS I USED TO ACHIEVE SUCCESS

First Means: Prayer

264 Because, as I have already said, I was driven to work for
God's greater glory and the salvation of souls, I shall now say
something of the means that the Lord showed me were the
best and most fitting to attain that goal.

The first means I have always employed and still do is
prayer. In my opinion, this is the greatest means that can be
used for the conversion of sinners, the perseverance of the
just, and the relief of the souls in purgatory. Hence in my
meditations, Masses, recitation of the breviary and other devotions, as well as in my aspirations, I always asked God and
the Blessed Virgin Mary for these three intentions.

265 I not only prayed myself but asked others to pray—
nuns, Sisters of Charity, Tertiaries,[1] and all virtuous and zealous folk.[2] I would ask them to attend Holy Mass, receive
Holy Communion and, both during Mass and after receiving
Holy Communion, to offer to the Eternal Father his most
holy Son; and in his holy Name and through his merits, to
ask for the three graces I have mentioned, namely, the conversion of sinners, the perseverance of the just, and the relief
of the poor souls in purgatory. I also asked them to make
visits to the Blessed Sacrament and to make the Way of the
Cross.

266 I also exhorted them to commend themselves earnestly
to the Blessed Virgin Mary and to pray to her for the same
three requests, availing themselves of the devotion to the
Holy Rosary, on which I preached to them, explaining a practical method of reciting it. Before beginning my sermon, I
would recite the rosary with all the people, both to teach
them how to pray it and, by saying it together, to obtain the
three aforesaid graces.[1] I likewise taught them the devotion
to the Sorrows of Mary and saw to it that on each day of the

week they meditated on one Sorrow, so that by the end of the week they would have meditated on all seven.[2]

267 I also prayed and had people pray to the saints in heaven that they might intercede with Jesus and Mary to obtain these same graces. I especially prayed to those saints who during their earthly lives had shown the greatest zeal for God's glory and the salvation of souls.

268 I never forgot to invoke St. Michael and the guardian angels—especially my own, and those of the kingdom, the province, the city in which I was preaching, and of each individual present.[1]

269 I have had visible knowledge of the protection of the holy guardian angels. I want to list here some of the aspirations I say every day. I have counseled others to say them, and they have told me that doing so has been of much benefit to them.[1]

> Who is like God?
> Who is like Jesus Christ?
> Who is like Mary, Virgin and Mother of God?
> Who is like the angels of heaven?
> Who is like the saints in glory?
> Who is like the just upon earth?
> Long live Jesus! Long live Mary Most Holy!
> Long live the holy law of God!
> Long live the holy evangelical counsels!
> Long live the holy sacraments of the Church!
> Long live the holy Sacrifice of the Mass!
> Long live the Blessed Sacrament of the Altar!
> Long live the Holy Rosary of Mary!
> Long live the grace of God!
> Long live the Christian virtues!
> Long live the works of mercy!
> Death to vices, faults, and sins!

270 *The Prayer I Said at the Beginning of Every Mission.*[1]

O Virgin Mother of God, mother and advocate of poor and unhappy sinners, you are well aware that I am your son and minister, formed in the furnace of your mercy and love.

I am like an arrow poised in your mighty hand. Release me, my Mother, with the full force of your arm, against the impious, sacrilegious, and cruel Ahab, wed to the base Jezebel.[2] I mean to say: release me against Satan, the prince of this world, who has made an alliance with the flesh.

271 May the victory be yours, my Mother; you shall overcome. Yes, you have the power to end all heresies, errors, and vices. And so, trusting in your most powerful protection, I begin to do battle not only against flesh and blood, but against the rulers of darkness, as the Apostle says,[1] taking up the shield of the Holy Rosary and armed with the two-edged sword of God's Word.[2]

272 You are Queen of the angels: command them, my Mother, to come to my aid. Surely you know how weak I am and how strong my enemies are.

You are Queen of the saints: command them to pray for me and tell them that the victory and triumph to be won will be for God's greater glory and the salvation of souls.

Lady, through your humility, crush the pride of Lucifer and his followers who have the audacity to claim the souls redeemed by the blood of Jesus, the Son of your virginal womb.

273 I also pronounced the following exorcism:[1]

Satan, with all your followers, I, a minister—however unworthy—of Jesus Christ and Mary Most Holy, command you to depart from here and go to the place where you belong. I command you to do so in the name of the Father,† who created you; in the name of the Son,† who has redeemed us from your tyranny; in the name of the Holy Spirit,† who has sanctified and consoled us. Amen.

I command you also in the name of Mary Most Holy, Virgin and Mother of the living God,† who has crushed your head.

Away, Satan! Away, you proud and envious one! May you never do anything to hinder the conversion and salvation of souls.

Chapter XVII

OTHER MEANS I MADE USE OF TO DO GOOD

Second Means: Instructing Children

274 I always bore in mind the old saying: "Pray to God and row for shore." Thus I took great care and worked energetically, as if everything depended on my work and, at the same time, I put all my trust in God because everything really does depend on Him, above all, the conversion of sinners, which is a work of grace and the greatest work of God.

275 *Catechizing children.* The first thing I saw to was the instruction of children in Christian doctrine—not only because I have always felt a strong inclination toward this kind of education but also because I have come to realize its prime importance. Knowledge of the catechism is the foundation for the whole edifice of religious and moral instruction. Moreover, children learn readily and are deeply impressed. Catechism preserves them from error, vice, and ignorance and more easily grounds them in virtue because they are more docile than adults. In the case of children, the only work required is that of planting, whereas adults require both weeding and planting.[1] There is yet another advantage: grownups are often won over by the little ones, and parents are won over by their children because children are like so many pieces of their parents' hearts. When the children receive a little holy card for their attendance and diligence, their parents and other adults read them at home out of curiosity, and this often results in their conversion, as I know from experience.

276 One of the things that has moved me most to teach children is the example of Jesus Christ and the saints. Jesus said, "Let the little children come to me and do not hinder them. It is to just such as these that the kingdom of God belongs" (Mark 10:14). Then he embraced them and blessed them, placing his hands on them. There is no doubt that a child whose innocence has been preserved through good instruc-

tion is a treasure more precious in God's eyes than all the kingdoms of this world.

277 The Apostles, who had been indoctrinated by Christ, catechized the small and the great alike, and so their sermons became so many basic statements of the mysteries of faith.

St. Denis, St. Clement of Alexandria—a most erudite man, the teacher of Origen—as well as Origen himself, were catechists, as were St. John Chrysostom, St. Augustine, and St. Gregory of Nyssa. St. Jerome, at the very time when he was being consulted from far and near as the oracle of the universe, was not ashamed to teach catechism to children. He spent his last days, which had otherwise been used so well in the service of the Church, in this humble occupation. He once told a widow, "Send me your children and I'll babble with them. I'll have less glory in men's eyes, but I'll be glorious in God's."[1]

278 In this respect, St. Gregory the Great surpassed St. Jerome in zeal. Rome, the capital of the world and the center of religion, was amazed to see that great pope, despite his illness, spending as much time as he could instructing young people. After giving solid food to the strong, he was not ashamed to provide milk for children.

279 The celebrated chancellor of Paris, Jean Gerson, dedicated himself constantly to catechizing children. When he was criticized for this, he replied that he could find no greater employment than in snatching these little souls from the hellish serpent and in watering these tender plants in the Church's garden.[1]

280 The Venerable Master John·of Avila, the apostle of Andalucía, was dedicated to the instruction of children. His disciples were also and strongly recommended the same dedication to schoolteachers. He used to say that "the winning of youth means the saving of the whole republic; for the little become the great, and their hand will govern the republic. A good education," he would say, "and the teaching of Christian doctrine is the fountain and source of the public happiness

and welfare, so much so that miseducating youth is like poisoning the common water supply."[1]

281 Father Diego de Guzmán, son of the Count of Bailén and a disciple of the Venerable Avila, spent the entire 83 years of his life in teaching Christian doctrine. He traveled through Spain and Italy with great zeal and effectiveness, at the cost of great personal pain and effort. To ensure the continuance of his work after his death, he founded a Congregation in Seville to continue teaching Christian doctrine as he had done.

282 St. Ignatius, St. Francis Xavier, and St. Francis Borgia also applied themselves to teaching Christian doctrine to children. Laínez and Salmerón, envoys to the Council of Trent, were ordered by St. Ignatius to teach catechism to children.
   St. Joseph Calasanctius and the Venerable César de Bus founded a Congregation to teach children Christian doctrine,[1] the Sisters of Christian Doctrine.[2]

283 Father Ignatius Martins, an eloquent orator who was preacher to the king of Portugal, abandoned preaching and dedicated his whole life to teaching children, a work in which he continued for a span of 18 years.[1]
   Father Edmond Auger, an apostolic preacher, who was called "the Gospel Trumpet" for his conversion of 40,000 heretics in France, was so deeply committed to teaching catechism that at his death it pleased God to allow him to be seen ascending into heaven accompanied by a host of angels and children. To Isaiah's question, "Where is the teacher of the little ones?"[2] one might well answer, "Here he is."[3]

284 In view of all these examples, as well as others I know but have omitted here, I was greatly encouraged in my own constant inclination to teach catechism to boys and girls. I have made it my occupation as a student, priest, administrator, missionary, and even as an archbishop.[1]

285 Because I love children and want them to be educated in Christian doctrine, I have written four catechisms: one for small children, from the time they begin talking until they

reach seven; one for country folk; another, more extensive one; and one fully explained and illustrated.[1]

286 The method I followed, based on what experience has taught me to be the best approach, I have described in the second volume of my *Well-Instructed Seminarian,* section 5, chapter 4.

Chapter XVIII

ADULT INSTRUCTION

The Third Means I Made Use of to Do Good

287 The most productive means I have used has been adult instruction. It has helped me rescue adults from an ignorance that is greater than one might imagine, even in the case of persons who hear sermons frequently. Preachers often take it for granted that their listeners are well instructed, while the fact is that instruction is precisely what most Catholics lack. The use of instruction has the further advantage of informing adults of their respective obligations and teaching them how to go about fulfilling them.

288 During a parish mission I gave these instructions every day except the first (which had its own assigned topic), as an introduction to the sermon just before we recited the Hail Mary together. As I was working alone, I had to do everything myself. This introduction lasted some 20 minutes, and the subject was always the Commandments of God's Law, which I explained at greater or lesser length, depending on how many days the mission or other service was to last. For the occasion I brought along a portfolio containing explanations of the commandments in general, as well as leaflets on individual commandments or topics related to each commandment.[1] I used these materials on the basis of the number of days I had to preach in the town and also on the basis of particular local customs or vices that needed to be corrected and virtues that needed to be fostered. For it was my practice, before I went to a town, to make inquiries in advance, and in

view of what I was told or discovered on my own, I applied
the proper remedy.

289 Despite all I knew about the predominant local vices, I
didn't begin talking about them at the very outset; on the
contrary, I saved such topics for later. I waited until I had
won my audience over, and then instead of being offended
when I told them about their vices and little idols, they took
my advice and mended their ways. I had noticed that at the
beginning of a mission many came for the novelty of it, to
see what I was going to talk about. If they had heard me reprehending them for their cherished vices, they would have
been cut to the quick, and in their irritation they would have
gone off upset, never to return, wishing a plague on the missionary, the mission, and everyone attending it.

290 It seems to me that in these troubled times a missionary
has to act like a man cooking snails. He starts by putting the
snails on the stove in a pot of cold water. Sensing the coolness
of the water, the snails come out of their shells. Then, as the
water heats up gradually to the boiling point, the snails are
killed and cooked. But if the cook were careless enough to
throw them at once into boiling water, they would retreat so
deeply into their shells that no one would be able to get them
out. This was the line I had to follow when dealing with sinners steeped in all sorts of vices, errors, blasphemies, and im-
pieties.

　　The first few days I would present virtue and truth in
the brightest and most winsome colors, without saying so
much as a word against vice and sinners. Seeing that they
were being treated with tolerance and kindness, people would
come back time and time again, so that afterwards, when I
was more outspoken with them, they took it well, were converted, and confessed their sins. I met quite a few who came
to the mission only out of curiosity, as well as others who
came out of mischief, to see whether they could catch me in
some slip; yet they were converted and made good confessions.

291 When I started preaching missions, in 1840, we were in
the midst of a civil war between the royalists and the constitutionalists, and so I had to be on my guard not to make any

political remarks pro or con regarding either party. There were members of each party in all the towns I preached in. I had to be very careful because some people came to the mission only to catch me in some slip of the tongue, like the spies who were sent to Jesus, our Redeemer, "to trap Him in his speech."[1] But, thank God, they never succeeded.

292 The times were so troubled that I not only had to avoid talking politics, but also I had to avoid calling the service I was holding a "mission." I had to call it, instead, a "novena" in honor of All Souls, or Our Lady of the Rosary, or the Blessed Sacrament, or a saint, so as not to upset the constitutionalists, who were in power in the towns I was preaching in. If the town was so large that nine days were not enough, I would lengthen the "novena" by as many days as I thought necessary.

On the first day of the service, I would begin with a sermon on the main theme of the entire mission; on the second day and on each day following, I would establish some doctrinal point; on the third day I would make a brief résumé of the doctrine I had just covered the day before, saying, for example:

293 Yesterday I explained such and such (going over the main points). This I did for three reasons: first, because when people hear the same matter again, no matter how briefly, it makes a deeper impression on them. For as St. Alphonsus Liguori says, simple folk have hard heads, and to impress things clearly on them you have to hit them over the head with several strokes.[1] Second, if someone had missed the day before because he had to stay home and take care of the home, the children, etc., he could learn what had been said and have a better idea of the connection between today's ideas and yesterday's. Besides, if those who attended the day before took home a mistaken version of what was said, this session is a good opportunity to correct it. A good number of people listen to things poorly and repeat them still more poorly, and in matters of doctrine an accurate understanding is very important. Third, this résumé serves as an introduction to the message of the day and, in addition to being more profitable for the listeners, lightens the task of the preacher,

who doesn't need to look for a new general or particular idea for an introduction.

Chapter XIX

SERMONS

The Fourth Means

294 Explaining points of doctrine serves to instruct the people; sermons serve to move them. Sermons should be chosen with the listener in mind. St. Alphonsus calls some sermon topics, such as the last things, necessary, while he calls others optional.

295 I regularly arranged my sermons in the following order:
First day, All Souls, the Blessed Virgin, etc., depending on the theme of the service.
Second day, the importance of being saved.
Third day, the seriousness of mortal sin.
Fourth day, the need for confession and the way to make a general confession.
Fifth day, death.
Sixth day, judgment.
Seventh day, hell.
Eighth day, eternity.
Ninth day, glory.
Tenth day, perseverance.

296 If more time was available, I added or inserted a few other themes, such as the Prodigal Son or God's mercy, final impenitence, the general judgment, the death of the just, the conversion of St. Augustine, scandal, the conversion of Mary Magdalene, the harm sin does to the sinner himself, venial sin, the near occasion of sin, devotion to the rosary, mental prayer, almsgiving, the Passion of Our Lord Jesus Christ, the Sorrows of Mary, etc.

297 From the very beginning, the style I aimed at was that of the Gospel: simple and clear. To achieve this aim I made

use of comparisons, likenesses, and examples from history and experience, most of them from Scripture. I had observed that one of the best attention-getters with all sorts of people, whether learned or ignorant, believers or unbelievers, was the use of comparisons drawn from things in nature.

298 I recall that in 1841 I was preaching a Septenary of the Seven Sorrows of the Blessed Virgin in a town that had a particularly unsavory reputation. In the midst of a sermon, I had just mentioned a most sublime truth and was going on to prove it from the authority of Sacred Scripture. The congregation was as still as a tomb.

Suddenly, a profane voice broke the silence: *"Quina garrofa que hi claves!"*[1] I went on as if I had heard nothing and said, "To give you a clearer idea of this most important truth, I will illustrate it by a comparison." After I had finished my explanation, the very same voice as before said loudly, *"Tens raó."*[2] The next day the man who had spoken came to see me and made a good general confession.

299 This and many other cases I could relate convinced me of the usefulness of natural comparisons. In this respect, God has so favored me that there is no subject I discuss without finding some natural comparison—without the slightest premeditation—and always such an apt one that it seems I have prepared it after long study. May you be blessed, my God, for enriching me with this gift, for it is yours, not mine. I know that of my own initiative I cannot say a word or have a single good thought! May it all be to your greater glory!

300 I have always been an avid reader of works by authors of sermons, especially of materials useful for preaching missions. I have read St. John Chrysostom, St. Alphonsus Liguori, Siniscalcqui, Barcia, and the Venerable John of Avila.[1] I noted that the last-mentioned author preached so clearly that everyone could understand him and nobody ever tired of listening to him, although his sermons sometimes lasted for two hours. Considering the number of specific examples that occurred to him as he spoke, it would have been very difficult for him to say what he did in less time.

301 Day and night his only thought was that of spreading God's glory through the reformation of morals and the conversion of sinners. The main object of his preaching was to retrieve sinners from their unhappy state by showing them the ugliness of sin, the wrath of God, the dreadful punishment that awaited impenitent sinners, and the reward that was offered to those who were truly repentant and contrite.

The Lord gave his words such power that, as the Venerable Luis of Granada says, "One day, in the midst of a sermon on the wickedness of those who for the love of beastly pleasure do not hesitate to offend the Lord our God, I heard him cite that passage in Jeremiah: 'Be amazed at this, O heavens.'[1] In all truth, he spoke with such great dread and spirit that I thought he made the very walls of the church tremble."

302 In the days when the Venerable Avila was preaching in Granada, another preacher, the most famous of his time, was also preaching there. People would walk away from the latter's sermons, crossing themselves in wonder at the many fine things so finely said. But when they had finished listening to the Venerable Avila, they all left with heads downcast, silent, without a single word to their neighbor, humbled and heartbroken by the sheer power of the truth and by the virtue and excellence of the preacher. With a single thought or cry, he moved the hearts of his listeners and set them on fire.

303 I have chosen to include something of this venerable father's work at this point because his style is the one that I have adopted and practiced the most, with the most gratifying results. May the Lord our God be glorified for letting me come to know the writings of this great master of preachers and father of good and most zealous priests!

304 Whenever I went to a town, I preached not only the daily mission sermon but also a separate sermon for the priests (unless they were making a retreat, in which case I preached to them daily both in the morning and in the evening). I also preached to all the nuns, Sisters of Charity and Tertiaries in the local convents, to the men of the St. Vincent de Paul Society, to women, prisoners, boys and girls, and to the sick. In a word, there was not a single pious or charitable

institution that I did not visit or preach in. As for the rest of my time, I spent it in the confessional, hearing general confessions throughout the morning and the afternoon.

305 May you be blessed, my God, for giving me the strength, health, and more besides, so that I was able to bear so great and continuous a burden of work. I am quite sure that without special help from heaven it would have been impossible for me to bear up under the tiring and prolonged work load I bore from 1840 to 1847, when I went to the Canary Islands with that virtuous and zealous man, Bishop Bonaventure Codina.[1]

Besides parish missions, I gave retreats to the clergy, nuns, students, laymen, and to boys and girls preparing for their first Holy Communion.

Chapter XX

THE SPIRITUAL EXERCISES OF ST. IGNATIUS

Fifth Means

306 As I have already mentioned elsewhere,[1] I have made the Spiritual Exercises every year of my life since I was a student. I first made them following the text of St. Ignatius when I was in Rome—once by myself, upon arriving in that city, and again in the Company of Jesus, before I had to leave it because of illness. The Jesuit Fathers themselves conducted these, which were the ones that made the most lasting impression on me.

307 When I had to leave the Jesuits because of illness, I was given a copy of the aforesaid Exercises of St. Ignatius, with explanations by Father Diertins, and I followed that text ever after when I gave the Exercises.[1] The esteemed clergy of Vich asked to borrow the book so as to have it reprinted. Trullás Printers handled the job.

308 The Exercises of St. Ignatius are one of the most power-

ful tools I have used in the conversion of priests, which is without doubt one of the most difficult of undertakings. Nevertheless, I have seen the most gratifying results in a great number of priests who have been truly converted, and not a few of them have turned out to be very zealous and fervent preachers. I have given these Exercises to the reverend clergy of Vich, Barcelona, Tarragona, Gerona, Solsona, Canarias, Mataro, Manresa, Pobla-Baga, Ripoll, Campdevanol, San Llorens del Piteus, etc.

309 I have also given them several times to the laity, to men and women separately, each in turn, and I have noticed that the results have been more solid and lasting than those of missions. For this reason I published a book entitled *The Exercises of St. Ignatius,* explained by me, which has been very popular and has produced and still is producing marvelous effects. By making the Exercises well, sinners are converted, and the just remain and are perfected in grace. May it all be for God's greater glory.[1] I should also like to mention that Her Majesty the Queen follows this book in making her annual Exercises and has counseled her ladies-in-waiting to do the same, following the same book.

Chapter XXI

BOOKS AND PAMPHLETS

Sixth Means

310 Experience has taught me that one of the most powerful forces for good is the press, although when abused it can also be one of the most potent weapons for evil. By means of the press so many good books and pamphlets are circulated that God should be praised for it. Not everyone wishes to or is able to hear the Word of God, but everyone can read or listen to the reading of a good book. Not everyone can go to church to hear God's Word, but a book can go to a person's house. The preacher can't always be preaching, but a book is always delivering the same message tirelessly and is always willing to repeat what it says. It is not offended if its reader

picks it up and puts it down a thousand times. It is always ready to accommodate itself to the wishes of its reader.

3 1 1 Reading good books has always been considered highly useful, but nowadays it is a real necessity. I say that it is nowadays a necessity because there is such a passion for reading that if people don't have good books they'll read bad ones. Books are the food of the soul, and just as the body is nourished by wholesome food and harmed by poisonous food, so it is with reading and the soul. If people read good books suited to their personal needs and circumstances, they will be nourished and grow. But if they read bad books, impious magazines, heretical booklets, and other pernicious literature, their beliefs will be corrupted and their morals perverted. Bad books begin by leading the mind astray and then go on to corrupt the heart; and as Christ Himself said, it is from a corrupt heart that all evils flow,[1] until one finally arrives at the stage of denying the very first truth, the existence of God, who is the origin of all truth: "The fool has said in his heart, 'There is no God.'"[2]

3 1 2 In our day, then, there is twice the need for circulating good books. But these books must be small because modern people rush about so much and are pressed on all sides by a thousand different demands—not to mention the concupiscence of the eyes and ears that has reached such a point that people have to see and hear everything and travel everywhere —so that a thick tome is just not going to be read. It will merely sit around gathering dust on the shelves of bookstores and libraries. It is because I am so convinced of this that, with the help of God's grace, I have published so many booklets and pamphlets.

3 1 3 The first booklet I published was one containing some spiritual counsels I had originally written for the nuns at Vich. I had just finished giving them a retreat, and to help them remember what I had preached about, I planned to leave them these counsels in writing. Before giving them a draft that each could copy by hand, I showed it to my dear friend, Dr. Jaime Passarell, canon of the cathedral of Vich. He told me that he would have it printed to save the nuns the

work of copying it. The booklet would then be useful both to them and to others. Since I held him in high esteem for his wisdom and virtue, I consented and it was printed. This is how I came to publish my first book.

314 Encouraged by the good results of this first book, I determined to write a second entitled *Advice to Young Ladies.* After this, I wrote a whole series of "advice" books: to *Parents, Children, Youth,* and others, as may be seen listed in the Religious Library's catalog.

315 As I was giving missions, I ran into all sorts of needs, and as each new need arose I wrote a booklet or pamphlet on the subject. If I noticed that risqué songs were popular in the town I was visiting, I published a song with a spiritual or moral message. This is why nearly all my early pamphlets were song sheets.

316 Another early publication of mine was a leaflet containing aids to overcome the habit of swearing. In those years when I was beginning to preach, there was so much serious cursing everywhere that it seemed all hell had been set loose on earth just to make men curse.

317 Impurity, too, was so far out of control that I wrote two pamphlets to help overcome it. Since devotion to the Blessed Virgin Mary is a powerful remedy against all ills, I started each pamphlet I wrote with the prayer that begins: "O Virgin and Mother of God," which can be found in nearly all my books and pamphlets.[1] I used the words "Virgin and Mother" because they reminded me of something I had come across in some summer reading I did as a student. I read in the life of St. Philip Neri (a two-volume work in quarto by Father Conciencia),[2] that the Saint always liked to join these words because they greatly honor Mary and incline her to help us. The rest of the prayer is an act of consecration to our Lady.

318 I could see for myself that this particular pamphlet was producing excellent results, so I resolved to write others as the need for them arose in society. I was always quite liberal

in distributing them, not only to adults but to boys and girls too. Following the local custom, children would come up to kiss the priest's hand and ask for a holy card; so I always arranged to have my pockets stuffed with leaflets. I would like to relate just one of the many anecdotes I could tell of how much God is glorified by the distribution of leaflets.

319 One afternoon as I was walking along a street in one of the larger cities of Spain, a little boy came up to me, kissed my hand, and asked me for a holy card, which I gave him. Very early the following day I went, as was my custom, to celebrate Mass in the church, after which I would ordinarily have taken my place in the confessional because there was always a large crowd waiting. After Mass, I knelt in the sanctuary to make my thanksgiving. I hadn't been there long, when a tall, heavy-set man with a large mustache and full beard approached me. He was holding his cape together with his hands, so that the only features I could make out were his nose and forehead. His eyes were closed and the rest of his face was covered by his eyebrows, mustache, and beard, as well as by the high fur collar of his cape. In a trembling, hoarse voice, he asked me whether I would be so good as to hear his confession. I told him that I would and asked him to go and wait for me in the sacristy, where I would join him after I finished my thanksgiving. Although there were other men and women waiting in line for confession, something told me that I should hear him apart from the rest because from his appearance I felt that was the right thing to do; and as things turned out, it was. I went to the sacristy where there was no one but the two of us and, even so, led him over to the farthest corner of the room.

320 I sat down and he knelt before me and began to cry so disconsolately that I didn't know what to say to quiet him. I asked him a number of questions to try to find out the cause of his suffering, and finally, amid tears, sighs, and sobs, he told me: "Father, yesterday you were walking along the street where I live, and as you were passing by the door of the house where I'm staying, a little boy ran out and kissed your hand. He asked you for a holy card, and you gave it to him. The boy walked away with it, very content, and after he

had held it for a while, he put it down on a table and ran off to play with the other boys. I was at home alone, watching all this, and my curiosity got the better of me. To pass the time, I picked up the card and read it. Father, I just can't tell you what I felt. It was like an arrow shot through my heart. I made up my mind then and there that I'd go to confession. I thought to myself, 'Since God chose to use that good man to give you a true knowledge of yourself, you should make your confession to him.' I've spent the whole night crying and examining my conscience and now here I am, waiting to confess my sins. Father, I'm a big sinner. I'm 50 years old and haven't been to confession since I was a child. I've been the ringleader of a very bad gang. Father, is there any hope of pardon for people like me?"

"Yes, sir," I said. "Yes, indeed. Have courage and trust in God's goodness and mercy. The good God has called you because He wants to save you, and you have done well not to harden your heart. You have carried out your resolution to make a good confession." He made his confession, I absolved him, and he was so happy that he couldn't speak.

321 Well then, if all the pamphlets and cards had resulted in just this one conversion, I would have thought the time well spent and I would have been satisfied for all the effort and money put into printing them. However, this was by no means the only case of someone's being converted by reading the pamphlets I have published.

322 In Villafranca del Panadés, four condemned convicts had refused to go to confession after three days of being brought to chapel; but after reading a pamphlet I had given to each of them, they thought it over, went to confession, received Viaticum, and died an edifying death.[1] Many—very many—have been converted by reading a pamphlet. My God, how good you are! You manage to find a way in all circumstances to shower your mercies on poor sinners. May you be blessed forever. Amen.

Chapter XXII

ON THE SAME SUBJECT (BOOKS AND PAMPHLETS), ON EVERYDAY CONVERSATIONS, ON MEDALS, PICTURES, ROSARIES, AND SCAPULARS

Seventh Means

323 Thanks be to God, all my books have had happy results, but the ones that I think have converted more people have been *The Straight Path* and *The Catechism Explained.* I meet a great number of people who attribute their conversion to reading these two books. Even here in the royal court, not a day goes by but that I meet someone who has resolved to change his life as a result of reading one of these books. It seems that everyone is looking for a copy, and readers can't put it down until they have finished it. People of all classes want a copy, and the demand has been so great that I have had to bring out a deluxe edition for the upper classes, which the Queen, King, Princess, ladies-in-waiting, and all the nobility have purchased. It is safe to say that among the upper classes there is no residence or palace without one or more deluxe copies of *The Straight Path.* The same is true of the regular edition among the other social classes.[1]

324 I don't know how I could have managed to write so many different books. You must have done it, Lord. I know that even this is putting it badly; I haven't written anything; you have done it all. My God, you have made use of me, a worthless instrument without the knowledge, talent, or time to do all this. But, unknown to me, you were giving me all the help I needed. May you be blessed for it, my God!

325 My object was always to seek God's greater glory and the salvation of souls; hence I chose to write in the form of books of counsel to all classes of society. But two classes were dearest to my heart: first, boys and girls. For them I published not only the four catechisms I have already mentioned but several other booklets and leaflets.

326 The other group that most claimed my attention was the clergy. If all those studying for service in the Church were men of genuine vocation, virtue, and studiousness, what good priests we'd have and how many converts we'd make! This was what I had in mind in publishing my two-volume work, *The Well-Instructed Seminarian,* which has pleased all its readers.[1] May it all be for God's greater honor and glory!

327 And because we have been created not only to know, love, and serve God but also to praise Him, I concluded that the clergy, in order to fulfill all their duties, needed to know plain chant. With this in mind, I wrote and published a book containing the shortest, easiest method for singing God's praises.[1]

328 In all the books I have published I have sought no financial gain, but only God's greater glory and the good of souls. I have never made a penny's profit from the works I have seen through the presses. On the contrary I have given away thousands upon thousands of free copies. I am still doing so today and hope to be doing so until I die; for I consider this to be the best alms one could possibly give nowadays.

329 In order to be able to give books away or to sell them as cheaply as possible, I planned on setting up a *Religious Press* under the protection of our Lady of Montserrat, patroness of Catalonia, and that of St. Michael.[1] I shared my plans with Fathers Caixal[2] and Palau,[3] who were then canons of the cathedral at Tarragona and are now Bishops of Urgel and Barcelona, respectively. They are still running it under the immediate direction of an administrator.

330 To form some idea of the past and present achievements of the Religious Library, all one has to do is visit its offices and presses and read the catalog of its publications. Even this will not tell the whole story because several of the works have been reprinted a number of times—some of them as much as 38 times—with many thousands of copies to each printing.

331 Through the offices of the Religious Library, both clergy and laity have been and are still able to purchase good

books, the best available and at the lowest prices. In fact, no press in Spain offers books printed as correctly or with the same quality of type and paper as those printed by Religious Library. I owe God countless thanks for having inspired me to undertake such an ambitious and advantageous enterprise.

332 While I am on the subject of books, I must mention the support given the Religious Library by the Academy of St. Michael, approved by His Holiness, Pius IX and by royal charter.[1] Their Majesties, the Queen and King are, in fact, members of its first ranks. The Academy's board of directors meets in Madrid every Sunday to carry out the objectives of its bylaws. There are a number of branches in Madrid and in all the major cities of Spain, and the amount of good they are doing is incalculable.

333 Good books and pamphlets always produce good effects, but never so much as when they are distributed during missions, where they not only back up the message preached to the people but help people persevere in the progress they have made. This is why I always give so much printed matter away during missions and other preaching engagements.

334 Another very effective way of doing good is taking part in familiar conversations with people. A great deal can be accomplished by this means. Among the early Jesuits there was a lay brother who went shopping every day, and as he made his rounds, the conversations he held with people were so effective that he converted more souls than any other missionary. I read this story as a student and liked it so much that I have followed the same practice as often as circumstances have permitted.[1]

335 If the subject of death came up or if a funeral bell was tolling, I seized the opportunity to talk about our human frailty and the uncertainty of our life and how we will have to render an account of our life to God when we die. Thunder and lightning would suggest the Judgment and I would speak of that great day. Standing by a blazing hearth, I would allude to the fires of hell. Once I was chatting with a pastor by the fireside in his kitchen, and the conversation I was

holding with him just as a pastime so moved him that the very next day he made a general confession to me of things he had never dared to confess before. As a result of that one conversation he was touched and genuinely converted.

336 While I was traveling I would strike up a conversation with those who chanced to join me about the various things we saw. If I happened to see some flowers, I would point to them and remark that, as these plants produced beautiful and fragrant flowers, we should produce virtues. The rose, for example, teaches us love, the lily symbolizes purity, the violet, humility, etc. We must, as the Apostle says, be "the good odor of Christ in every place."[1] If I saw a tree laden with fruit, I would remark that we, too, should bear the fruit of good works, so not to end up like the two fig trees in the Gospel.[2] If we passed by a river, I would say that the running water reminds us that we are passing on toward eternity. If we heard birds singing or music being played, I would refer to the new and everlasting song of heaven, etc. I have personally witnessed the great value of conversations like these; their effect was like that of the conversation Christ held with the two travelers on the road to Emmaus.[3] I also found that they had the further advantage of avoiding useless talk and grumbling.[4]

337 I found that another powerful means for doing good was giving away rosaries and teaching people how to use them. I also gave away medals and told people to wear them and kiss them morning and night. I did the same with scapulars, explaining their meaning and how they are to be worn.

338 I also found that I could encourage piety by obtaining faculties to bless pictures, rosaries, medals, and scapulars. When people knew that I had these faculties, they would buy religious objects and, on the appointed day, bring them to the mission where I would bless them from the pulpit. Besides encouraging their fervor, this would also give them a souvenir of the mission and a reminder of all that was said and done there.

339 I also wrote a book on the origin of the scapular and on the graces and indulgences attached to wearing it. Many mem-

bers of the royal court have been enrolled in it, especially the queen, the king, the prince, and the two infantas, and all the ladies of the court.[1]

Chapter XXIII

VIRTUES I CONSIDER ESSENTIAL FOR AN EFFECTIVE MINISTRY. THE FIRST VIRTUE I STROVE FOR: HUMILITY

340 Thus far, I have been speaking of the ordinary means I made use of to produce fruit. Now I would like to say something about the virtues I know are necessary for any missionary in order to bear fruit.

Cicero, speaking of the orator, says that he should be proficient in all the arts and sciences.[1] In a similar vein, I would say that the apostolic missionary should be a model of all the virtues: he should, in fact, be virtue personified. Following Christ's example, he should first practice, then preach. "He began to do and teach."[2] By his actions, the missionary should be able to say with the Apostle, "Be imitators of me, as I am of Christ."[3]

341 I knew that if I was to acquire the virtues I needed in order to become a truly apostolic missionary, I would have to begin with humility, which I regard as the foundation for all other virtues.[1] From the time I entered the seminary at Vich to study philosophy, I began to make a particular examen of this virtue of humility, and I really needed to because I had been so preoccupied in Barcelona with sketches, machines, and other such foolishness that my head was quite swollen with vanity and my tainted heart was flattered at hearing all the praises and compliments I received. My God, forgive me; I am truly sorry for it. The memory of my vanity has brought many a bitter tear to my eyes. But you, my God, have humbled me and I can do no less than thank you in the words of the royal Prophet: "It is good for me that you have humbled me."[2] Yes, Lord, you have humbled me and I have gone on humbling myself, with your help.

342 At the beginning of my stay in Vich I was undergoing an experience not unlike what goes on in a blacksmith's shop. The smith thrusts an iron bar into the furnace, and when it is white-hot he draws it out, places it on the anvil, and begins to hammer it. His assistant joins in, and the two of them keep alternating hammer-blows in a sort of rhythmic dance until the iron takes the shape the smith had planned. You, my Lord and Master, thrust my heart into the furnace of the Spiritual Exercises and frequent reception of the Sacraments; and after thus setting my heart on fire with love for you and the Blessed Virgin Mary, you began to hammer away at me with humiliations, and I, too, began hammering away with my particular examen on this virtue that I needed so badly.[1]

343 I would often repeat St. Augustine's prayer, "May I know thee; may I know myself,"[1] and St. Francis's, "Who art thou and who am I?" And I could imagine the Lord telling me, "I am who am, and you are who are not; you are nothing and less than nothing, since nothingness has not sinned and you have."[2]

344 I have recognized quite clearly that all that I can call truly my own is sin. If I am or have anything else, I have received it all from God. My physical being is not mine, it comes from God. He it is who created me, keeps me in being, and, through physical concurrence, sets me in motion. Without water, not even the best-built water mill can turn; I have come to know that this is true of me even in my physical and natural being.

345 The same is all the more true in the spiritual and supernatural orders. I realize that I cannot call upon the name of Jesus, nor have a single good thought, without the help of God. For without Him I can do absolutely nothing. Yet, despite all I know, how many distractions I have!

346 I know that in the order of grace I am like a man who can throw himself into a deep pit but cannot get out again by his own efforts. So it is with me; I can sin but can't get out of sin without the help of God and the merits of Jesus Christ. I

can be damned on my own, but I can't be saved without God's goodness and mercy.

347 I have come to know that the virtue of humility consists in this: in realizing that I am nothing, can do nothing but sin, and depend on God in everything—being, conservation, movement, and grace—and I am most happy to be dependent on God rather than on myself. May I escape the fate of Lucifer, who clearly saw that his whole being, natural and supernatural, depended on God, and yet fell through pride. For his clear knowledge was merely speculative, and he set his will against it, desiring to be like God not through grace, but through his own power.

348 I realized from the outset that my knowledge is practical only when I feel that I have nothing to boast of or be vain about because, of myself, I am nothing, have nothing, am worth nothing, can do nothing, and do nothing. I am like a saw in the carpenter's hands.

349 I understood, too, that I should feel nothing when I am scorned, since being nothing, I deserve nothing. And I have put this knowledge into practice, so that I am neither elated by esteem or honor nor cast down by censure or dishonor.

350 I have come to see that a truly humble man must be like a stone that, even if it is hoisted to the very top of a building, always gravitates toward the bottom. I have read many ascetical authors on the subject of humility, to gain a clearer idea of its nature and learn the means they suggest for acquiring it.[1] I used to read the lives of the saints most distinguished for this virtue, to see how they practiced it, because of my great desire to achieve humility.

351 With this in mind, I made humility the object of my particular examen and wrote down my resolutions, arranging them in the order in which they are presented in my booklet, *The Dove.*[1] I have made this examen noon and night for the past fifteen years and I am still not humble.[2] Even when I was doing my best, I would notice some new outgrowth of vanity in me that had to be cut back instantly—some feeling

of complacency in something that had turned out well, or some vain word that slipped out, which I would have to regret, repent, confess, and do penance for.

352 I understood quite clearly that our Lord wanted me to be humble and that He was helping me greatly in this direction by supplying me with motives for humbling myself. During my early years as a missionary, I was very much persecuted everywhere I went, and to tell the truth this can be very humiliating. All sorts of ugly calumnies were spread about me. People said I'd stolen a mule, and who knows what other nonsense. In every town I went to, the only things to be heard about me during the first half of the mission or other service were silly stories, lies, and calumnies. Thus I had much to suffer and to offer God, and at the same time a rich opportunity to practice humility, patience, meekness, charity, and other virtues.

353 This lasted throughout the first half of the mission, and it was the same wherever I went. But from the middle of the mission to the end, everything changed completely. Then the devil would try the opposite approach. Everyone would say that I was a saint and thus I would be tempted to become puffed up with vanity. But our Lord took good care of me. During the closing days of the mission large crowds would come to the sermons, confession, Communion, and other services. One could see the rich results and hear my praises on every side. But in those very days the Lord allowed me to feel a sadness so great that I can only explain it by saying that it was a special providence of God, letting this sadness press upon me like ballast, so that the winds of vanity could not carry me away.

354 My God, may you be blessed for taking such good care of me. How many times I would have lost the fruits of all my labors if you had not guarded me. Lord, I would have been like a hen that lays an egg. She cackles, the farmer comes and takes the egg away, and thus, although she lays many eggs a year, she loses them all by her cackling. My God, if you hadn't silenced me when I felt like talking about my sermons, etc., I would have been like that foolish hen, cackling and not only

losing all the good of it, but gaining a well-deserved punishment. For you have said, "I will not give my glory to another,"[1] and I, by talking about it, would have given your glory to the demon of vanity. Then you would have had to chastise me, and justly, Lord, for giving the credit not to you, but to your archenemy, the devil. When all is said and done, Lord, only you know whether or not the devil has managed to pilfer something in spite of all the powerful help you gave me. Have mercy on me, Lord!

355 So as not to be carried away by vanity, I strove to keep in mind the twelve degrees of humility listed by St. Benedict and approved by St. Thomas (IIa, IIae, q. 161, a. 6):

First, to be humble inwardly and outwardly, in heart and in body, with eyes turned toward the ground—for that is what the word *humi-litas* (ground-liness) means.

Second, to speak sparingly, reasonably, and quietly.

Third, not to be overly ready to laugh.

Fourth, not to speak unless you are spoken to.

Fifth, not to do your regular work differently from the way others do.

Sixth, to consider yourself the lowest of all and say so sincerely.

Seventh, to think yourself unworthy and of no use for anything.

Eighth, to know your defects and frankly admit them.

Ninth, to show prompt obedience in hard tasks and patient obedience in extremely harsh tasks.

Tenth, to obey and be subject to superiors.

Eleventh, to do nothing of your own will.

Twelfth, to fear God and keep His holy Law always uppermost in your mind.[1]

356 Even more than the teaching contained in these twelve degrees I strove to imitate Jesus, who tells all of us, "Learn of me, because I am meek and humble of heart, and you will find rest for your souls."[1] And so I constantly thought on Jesus—in the crib, in the carpenter's shop, on Calvary. I meditated on his words, his sermons, his actions; on the way He ate, dressed, and traveled from town to town. I took courage from his example and would ask myself, "How would Jesus

act in this case?" Striving to imitate Him filled me with contentment and joy because I was pleased to think that my model was also my Father, my Master, and my Lord. My God, how good you are! You gave me these holy inspirations to help me imitate you and be humble. May you be praised, my God, for if you had given anyone else the grace and help you have given me, how different they would have been from what I am!

Chapter XXIV

THE SECOND VIRTUE I STROVE FOR: POVERTY[1]

357 Seeing that the Lord, out of sheer good will and no merit on my part, was calling me to stem the torrent of corruption and cure the ills of a moribund society, I thought that I should dedicate myself to studying and gaining a thorough knowledge of the maladies of this social body. I did so, in fact, and found that this world is nothing but the love of riches, the love of honor, and the love of sensual pleasure. The human race has always been bent on this threefold lust,[2] but in our day the thirst for material things is drying up the heart and bowels of modern societies.

358 I see that we live in a century that not only adores the golden calf as did the ancient Hebrews[1] but also worships gold so avidly that it has pulled down the most generous of all virtues from their pedestals. I have seen this era as one in which selfishness has made men forget their most sacred duties to their neighbors and brothers—for all of us are images of God, children of God, redeemed by the Precious Blood of Jesus Christ, and destined for heaven.

359 I believed that this dreadful giant, which worldlings call all-powerful, had to be confronted with the holy virtue of poverty. So wherever I encountered greed, I countered it with poverty. I had nothing, wanted nothing, refused everything.[1] I was content with the clothes I had on and the food that was set before me. I carried all I had in a bandanna. The contents

of my luggage were a full-year breviary, a sheaf of sermons, a pair of socks, and an extra shirt—nothing more.

360 I never carried money or wanted any. One day I had a shock. I put my hand into my coat pocket and thought I felt a coin. Horrified, I took it out and was much relieved to discover that it wasn't a coin but a medal someone had given me long ago. I felt as if I had come back to life from the dead, so great was the horror I felt for money.

361 I had no money, but then I had no need of it. I didn't need it for horses, carriage, or train because I always traveled on foot, even though I did have to make some quite long little journeys, as I shall tell later. I didn't need it for meals because I begged for them wherever I went. Nor did I need it for clothes because the Lord preserved my clothes and shoes almost the way he did the clothes of the Hebrews in the desert. I knew quite clearly that it was God's will for me not to have any money, nor to accept anything but the meal that was set before me, never carrying any provisions.

362 I knew that people were deeply impressed by this detachment, and for that reason I was determined to maintain the position I had taken. To encourage myself, I would recall Christ's teaching on the matter and meditate on it constantly, especially those words, "Blessed are the poor in spirit, for theirs is the kingdom of heaven.... If you would be perfect, go, sell what you have, give it to the poor and come, follow me.... No one can be my disciple unless he renounces all things."[1]

363 I always remembered that Jesus had become poor Himself; he chose to be born, to live, and to die in the utmost poverty. I thought of how Mary, too, had always wanted to be poor. And I thought, too, of how the Apostles left everything to follow Jesus Christ. Sometimes the Lord made me feel the pinch of poverty but only for a short time. Then He would console me with whatever I needed, and the joy I experienced in feeling poverty was so great that the rich could never enjoy all their riches as much as I enjoyed my beloved poverty.[1]

364 I have observed one thing, and the least I can do is set it down here: When one is poor and really wants to be poor, freely and not by force, then he enjoys the sweetness of poverty. Moreover, God will take care of him in one of two ways —either by moving the hearts of those who have something to give so that they will give it to him, or else by helping him live without eating. I have experienced both.

365 I am going to list here just a few of the things that happened to me. Once I was on my way from Vich to Campdevànol to preach the Spiritual Exercises to some priests who had joined Canon Soler in the rectory. It was near the end of July and the weather was really hot. I was hungry and thirsty, and as I was passing the Inn of San Quirico de Besora, the proprietress asked me to come in and have something to eat and drink.[1] I answered that I didn't have any money to pay for it. She told me I could eat and drink as much as I needed and she'd give it to me gladly. I accepted.

366 Once I was traveling from Igualada to Barcelona. As I was passing the King's Mill Inn, at noon, a poor man took pity on me and asked me into the inn, where he spent four quarters to buy me a plate of beans. I ate them gladly and arrived perfectly well in Barcelona that same afternoon.[1]

367 On another occasion I was on my way back from giving a mission in the town of Baga. I passed through Badella, Montaña de Santa María, Espinalbet, and Pla d'en Llonch, as far as San Lorenzo dels Piteus. I walked all the way over the most rugged roads and had to cross swollen rivers and creeks.[1] In truth, crossing the rivers pained me the most—yes, even more than not eating; yet even in this the Lord was favoring me.

368 On one occasion I had to cross the river Besós, which was then quite swollen with water. I was about to take off my shoes when a little boy I'd never met before came up to me and said, "Don't take off your shoes; I'll take you across." "You'll take me across? You're so small you couldn't even get me up on your shoulders, let alone carry me across."

Nevertheless, he carried me across easily, without getting me wet at all.

369 I once found that the stream on the other side of Manresa had risen so high that the stepping stones across it were covered with water.[1] So that I would not have to take my shoes off, I decided to leap from stone to stone, coming down as hard as I could on each stone. With each step I took, the water splashed away and by continuing to leap like this I got to the other side without getting wet.

370 I had observed that the holy virtue of poverty not only edified people and upset the idol of mammon but also helped me greatly to grow in humility and advance in perfection. I can sum up what I learned by experience in the following comparison: The virtues are like the strings on a harp. Poverty is the shortest and thinnest chord and hence gives the highest sound. The shorter we are in life's conveniences, the higher we reach on the scale of perfection. Thus we see that Jesus spent 40 days and nights without anything to eat. He and his Apostles ate barley loaves, and they even ran out of these at times. Once the Apostles were so short of food that they took ears of grain and rubbed them in their hands to kill their hunger with the grains. They were even criticized for this by the Pharisees because they did it on a sabbath.[1]

371 Furthermore, this lack of resources abates pride, banishes arrogance, clears a path for humility, and disposes the heart to receive new graces. Thus it makes us ascend in perfection, just as lighter liquids rise to the top and heavier liquids sink to the bottom. O my Savior, make your ministers understand the worth of the virtue of poverty. Make them love it and practice it as you have taught us to, in deeds as well as in words. How perfect we would all be if only we practiced it well. What a great deal of good we would do and how many souls would be saved! On the other hand, if your ministers do not practice poverty, souls are not saved and the ministers themselves bring about their own condemnation out of avarice, as Judas did.

Chapter XXV

THE THIRD VIRTUE: MEEKNESS

372 I knew that the virtue an apostolic missionary needs most, after humility and poverty, is meekness.[1] Jesus told his beloved disciples, "Learn of me, for I am meek and humble of heart, and you will find rest for your souls."[2] Humility is like the root of the tree, and meekness is its fruit. St. Bernard tells us that we please God by humility and our neighbor by meekness. In the Sermon on the Mount, Jesus said, "Blessed are the meek, for they shall possess the land"[3]—and not just the promised land of those living in heaven but also the earthly hearts of men.

373 There is no virtue so attractive as meekness. If you stand by a fishpond and throw in little pieces of bread, the fish will crowd about the bank and come fearlessly up to your feet; but if you throw rocks instead, they will all swim away and hide. Men are much the same; treat them meekly and they will all show up at sermons and in the confessional; but if you treat them harshly they will be uncomfortable, stay away from the mission, and murmur against the minister of the Lord.

374 Meekness is one sign of a vocation to be an apostolic missionary. When God sent Moses, he gave him the grace and virtue of meekness. Jesus Christ was meekness itself, and because of this virtue He is called the Lamb. The prophets foretold that He would be so mild that He would neither break the bruised reed nor quench the smoking flax;[1] that he would be persecuted, calumniated, and covered with reproaches and yet remain as one without a tongue and say nothing.[2] What patience and meekness! Yes, by his labors, his suffering, his silence and death on the Cross, He redeemed us and taught us how we must act to save the souls He has entrusted to us.[3]

375 The Apostles, who were taught by the Divine Master Himself, all had the virtue of meekness, practiced it them-

selves, and taught others, especially priests, to practice it. Thus St. James says to any of us who thinks he is wise and understanding enough to teach others, "Let him show this in practice through a humility filled with good sense. Should you instead nurse bitter jealousy and selfish ambition in your hearts, at least refrain from arrogant and false claims against the truth. Wisdom like this does not come from above. It is earthbound, a kind of animal, even devilish, cunning."[1]

376 The first time I read these words of the Apostles I was horrified to learn that he called knowledge without meekness "devilish." Good God! Devilish! Yes, it is devilish, for experience has taught me that a bitter zeal is a weapon that the devil uses, and that the priest who works without meekness serves Satan, not Christ. When such a man preaches, he frightens away his listeners; when he hears confessions, he frightens away his penitents (and if they do confess their sins they do so badly because they are embarrassed and hide their sins out of fear). I have listened to many general confessions of penitents who had hidden their sins because of so-called confessors who had harshly reprimanded them.

377 One May I was conducting services for the Month of Mary. Large crowds were coming to hear the sermons and go to confession. In the same chapel where I was hearing confessions, another wise and very zealous priest was also hearing confessions. Age and long illness had made him short-tempered and so ill-natured that all he ever did was scold people. He cut his penitents short and so upset them that they dared not tell him their sins, and so they made bad confessions. They left his confessional in such a disturbed state that to ease their consciences they would come over and confess their sins to me.

378 Since bad temper and anger—the lack of meekness—often masquerade as zeal, I made a prolonged study of the distinction between the two so as not to make mistakes in a matter that can make such a crucial difference. I have found that the function of zeal is to abhor, flee, impede, detest, renounce, combat, and overthrow, if possible, everything that is contrary to God, his will and glory, and the hallowing of

his Name. As David says, "I have hated and detested iniquity; but I have loved your law."[1]

379 I have observed that true zeal sets us on fire for the purity of souls, the spouses of Christ, as the Apostle tells the Corinthians: "I am jealous of you with the jealousy of God Himself, since I have given you in marriage to one husband, presenting you as a chaste virgin to Christ."[1] And he says the same in another letter: "I daily die for your glory."[2] "Who is weak that I am not affected by it? Who is scandalized that I am not aflame with indignation?"[3]

380 The Church Fathers illustrate this matter by a comparison with the hen.[1] Consider, they tell us, the great love, care, and zeal a hen has for her chicks. The hen is by nature a timid, cowardly, and fearful animal, but when she is brooding she has a lion's heart; her head is always aloft, her eyes are always on the alert, always looking about for the least sight of danger to her chicks. No matter how great the foe, she rushes to their defense. She lives in a perpetual state of care that she shows by her constant clucking. So great is her love for her brood that she always goes about looking sick and discolored. Lord, what a curious lesson of zeal you teach me in this example of the hen!

381 I have learned that zeal is an ardent and violent love that needs to be wisely controlled. Otherwise it might go beyond the limits of modesty and discretion. Not because divine love, however violent, can be excessive in itself, nor in the movements and inclinations it gives to our spirits, but because our understanding fails to choose the proper means or else uses them in a disorderly manner. Uncontrolled zeal takes us over rough and wild roads; moved by anger it fails to keep within the bounds of reason and pushes the heart into disorder. This is how zeal acts indiscreetly, intemperately, so that it becomes evil and reprehensible.

382 When David sent Joab and his army against his rebel son, Absalom, he charged Joab not to touch him. But Joab, in the heat of battle, like a fury in his lust for victory, slew poor Absalom with his own hand.[1] God sends the missionary

to do battle against vice and sin but charges him most clearly to pardon the sinner, to bring this rebel son home alive so that he may be converted, live in grace, and come to enjoy eternal glory.

383 My God, give me a zeal that is discreet and prudent so that I may do everything strongly yet sweetly, meekly yet thoroughly. I hope to act in all things with a holy prudence, and to this end I shall try to remember that prudence is born in man along with his natural reason, is nurtured by study, strengthened by age, clarified by consulting those who are wise, and perfected in daily experience.

Chapter XXVI

THE FOURTH VIRTUE: MODESTY

384 The missionary, I would tell myself, is a spectacle to God, the angels, and men.[1] Hence he must be very circumspect and guarded in all his words, actions, and bearing. And so I resolved, both at home and away, to speak very little and carefully weigh the words I did speak because people take in everything and often in a sense quite different from what one said.

385 I resolved that in speaking I would avoid all those manual gestures that people in some quarters laughingly call "shadow-boxing." So I made up my mind that when I had to speak I would be brief, quiet, and serious and avoid touching my face, chin, or head—much less my nose. I would avoid grimacing, as well as poking fun, scorn, or ridicule at anyone because I knew that a missionary can lose much of the authority, respect, and reverence he needs through the levity and lack of self-control and modesty that lead him to indulge in such coarse displays. Besides, they only point to a man's lack of virtue and show that he has had little or no education.[1]

386 I was convinced, too, that a missionary should be at peace with everyone, as the Apostle Paul tells us.[1] Thus I never quarreled with anyone but strove to be kind with all.

I avoided all clowning and disliked silly and mocking talk. Although I always appeared joyful, pleasant, and kind, I disliked laughing because I remembered that Jesus was never seen laughing, although He did cry on occasion. I also remembered the proverb, "A fool raises his voice in laughter, but a prudent man at the most smiles gently."[2]

387 It is well known that modesty is the virtue that teaches us to do all things in a fitting manner. Because we should do all things just as Jesus Christ did, I used to ask myself in every situation, and still do, how Jesus would have acted. How carefully and with what purity and rightness of intention He did everything: preaching, eating, dealing with all sorts of people, praying! Thus, with the Lord's help, I resolved to imitate Jesus Christ in all things so as to be able to say by my actions, if not in so many words, "Be imitators of me as I am of Christ."[1]

388 I understood, my God, how important it is for a missionary's effectiveness that he not only be beyond reproach, but appear so to everyone because people pay more attention to what they see in a missionary than to what they hear him say. This is why it was said of Jesus, the model of missionaries, "He began to *do* and teach."[1] Doing comes first, then teaching.

389 My God, you know that, despite all my proposals and resolutions, I must have failed against the holy virtue of modesty. You know whether or not someone has taken scandal at my failure to observe this virtue.

Pardon me, my God. I give you my word that I shall put the Apostle's words into action and strive to let my modesty be known to all men;[1] and my modesty will be that of Jesus Christ, as the same Apostle exhorts us.[2] My Jesus, I give you my word that I shall also imitate the humble St. Francis of Assisi, whose modesty was a sermon in itself; who converted people by his good example. Jesus, love of my heart, I love you and want to draw everyone to your most holy love.

Chapter XXVII

THE FIFTH VIRTUE: MORTIFICATION

390 I knew that I could not practice modesty without the virtue of mortification, so with God's grace, I bent all my forces on acquiring that, cost what it might.[1]

391 In the first place, then, I strove to deprive myself of every pleasure in order to give pleasure to God. Without knowing how, I felt obliged to fulfill what was a mere proposal. My mind was faced with choosing between my pleasure and God's, and because my mind saw the glaring inequality between the two, even in the slightest matter, I would be forced to choose what then seemed more pleasing to God. I would joyfully abstain from the pleasure in question, to give pleasure to God. This is still the way it is with me in all things: eating, drinking, resting, talking, looking, hearing, going somewhere, etc.[1]

392 God's grace has greatly helped me in practicing mortification. I now know that mortification has been an essential need for me in working effectively for souls and in praying as I ought.

393 I have received special encouragement in practicing mortification from considering the example set by Jesus, Mary, and the Saints. I have read their lives carefully, with an eye to how they practiced mortification, and I have taken many notes from some of them such as St. Bernard and St. Peter of Alcántara. I read of St. Philip Neri that after 30 years of hearing the confession of one of Rome's most famous beauties he had no idea what she looked like.[1]

394 In my own case I can vouch for the fact that I know the many women who go to confession to me by their voice, rather than by their appearance. The fact is, I never look women in the face because it makes me blush and I get embarrassed. Not that they cause me temptations—thank God, I no longer have any[1]—just a sort of blushing I can't explain.

Thus I quite naturally and unconsciously observe that oft-repeated maxim of the Fathers, "Let your conversation with women be brief and to the point, with eyes downcast." I hardly know how to prolong a conversation with a woman, however good she might be. In a few serious words I say what has to be said concerning her case; then I send her off immediately, without looking to see whether she is poor or rich, beautiful or ugly.

395 When I was giving missions throughout Catalonia, I was a guest in rectories, where I stayed during the mission, and I can't remember ever looking at the face of any woman, even if she happened to be the priest's housekeeper, servant, or relative. Thus, it has happened that, on my return to Vich or some other town after an absence of some time, a woman would come up to me and say, "Father Claret, don't you recognize me? I'm the housekeeper at such-and-such a parish, where you stayed several days giving a mission." Of course I couldn't recognize her, never having looked at her, and so, with eyes downcast, I would just ask, "And Father so-and-so, the pastor—he's well, I hope?"

396 I had another experience that I know would have been impossible without a very special grace from God. During my six years and two months' stay in Cuba, I confirmed over 300,000 people, more of them women than men and more of these younger than older. But if someone were to ask me to describe the typical face and figure of the women of the island, I would have to say I could not, despite the fact that I had confirmed so many of them. I simply took a rapid glance at where their forehead was and then closed my eyes and kept them closed while I confirmed them.

397 Besides this natural blushing of mine in the presence of women, which prevents me from looking at them, I have the further reason of wanting to benefit the people. I remember reading years ago[1] that a famous preacher went to a town where he preached so effectively that afterwards people were saying, "What a holy man!" But one malicious wag remarked, "He may be a saint, but he certainly had an eye for the women!" This remark was enough to undo all the good re-

sults the preacher had gained in that town and canceled all the fruits of his preaching there.

398 I have also noticed that people form a poor opinion of a priest who does not mortify his eyes. In reading of Jesus Christ, I observed that He was always very mortified and modest in his glances. The evangelists are always careful to note the number of times He lifted up his eyes, as if it were something most unusual.[1]

399 I always strove to mortify my sense of *hearing*. Thus, I took no pleasure in useless conversations or idle words. I couldn't abide or tolerate uncharitable conversations; if someone started one, I would either leave, change the subject, or frown in disapproval. I also disliked listening to conversations about food, drink, money, worldly things, or politics. I didn't care for reading newspapers and would say that I preferred reading a chapter from the Holy Bible, in which I would read the truth, to reading newspapers, which are ordinarily full of lies and trivia.

400 I strove continuously to mortify myself in *speaking*. All the things I didn't like hearing, I didn't like talking about, either. I resolved never to talk about what I had said in my sermons.[1] I knew well enough how I myself disliked hearing others prate about their delivery, and I thought that I would only displease others if I spoke of such things. This is what led me to resolve never to talk about my preaching but to preach as well as I could and leave the rest in God's hands. If anyone offered me some advice on my preaching, I would accept it gratefully, without excusing my practice or giving reasons for it. Then I would try to correct any fault as best I could.

401 I have already pointed out that some people act like hens who, having laid an egg, begin to cackle and so lose it. This is much like the case of some ill-advised priests who, after they have done some good deed or heard confessions or given a sermon, go around looking for little tidbits to satisfy their vanity. They talk complacently about what they've said or how they've said it. Just as I myself am disgusted lis-

tening to such talk, I can well imagine that I would disgust others if I were to do the same. So I resolved never at all to talk about these things.

402 One thing I really couldn't bear was to hear any talk about things heard in the confessional, not only because of the danger of breaking the seal of confession but also because of the very bad impression such talk makes on people. So I resolved never to speak of topics or persons involved in confession, of how long it had been since someone had made his last confession, or whether or not someone had made a general confession. In short, I couldn't endure hearing priests talk about persons, topics, or times in connection with confession. If someone came to ask my opinion, I couldn't bear to hear him start, "I have this case—what shall I do?" I would tell him to express himself always in the third person, e.g., "Suppose a confessor was faced with such and such a problem; what should he do to solve it?"

403 One thing that the Lord gave me to understand is that it is important for a missionary to deny himself in taking food and drink. The Italians have a saying to the effect that no one gives credit to saints who like to eat. People would like to think of missionaries as men who are more heavenly than earthly and that we are like saints' statues that don't need to eat or drink. In this respect, our Lord has given me the very special grace of being able to get along without eating, or with eating very little.

404 I had three reasons for not eating. First, because I was able not to—I had no appetite, especially when I had to do a lot of preaching or had to hear large numbers of confessions. Second, on certain occasions when I did have some appetite, I wouldn't eat, especially when I was about to start on a trip, so as not to be heavy on my feet. Finally, I abstained from eating in order to edify people because I noticed that they were always watching me. Thus I ate very little even though I was hungry.

405 Whenever I did eat what was set before me, I always took very little and the poorest that was offered. If I arrived

at a rectory at an inconvenient hour, I asked the cook for a little soup and an egg—nothing more. For I never ate meat then and I still don't. Not that I wouldn't like it, but I know that abstaining from it is very edifying. The same goes for wine. Of course I like wine, but I haven't taken any for years, outside of the ablutions at Mass. I never drink spirits or liquor, either, although I like them and have tasted them in the past. I have come to know that abstaining from food and drink is very edifying and is much needed to counteract the sad excesses that take place at table nowadays.

406 I was in Segovia on September 4, 1859 and while I was making my meditation, at 4:25 in the morning, Jesus told me, "You must teach your missionaries mortification in eating and drinking, Anthony." A few minutes later the Blessed Virgin said, "If you do, you will have great results, Anthony."

407 At that time I was preaching a mission in the cathedral of Segovia to priests, nuns, and laity. One day, as we were at table together, someone told the story of how the former bishop, a very zealous man, had exhorted a group of priests to go out and give missions, which they did. After walking for a good stretch they were hungry and thirsty and, since they had brought some food along with them, they sat down to have lunch. While they were eating, a delegation from the town to which they were going arrived to greet them. But when the delegation found them all eating, the priests lost so much prestige in the eyes of the delegation that their mission proved totally ineffectual. Thus the story went. I have no idea why it was told, but as far as I was concerned it came to me as a confirmation of what Jesus and Mary had told me.

408 Past experience has shown me how edifying this practice can be in a missionary, and I still find it useful today. Many banquets are held at the palace—there were even more at an earlier date—and I am always one of the invited guests. If I can, I excuse myself from attending; if this doesn't work, I attend. On these days, however, I eat the least. It is my custom to take only a spoonful of soup and one small piece of fruit—nothing more. I drink no wine, only water. Everyone sees me, of course, and all are highly edified.

409 I have been told that before I arrived in Madrid there were some excesses at table. Indeed, it is no wonder because such a variety of rich courses, exquisite dishes, and excellent wines were served, all an invitation to over-indulgence. But since I have been forced by duty to attend,[1] I have not noticed the slightest display of intemperance. On the contrary, it seems to me that the other guests take less than they need when they see that I am not eating. Often while we are still at table the guests seated on either side talk to me about spiritual matters and want to know what church I hear confessions in so that they can go to confession there.

410 To give still greater edification, I have refrained from smoking or taking snuff. Furthermore, I have never said or even hinted that I prefer any one thing to another. This, of course, is an old habit with me. The Lord had already given me this heavenly blessing while my dear mother (R.I.P.) was still alive. She died without ever knowing what I liked best. Because she loved me so much and wanted to please me, she would sometimes ask me whether I liked this or that. I would answer that whatever she chose for me was what I liked best. Then she would say, "I know, but there is always something we like better than something else." I would still tell her that what she gave me was what I liked best. Naturally I, like everyone else, prefer some things to others; but the spiritual joy I feel in doing the will of others is far greater than that of any particular physical preference, so that I was telling my mother the truth.[1]

411 Besides mortifying myself in sight, hearing, speech, taste, and smell, I also strove to practice some particular acts of mortification. On Mondays, Wednesdays, and Fridays I took the discipline. On Tuesdays, Thursdays, and Saturdays I wore the cilice. If circumstances were such that I couldn't take the discipline, I would do some equivalent penance such as praying with my arms outstretched in the form of a cross or kneeling on my fingers.

412 I am well aware that worldly people, who lack the spirit of Jesus Christ, ridicule or even condemn such mortifications; but I remember the teaching of St. John of the Cross con-

cerning this. He says that if anyone tells you that you can be perfect without practicing external mortification, you should pay him no heed. Even if he worked miracles to confirm what he says, you should regard them as illusions.[1]

413 I can see that St. Paul mortified himself and said so publicly: "I chastise my body and bring it into subjection, lest having preached to others I myself become a castaway."[1] All the saints down to this day have done so. Rodríguez relates that the Blessed Virgin told St. Elizabeth of Hungary that ordinarily no spiritual grace comes to the soul except by means of prayer and bodily affliction.[2] There is a maxim, "Give me blood and I will give you spirit." Woe to those who are enemies of the scourging and cross of Christ!

Chapter XXVIII

THE VIRTUE OF MORTIFICATION (CONTINUED)

414 I know that in a single act of mortification one may practice many other virtues, depending on the different intentions one has in performing each act. Thus, for example:

(1) One who mortifies his body to check concupiscence performs an act of the virtue of *temperance.*

(2) If he does so to set his life in proper order, he performs an act of the virtue of *prudence.*

(3) If he does so to make satisfaction for his past sins, he performs an act of *justice.*

(4) If he does so to overcome difficulties in his spiritual life, he performs an act of *fortitude.*

(5) If he does so to offer sacrifice to God by depriving himself of something pleasant and doing something bitter or repugnant to himself, he performs an act of the virtue of *religion.*

415 (6) If he does so to receive greater enlightenment in understanding the attributes of God, he performs an act of *faith.*

(7) If he does so to make his salvation more secure, he performs an act of *hope.*

(8) If he does so to help convert sinners or to free the souls in purgatory, he performs an act of fraternal *charity*.

(9) If he does so to have more to give the poor, he performs an act of the virtue of *mercy*.

(10) If he does so to please God more and more, he performs an act of *love of God*.

In every act of mortification I can practice all ten of these virtues, depending on the intention I form in doing the action.

416 The greater the sacrifice involved, the more meritorious, splendid, winsome, and overwhelming is any act of virtue.

417 A man who is base, vile, stingy, and cowardly never sacrifices—nor can he because he never resists the slightest whim or urging of his concupiscence. All that his concupiscence asks for—if it is within his power to grant or refuse it—he grants, refusing nothing to his passion. Because he is a cringing coward, he lets himself be overcome and gives in to it. In a fight between a brave man and a coward, the brave man wins. In a fight between vice and a man of vice, vice wins and pins the man down. This is why continence and chastity are praised so highly: because they enable a man to abstain from the pleasures and delights that nature and passion offer him.

418 A man's merit will be greater depending on the greater the pleasure he abstains from, the greater the repugnance he has to overcome, the greater the intensity and length of the pain he has to bear, the greater the human respect he has to set aside, and the greater the sacrifices he has to make—provided he does all and bears all for the love of virtue and the greater glory of God.

419 I resolved that in my outward bearing I would be modest and recollected; that in my inner being I would be continuously and fervently absorbed with God; that in my work I would be patient, silent, and long-suffering. I proposed, furthermore, to fulfill the law of God and the Church exactly, as well as the duties that God demands of my state; to do good to all men; to shun sins, faults, and imperfections; and to practice the virtues.

420 In all of life's disagreeable, sad, and humiliating events, I always remind myself that they come from God's hand, for my betterment. And so, as soon as I think of it, I manage to turn to God in silent resignation to his holy will, remembering that our Lord has said that not a hair can fall from my head unless it is the will of the Heavenly Father, who loves me so much.[1]

421 I know that 300 years of faithful service to God are rewarded, and more than rewarded, by one hour of pain that I am allowed to suffer, so great is its worth. Jesus, my Master! It is the man who is tried, persecuted, and deprived of friends; the man who bears the outer cross of work and the inner cross of spiritual dryness; the man who holds his tongue, suffers and endures out of love; this is the man you love, the man who pleases you and counts in your esteem.[1]

422 Thus it is that I have resolved never to vindicate, excuse, or defend myself whenever I am censured, misjudged, and persecuted because I would then be the loser in the eyes of God and of men. Yes, men would shape even the truth of my reasons into weapons to turn against me.

423 I believe that everything comes from God and that God expects of me the tribute of suffering patiently for his love's sake every injury to my body, soul, and honor. I believe that I do the most for God's greater glory when I hold my tongue and suffer like Jesus, who died on the cross, deprived of everything.

424 Doing and suffering are the greatest proofs of love.

425 God became man. But what kind of man? What sort of birth, life, and death did He have? "I am a worm and no man, scorned by men and despised by the people."[1] Jesus is God and man, and yet his Godhood is of no help to his manhood in his pain and suffering, any more than the soul of a just man in heaven is of any help to his body that lies rotting in the earth.

426 God gave the martyrs his special assistance, but this very

same God abandoned Jesus, the man of sorrows, in the midst of his sufferings and great pain. Christ's body was far more delicate than ours and hence felt pain more than we do. Well then, who can even imagine what Jesus suffered? His whole life passed before Him. How much He must have suffered out of love for us. Such an intense and prolonged agony!

427 Jesus, my Life, I know and fully realize that suffering, sorrow, and work are the badge of the apostolate. With the help of your grace, my Lord and Father, I will embrace them and declare that I am ready to drink the cup of inner torment and the baptism of outer pain. And so I say, "God forbid that I should glory, save in the cross on which you were nailed for me and on which I, too, would be nailed for you."[1] So be it.

Chapter XXIX

VIRTUES OF JESUS THAT I RESOLVED TO IMITATE

In this chapter, Claret presents a concretely detailed synthesis of his image of Jesus, the model of missionaries: a series of facets of Christ's life that the Saint resolved to live as literally as possible.

428 (1) Humility, obedience, meekness, and love are the virtues that shine through the Cross and the Blessed Sacrament of the Altar. O my Jesus, help me imitate you!

429 (2) *Clothing.* Throughout his life, He had only a coarse tunic, woven by his mother, and a cloak.[1] They even stripped Him of these so that He died naked, unshod, and uncovered.

430 (3) *Food.* He took only bread and water during the entire 30 years of his hidden life. In the desert, at the end of 40 days of rigorous fasting, the angels brought Him bread and water, as they had done to Elijah. During the remaining years of his public life, He ate what was set before Him and conformed to custom. The meal that He and the Apostles shared

was barley loaves and broiled fish, and sometimes they didn't even have this because they plucked ears of grain to ease their hunger and were criticized for it.[1]

On the cross He said "I thirst," but they only gave Him gall and vinegar,[2] to his greater torment.

431 (4) *House.* He had none. The birds have nests and the foxes have lairs, but Jesus doesn't even have a stone on which to lay his head.[1] For his birth, He had a manger; for his death, He had a cross. To survive, He had to flee to Egypt as an exile. For the rest, He lived in Nazareth or any place He happened to be.

432 (5) *Travels.* He always went on foot. The only time He rode on an ass was at his entry into Jerusalem, in order to fulfill the prophecies concerning Him.[1]

433 (6) *Money.* He had none. To pay the tribute tax He performed a miracle, taking what was needed from the mouth of a fish.[1] If pious people offered an alms, not He, but Judas, the only wicked Apostle, kept it.

434 (7) *By day* He preached and cured the sick, and by night He prayed. "And He spent the night in communion with God."[1]

435 (8) *Jesus* was the friend of children, the poor, the sick, and sinners.

436 (9) *He sought not his own glory,* but that of his heavenly Father.[1] Everything He did was done to fulfill his Father's will and to save souls, the beloved sheep for whom He, their Good Shepherd, gave his life.

437 O my Jesus, give me your holy grace so that I may imitate you perfectly in practicing all the virtues. As you well know, I can do all things with you and absolutely nothing without you.

Chapter XXX

THE VIRTUE OF LOVE OF GOD
AND NEIGHBOR

438 Love is the most necessary of all the virtues. Yes, I say it and will say it a thousand times: the virtue an apostolic missionary needs most of all is love. He must love God, Jesus Christ, the Blessed Virgin Mary, and his neighbors. If he lacks this love, all his talents, however fine in themselves, are for nothing. But if, together with his natural endowments, he has much love, he has everything.[1]

439 Love in a man who preaches the Word of God is like fire in a musket. If a man were to throw a bullet with his hands, he would hardly make a dent in anything; but if he takes this same bullet and ignites some gunpowder behind it, it can kill. It is much the same with the Word of God. If God's Word is spoken only naturally, it does very little; but if it is spoken by a priest who is filled with the fire of charity— the fire of love of God and neighbor—it will wound vices, kill sins, convert sinners, and work wonders. We can see this in the case of St. Peter, who walked out of the upper room afire with the love he had received from the Holy Spirit, with the result that through just two sermons he converted 8,000 people, three in the first sermon and five in the second.[1]

440 The same Holy Spirit, by appearing in the form of tongues of fire above the Apostles on Pentecost, showed us this truth quite clearly: an apostolic missionary must have both heart and tongue ablaze with charity. One day the Venerable Avila was asked by a young priest what he should do to become a good preacher. His ready answer was, "Love much."[1] And both experience and the history of the Church teach us that the greatest preachers have always been the most fervent lovers.

441 In truth, the fire of love acts in a minister of the Lord in much the same way that material fire acts in the engine of a locomotive or a ship: it enables them to move the heaviest

cargo with the greatest of ease.[1] What good would either of these two huge machines be without fire and steam to move them? None at all. What good is a priest who has finished all his studies and holds degrees in theology and canon and civil law if he lacks the fire of love? None at all. He is no good for others because he is like a locomotive without steam. Instead of being a help, as he should, he may only be a hindrance. He is no good even for himself. As St. Paul says, "If I speak with human tongues and angelic as well, but do not have love, I am a noisy gong, a clanging cymbal."[2]

442 Thoroughly convinced that to be a good missionary it is both useful and essential to have love, I have searched for this hidden treasure and would sell everything in order to find it. I studied the means to acquire it and discovered the following: (1) keeping the commandments of God's law, (2) practicing the evangelical counsels, (3) corresponding faithfully with divine inspirations, (4) making one's meditation well.[1]

443 (5) Asking and begging for love continuously and incessantly, without flagging or growing tired of asking for it, however late it seems in coming.[1] Praying to Jesus and Mary and, above all, asking our Father who is in heaven, through the merits of Jesus and Mary, in the sure hope that that good Father will give the Holy Spirit to those who keep asking thus.[2]

444 (6) Hungering and thirsting after this love. Just as a man who is physically hungry and thirsty is always thinking of ways to satisfy his craving and asks for food and drink wherever he thinks he can get them, I am resolved to do so by my sighs and burning desires. I turn to the Lord and ask Him with all my heart, "O my Lord, you are my love, my honor, my hope, and my refuge! You are my life, my glory, my goal! O my love, my happiness, my sustainer! O my delight, my reformer, my master, my Father! O my love!"

445 Lord, I want to know nothing but your holy will, that I may do it, and do it, Lord, as perfectly as possible. I want nothing but you yourself, Lord, and in you—and only through and for you—all other things. For you are all I need. You are

my Father, my friend, my brother, my spouse, my all. I love you, my Father, my strength, my refuge, and my consoler. Make me love you, Father, as you love me and wish me to love you. I know, my Father, that I do not love you as I ought, but I am quite sure that a day will come when I will love you as much as I desire to because you will grant me the love I ask through Jesus and Mary.

446 My Jesus, there is one thing I ask that I know you will grant. Yes, my Jesus, I ask you for love, for great flames of that fire you brought down from heaven to earth. May that sacred fire enkindle, burn, melt, and pour me into the mold of God's will.

447 Mary, my Mother, Mother of Divine Love,[1] I can ask for nothing more pleasing to you, nor anything that you are more ready to grant, than the love of God. Grant me this, my Mother and my love. Mother, I am hungry and thirsty for love; help me, satisfy my need. O Heart of Mary, furnace and instrument of love, kindle in me the love of God and neighbor.

448 My neighbor, I love and cherish you for a thousand reasons. I love you because God wants me to love you; because God commands me to love you; because God himself loves you. I love you because God has created you in his image for the life of heaven. I love you because you have been ransomed by the blood of Jesus Christ. I love you because of all that Jesus Christ has done and suffered for you. To prove my love for you, I will strive and suffer; I will undergo any work or pain, even death, if necessary, for your sake. I love you because Mary, my dear Mother, loves you, and because all the angels and saints of heaven love you. I love you and out of love for you I will free you from sins and the pains of hell; I will teach you the evils you must avoid and the virtues you must practice; and I will accompany you along the road of good works and of heaven.

449 Here I seem to hear a voice that says, "Man needs someone to help him understand his being, to instruct him in his duties, to guide him in virtue, to renew his heart, to restore him to his dignity and, to some extent, his rights,[1] and all

this is done through the Word."[2] The Word has been, is, and will always be queen of the world.

450 The Word of God brought all things out of nothingness. The divine Word of Jesus Christ restored all things. Christ told his Apostles, "Go out into the world and preach the Gospel to every creature."[1] St. Paul told his disciple Timothy, "Preach the Word."[2] Society is perishing for no other reason than that it has withdrawn from the Church's Word, which is the Word of life and the Word of God. Societies have become weak and are starving because they have ceased to receive the daily bread of God's Word. Every plan of salvation will be sterile unless there is a return to the fullness of the great, catholic Word.

451 The right to speak out and teach the nations, which the Church received from God himself in the person of the Apostles, has been usurped by a mob of obscure journalists and utterly ignorant charlatans.

452 The ministry of the Word—at once the most exalted and invincible of all ministries because it has overcome the world —has been converted everywhere from a ministry of salvation into a wretched ministry of ruin. And just as nothing or no one could hold back its triumphs in apostolic times, so nothing or no one can hold back its ravages today unless it is confronted by the preaching of priests and a flood of good books and other holy and wholesome writings.

453 O my God, I give you my word that I shall do this: I shall preach, write, and circulate good books and pamphlets in abundance, so as to drown evil in a flood of good.

Chapter XXXI

TOWNS I HAVE PREACHED IN AND PERSECUTIONS I HAVE SUFFERED

454 Thus far I have described the means I considered essential for me to use and the virtues I must possess if I were to

achieve any success in the towns to which bishops sent me (for I desired to go nowhere unless under obedience). Now I will say something about the towns I went to and what I did there.[1]

From early in 1840, after my return from Rome, until early in 1848, when I left Madrid to go to the Canary Islands with His Excellency Msgr. Codina, the bishop of those islands, I preached in the following towns: Viladrau, Seva, Espinelvas, Artés, Igualada, Santa Coloma de Queralt, Prats del Rey, Calaf, Calldetenas, Vallfogona, Vidrá, San Quirico, Montesquíu, Olot, Olost, Figueras, Bañolas, San Feliu de Guíxols, Lloret, Calella, Malgrat, Arenys de Mar.

455 Arenys de Munt, Mataró, Teyá, Masnou, Badalona, Barcelona, San Andrés, Granollers, Hospitalet, Villanueva, Manresa, Sampedor, Sallent, Balsareny, Horta, Calders, Moyá, Vich, Gurb, Santa Eulalia, San Feliu, Estany, Oló, San Juan de Oló, Pruit, San Feliu de Pallarols, Piera, Pobla de Lillet, Bagá, San Jaime de Frontanyá, Solsona, Anglesola, San Lorenzo del Piteus, Lérida, Tarragona, Torredembarra, Altafulla, Constantí, La Selva, Valls, Alforja, Falset, Pont de Armentera, Barbará, Montblanch, Vimbodí, Vinaixa, Espluga de Francoli, Cornudella, Prades, Vilanova de Prades, and many, many more.

456 I didn't travel directly from one town to the next. On the contrary, I would go to one town and when I had finished there, I would go to another town a good distance away. I did so either because the townspeople had requested my services of my superior, the Bishop of Vich, whom I always obeyed with the utmost deference, or because it was demanded by those turbulent times, when the ministers of religion or any good cause were being so greatly persecuted.

457 At each town I preached in, the first half of the service was marked by persecutions and calumnies by the wicked of the town. Halfway through the mission these people would be converted and everyone would sing my praises. Then the government and the higher officials would begin persecuting me. This is why my bishop made me go from one town to another town far away. In this way, the government's perse-

cution of me became something of a joke because by the time a warrant had been put out against me in one province of Catalonia, I had already finished the mission there and gone off to another province. And by the time they got around to persecuting me there, I was already off to yet another province. Despite all the government's efforts to pursue and apprehend me, they were never able to succeed.

458 General Manzano[1] himself told me later, when we were both in Cuba (I as Archbishop and he as Governor General of the city of Santiago), that he had been commissioned to arrest me, not because the government had any charge against me—since I never meddled in politics—but because they were worried at the crowds that gathered from all over whenever I preached. Furthermore they were afraid that, because of the immense prestige in which I was held, my least insinuation might cause a general uprising. Hence they sought to take me but could never catch me, either because of my strategy of moving so far away or because our Lord didn't want them to—and this was the main reason. The Lord wanted me to preach the Word of God to these people, while the devil was hard at work trying to corrupt them with dances, theatres, military maneuvers, platoons, books, evil magazines, etc.

459 On Sundays and feast days, in many of the towns, the men had to bear arms and take part in military maneuvers and so could not attend Mass or other religious services, as was their custom. Good deeds were hindered and bad deeds of all sorts were encouraged. Everywhere you turned you could see nothing but scandals and outrages and hear nothing but blasphemies and lies. It seemed as if all hell had broken loose.

460 During that whole seven years, I was on the go from one town to another. I traveled alone and on foot. I had a canvas-backed map of Catalonia that I always carried with me, and on it I would mark the distances I traveled, as well as any resting places. I would walk for five hours in the morning and another five in the afternoon. Sometimes I had to walk through rain, other times through snow, or under the broiling sun of a summer's day. Summer caused me the most

suffering because I always wore the same cassock and rain-coat in summer as I wore in winter—and it got very hot. Furthermore my shoes and heavy woolen socks caused my feet to blister so badly that I sometimes had to walk with a limp. The snow also gave me a chance to practice patience, for when high snowdrifts covered the roads I couldn't recognize the landscape, and in trying to cross the drifts I would sometimes get buried in snow-filled ditches.[1]

461 Because I always went on foot, I would fall in with mule-drivers and ordinary folk, and so I had a chance to talk with them about God and instruct them in their religion. This had the added advantage of helping take our minds off the road and giving us a great deal of consolation. Once when I was traveling from Bañolas to Figueras[1] to preach a mission, I had to cross a river that had a large boulder in the middle. A large plank led from one side to the boulder, and another led from the boulder to the other side. I was crossing the river with some other people during a heavy gale. The wind blew so violently that it carried away the plank in front of me, as well as the man who was standing on it, and threw both into the river. There I was, stranded on that boulder in the middle of the river, leaning on my walking stick and fighting the blast, until a stranger waded the river, hoisted me on his shoulders, and carried me to the other side. I continued my journey but had to fight a wind so fierce that it blew me off the road more than once. Anyone who has traveled through Ampurdán knows what a wind races through the place—enough to make the sandy hills of Pegú shift their place.

462 I had to suffer not only heat and cold, snow and mud, rain and wind, rivers and seas (as I did from San Feliu to Tosa, sailing the white-caps against the tide),[1] but the demons as well, who persecuted me terribly. Once they caused a boulder to fall as I was passing. Again, on a Sunday evening in the town of Serreal, the church was packed with people and Satan dislodged a large stone from the main arch and made it fall to the floor, where it broke into a thousand pieces. Yet no one was hurt, despite the fact that it fell into the very center of the congregation. This event was a source of admiration to all present.[2]

463 Sometimes while I was preaching and the people were in a state of deep compunction, Satan would appear in the form of a terrified peasant, shouting that there was a fire in the town. Knowing his trick, and seeing that the congregation was becoming alarmed at the news, I would announce from the pulpit, "Keep calm. There's no such fire; it's only a trick of the enemy. But to put your minds at ease, send one person to see where this fire is supposed to be burning. If there is one, I'll get up and go with you myself. But I assure you there's no such fire. It's only a snare of the devil to prevent you from growing in holiness." And so it was. When I was engaged in open-air preaching, the devil would threaten us with storms. Sometimes he would afflict me with terrible maladies; but oddly enough, as soon as I realized that the malady was the work of the enemy, I was totally cured without any medical aid.[1]

464 If hell's persecution was great, heaven's protection was far greater. I experienced the visible protection of the Blessed Virgin and of the angels and saints, who guided me through unknown paths, freed me from thieves and murderers, and brought me to a place of safety without my ever knowing how. Many times the word went out that I had been murdered, and good souls were already having Masses said for me. May God reward them.

465 In the midst of all these turns of events I somehow got through. I had some good times and some so bitter that they made me weary of life. At such times the only thoughts and words I could summon up were about heaven, and this consoled and encouraged me greatly. I never refused suffering; rather, I loved it and even wanted to die for Jesus' sake. I did not rashly place myself in danger, but I was glad when my superior sent me to dangerous places, realizing that I might have the joy of dying for Jesus Christ.

466 In the province of Tarragona I was loved by nearly all the people, but there were a few who wished me dead. The archbishop knew this,[1] and one day as we were talking about this possibility, I told him, "Your Excellency, this in no way frightens me or holds me back. Send me anywhere in your di-

ocese and I'll go there gladly, even if I knew that the road was lined with two rows of murderers waiting for me with daggers drawn. I would gladly walk on, thinking it a gain to die.[2] My gain would be to die at the hands of those who hate Jesus Christ."

467 I have always wanted to die a poor man in some hospital, or on the scaffold as a martyr, or to be put to death by the enemies of the holy religion we profess and preach, thus sealing the virtues and truths I have preached and taught with my blood.

Chapter XXXII

TOPICS I PREACHED ON, AND THE CARE I TOOK IN PRESENTING THEM

468 In all of the towns I mentioned in the last chapter, and in others I have not mentioned, I preached various services under different titles. Although they weren't called "missions," because we weren't allowed to call them that, nevertheless the subjects I preached on were really mission topics. The services were labeled, variously, Lent, Month of Mary; Fortnight of the Rosary; Novena for All Souls; Octave of the Blessed Sacrament; Septenary of the Seven Sorrows; etc. Such were the titles we usually gave these services, and although they were nominally a "novena," we lengthened the number of days if we needed to.[1]

469 In each of the towns I mentioned, one or more of these services had been held that year or some recent year and had always been quite fruitful. There had been conversions of all sorts everywhere—mass conversions, great and extraordinary conversions. At the beginning of the mission everyone would come to hear me: some in good faith, others out of curiosity, and others out of sheer malice, to see if they could trap me in my speech.

470 During the opening service I never made a frontal attack on the vices and errors of the town I was visiting. Instead I al-

ways talked to them about the Blessed Virgin, the love of God, etc. As the wicked and corrupt saw that I was not attacking them, but was all love, sweetness, and charity in my speech, they were interested and felt like coming again. As I started talking about the last things that pertain to all of us, they were not offended. Finally, they underwent a complete change of heart. During the last days of the mission I was able to speak with complete freedom about their predominant vices and failings.

471 I believed that a certain class of sinners must be caught after the fashion of a man cooking snails. He puts them in a pot of cold water, which they like, and hence they come out of their shells as far as they can. The cook, in the meantime, has to see to it that the water heats up only a little at a time so that the snails die without sensing it and thus are cooked. If the cook were careless enough to throw the snails directly into hot water, they would withdraw into their shells and nobody would be able to get them out. It is much the same with sinners. If a missionary starts by blasting away at them with fire and brimstone, at the sound of that blast those who have come out of curiosity or malice will withdraw into the shell of their obstinacy and, far from being converted, will spend all their time and energy discrediting the missionary and ridiculing everyone who goes to listen to him. But if they are treated with sweetness, kindness, and love, they will be won over.

472 Among the many sinners who were converted, one deserves to be singled out: Don Miguel Ribas, a landowner from Alforja, a town in the archdiocese of Tarragona. This gentleman had formerly lived a very orderly life. Every year he made the Spiritual Exercises in the monastery of the Franciscan Missionaries of Escornalbou, where one of his cousins was a friar. When the Fathers saw the disastrous times that were fast approaching, they thought that they might prudently entrust certain documents to his safekeeping. But he interpreted their action in such a bad sense that he would never credit the word of a priest again. He gathered together his own little band of proselytes, who in a short while outstripped their master in wickedness.

473 His dogmatic and moral teaching was simple; it consisted in not obeying anyone. Children should not obey their parents; wives, their husbands; subjects, their superiors. Everyone was obliged to receive Communion daily, but without the inconvenience of fasting, etc., etc. At length Don Miguel was converted and, after offering to retract his errors, did so in a public document that was notarized in the parish rectory in the presence of 11 witnesses chosen from among the outstanding local citizenry, in accordance with the dispositions of the Archbishop of Tarragona.[1]

474 In every town I preached in, I spoke not only to the laity but also—depending on the amount of time I had at my disposal—to priests, students, nuns and sisters, the sick in various hospitals, and prisoners. In any event, I regularly preached to the priests for ten days, morning and evening, and directed them in the Spiritual Exercises.

475 As I traveled from town to town, I would think about some means for making the results of the mission or retreat more lasting. It occurred to me that one very effective means might be to give the people in writing what I had given them in preaching. This was the line of reasoning that led me to start writing small books and pamphlets for all states in life, entitled "Advice to ..."—priests, parents, etc. The effects of these books and pamphlets were truly gratifying.

476 In order to distribute them more widely, I hit upon the idea of founding the Religious Library. With the help of God and the protection of our Lady of Montserrat, I was joined in this enterprise by Don José Caixal and Don Antonio Palau, both canons of Tarragona at the time, who have since become the Bishops of Urgel and Barcelona, respectively. Since I was then giving missions in the surrounding dioceses, I consulted them on this project, as men who were wise and zealous for the greater glory of God, and they were a great help to me. Thus it was that as early as December, 1848, while I was in the Canary Islands, the Religious Library issued its first volume, my *Catechism Explained*. It has continued issuing new works to this very day, and its catalog of publications has grown considerably. Some of these publications have had

not only a large first printing but also numerous reprints—
The Straight Path, for example, now in its thirty-ninth printing. May it all be for the greater glory of God and of the Blessed Virgin Mary, and for the salvation of souls. Amen.

Chapter XXXIII

PREACHING MISSIONS IN
THE CANARY ISLANDS

477 The world has always striven to hinder and persecute
me, but our Lord has taken care of me and frustrated all its
evil designs. During the month of August, 1847, a number of
bands of men called "The Early Risers" began to spring up
all over Catalonia.[1] The newspapers put it out that the lead-
ers of these groups would do nothing without consulting
Father Claret first. This was only a move of theirs to discredit
my name and to invent some pretext for apprehending me
and putting an end to my preaching. But God our Lord arranged matters so as to snatch me from their clutches. He
sent me to preach in the Canary Islands, as I shall now relate.

478 I happened to be in Manresa, preaching to the Daughters
of Charity in the local hospital, when the Mother Superior
told me that Father Codina had been elected Bishop of the
Canary Islands.[1] She asked me whether I would like to go to
the islands to preach. I told her that I had no preference or
will of my own; that the only thing I liked was going wherever my superior in Vich sent me. If he told me to go to the
Canary Islands, I'd go there as I would to any other place.
That was all there was to it.

479 The good sister took it upon herself to write to the
bishop-elect and tell him what I had said. He, in turn, immediately wrote to Vich, and the Bishop of Vich wrote to me,
telling me to put myself at the disposal of the bishop-elect of
the Canary Islands. The latter was in Madrid and summoned
me at the beginning of January, 1847, and I went. During the
time it took to complete arrangements for the voyage, I was a
guest in the house of Father José Ramírez y Cortés, an ex-

emplary and zealous priest.[1] I attended the consecration of Bishop Codina and throughout my stay in the capital I busied myself preaching and hearing the confessions of poor patients in the General Hospital.[2]

480 We left Madrid for Seville, Jérez, and Cádiz, where I preached. From there we set sail for the Canary Islands.[1] Around the beginning of February, we arrived at Tenerife,[2] where I preached on Sunday, embarking from there on Monday for Grand Canary Island. Here I conducted the Spiritual Exercises for the priests, in a drawing room of the episcopal residence, with the bishop presiding at all the sessions. I also gave a retreat to all the seminarians and preached missions in all the parishes of Grand Canary Island.

481 I often had to preach in public squares because the crowds who gathered for the mission in every town were too large to fit in the churches. With such huge crowds I always preferred preaching in public squares, for obvious reasons.

482 My most time-consuming task was hearing all the confessions because everyone wanted to make a general confession of his life. To be able to do this, I asked the other priests to help me and explained to them a procedure for doing the job both quickly and thoroughly. I wanted to avoid having penitents quarreling over their place in line, and so, as they arrived, I had them form in groups of eight, four men and four women. Then I had them bless themselves and say the Confiteor and all the preliminary prayers for confession along with me. I found this most helpful, for otherwise I would have had to spend a great deal more time waiting for them to say all these prayers individually. This way, after they had said the prayers in common, they could begin their confession directly, when their turn came. And so we not only saved time and avoided squabbles but also avoided having crowds of people pressed up against the confessional.

483 Whenever I finished a mission, all the townspeople would accompany me on my departure; and the people from the next town would come out to receive me—one group bidding me farewell amid tears and the other welcoming me with

joy. If I tried to relate all the things that happened to me in those towns, I'd never be able to finish. I will relate just one of my experiences so that the missionaries may learn from it.[1]

484 After I had finished giving missions on Grand Canary Island, the bishop asked me to go to Lanzarote. He decided that his brother, Father Salvador, a Capuchin, should accompany me there to help with confessions because there were very few clergy on the island.[1] Well, it happened that the priest in question was very fat, and as it was a trip of some two leagues inland from the port to the capital, he asked me, "How are we ever going to make it? Do you want to walk or ride?"

I answered, "You know I never ride, but always go on foot."

"Well," he said, "If you won't ride, neither will I."

I told him, "You can plainly see what a burden it would be for you to walk that far. I can't permit it. Since you won't ride unless I ride, then I'll ride so that you can, too."

485 Presently they brought us a big camel and the two of us got up on it. Shortly before we arrived at the town, we got down and walked the rest of the way into town, where I started preaching the mission. As we were saying our goodbyes after the mission, a man asked me, "Are you the missionary who preached on Grand Canary Island?" I said that I was. "Well," he said, "people here were saying it couldn't be you because that missionary said he always went on foot and you came here on camelback. That's why I heard someone say, 'I'm not going to hear him talk because he's not the missionary from Grand Canary Island.'"

486 Toward the beginning of May, 1849, I left the Islands. The bishop wanted to give me a new hat and coat, but I wouldn't hear of it. All I took away with me were five big rips in my old coat, which I got from the crowds that always used to press about me as I went from town to town. I spent 15 months in those islands and worked every day, with God's help. I had no appetite whatsoever, and I underwent a few trials, but I did it all gladly because I knew that it was the

will of the Lord and the Blessed Virgin Mary, and, further-more, because so many souls were converted and saved.[1]

487 My God, how good you are! What unexpected means you use to convert sinners. The worldly sought to discredit me in Catalonia, and yet this was the very thing you took advantage of to send me to the Canary Islands.[1] Thus you freed me from the prison that was planned for me and took me to those islands to pasture those sheep of your heavenly Father's flock, for whom I would gladly have laid down my life to see them living the life of grace. Blessed be your love and the great providence you have always shown me. Now and forever I shall sing your eternal mercies.[2] Amen.

Chapter XXXIV

THE CONGREGATION OF THE IMMACULATE HEART OF MARY

488 Toward the middle of May I arrived in Barcelona[1] and returned to Vich where I discussed with Canons Soler[2] and Passarell[3] my plan to form a congregation of priests who would both be, and be called, Sons of the Immaculate Heart of Mary.[4] Both of them approved of my plan and the former, who was rector of the seminary of Vich, told me that as soon as the seminarians went home for the summer vacation we could meet in the seminary and live there until God would find some other place for us.

489 I presented the same plan to the Bishop of Vich, Dr. Luciano Casadevall, who had always been very fond of me. He was enthusiastic in his praise of the idea and agreed that we should live in the seminary during the summer vacation, while he, in the meantime, could have the Monastery of Our Lady of Mercy rehabilitated because the government had left it at his disposal. And so he did.[1]

While the bishop was in the process of putting the monastery in order, I talked with a number of priests whom the Lord had given the same spirit that motivated me. These were Fathers Stephen Sala, Joseph Xifré, Dominic Fábregas, Manuel

Vilaró, and Jaime Clotet.[2] I, Anthony Claret, was last of all. And, indeed, they were all better educated and more virtuous than I so that I felt happy and content to consider myself their servant.[3]

490 On July 16, 1849, after we had gathered together in the seminary with the approval of the bishop and the rector, we commenced our own Spiritual Exercises, which we followed with all exactness and fervor.[1] Because July 16 is the Feast of the Holy Cross and of Our Lady of Mt. Carmel, I based my first sermon on those words of the twenty-third Psalm: "Your rod and your staff give me courage" (v. 4), alluding to the devotion and confidence we should place in the Holy Cross and the Blessed Virgin Mary and applying it also to the project we were beginning.[2] We left those Exercises full of fervor, bound and determined to persevere, and, thanks be to God and Mary, all have persevered. Two have already gone to the glory of heaven, enjoying God and the reward of their apostolic labors and praying for their brethren.[3]

491 Thus we had begun and thus we continued, living together strictly in community. All of us were going out regularly to work in the sacred ministry. At the end of the Spiritual Exercises I gave to the tiny, newborn community, I was asked to give another set of Exercises to the clergy of Vich in the seminary chapel. On August 11, as I was coming down from the pulpit after the closing service, lo and behold, I was called to the bishop's palace. When I arrived there, he handed me a letter dated August 4, containing my royal appointment as Archbishop of Cuba. I was struck dead by the news. I said that I would by no means accept and begged the bishop to be good enough to answer for me, telling them that I would by no manner of means accept.

492 My God, may you be blessed for condescending to choose your humble servants to be Sons of the Immaculate Heart of your Mother!

493 Most Blessed Mother, may the courtesy of your Immaculate Heart, in accepting us as your Sons, be praised a thousand times! Mother, make us cooperate with such kindness

by becoming daily more humble, fervent, and zealous for the salvation of souls.

494 I tell myself: A Son of the Immaculate Heart of Mary is a man on fire with love, who spreads its flames wherever he goes. He desires mightily and strives by all means possible to set the whole world on fire with God's love. Nothing daunts him; he delights in privations, welcomes work, embraces sacrifices, smiles at slander, and rejoices in suffering. His only concern is how he can best follow Jesus Christ and imitate Him in working, suffering, and striving constantly and single-mindedly for the greater glory of God and the salvation of souls.[1]

Chapter XXXV

ACCEPTING THE NOMINATION AS ARCHBISHOP OF SANTIAGO, CUBA

495 Overwhelmed by the nomination, I had no desire to accept it because I considered myself unworthy and incapable of such a great dignity, for which I lacked both the necessary knowledge and virtue. Even after prolonged reflection on the matter, I concluded that, even if I had the required knowledge and virtue, it would be wrong for me to abandon the Religious Library and the Congregation, which were just coming into being.[1] Therefore I forcefully rejected all the overtures of the Papal Nuncio, Monsignor Brunelli,[2] as well as those of the Attorney General of Spain, Don Lorenzo Arrazola.[3] When both of these gentlemen, the Nuncio and the Attorney General, saw that they were getting nowhere with me, they decided to work through my superior, the Bishop of Vich, whom I always obeyed blindly, and he, in turn, formally commanded me to accept.[4]

496 This order shook me deeply: on the one hand, I didn't dare accept; on the other, I wanted to obey. I begged the bishop to allow me a few days of prayer to think things over before giving my answer, which he did. Then I called together Fathers Jaime Soler, Jaime Passarell, Pedro Bach, and Stephen

Sala, all of them very wise and virtuous priests whom I trusted implicitly, and begged them to commend me to God. I told them that I hoped they would be good enough to tell me, on the last day of the retreat I was about to begin, what I should do—whether to accept the appointment as the bishop had commanded or to oppose it completely. When the appointed day arrived, after conferring among themselves, they concluded that it was God's will that I accept the nomination. And so I did, on the fourth day of October, two months after I had been elected.

497 Once I had accepted Her Majesty's choice of my humble person, the customary formalities were immediately set in motion and the dispatch was sent to Rome. Meanwhile, I went back to the work I had been doing before: giving retreats to the clergy, students, nuns, and laity. During this period I conducted the Spiritual Exercises for the clergy of Gerona and gave a mission in that city, preaching every day from a balcony in the Casa Pastors to a huge crowd that filled not only the plaza, staircase, and porch of the cathedral but also the adjoining streets, as well as to all the people who were standing in the balconies, at the windows, and on the rooftops of the houses roundabout.[1]

498 During these days, God our Lord made me understand some very special things for his greater glory and the good of souls.[1] My election was proclaimed in consistory, the Papal Bull from Rome was delivered to Madrid and duly dispatched, and it was brought from Madrid to Vich by two exemplary priests, Fathers Fermin de la Cruz and Andrew Novoa. Meanwhile, I prepared myself by a retreat of several days, during which I drew up a plan of life that I would follow in my new assignment.[2] Thus prepared and disposed, I was consecrated in Vich, as I shall describe, God willing, in Part Three of this work.

NOTES TO PART TWO

Chapter I

113.1 Every day he read two chapters of the Bible—four in Lent—following Bishop Corcuera's advice. Throughout his life he was faithful to this reading and recommended it to others. He published a number of editions of the Bible so as to put it within the reach of all.

114.1 The Saint drew up two other lists of vocational texts that in part coincide with those in the *Autobiography* and in part complement it. These passages from Isaiah, culminating in the call of the Servant of Yahweh, were interiorized in the Saint's heart by the Holy Spirit, to make him understand the mission to which he had been predestined.

116.1 "You will seek but never find them, those enemies of yours. They shall be destroyed and brought to nothing, those who made war on you" (Isa. 41:12) is also cited in *Autob. Documents* III and IV and in *Writings,* pp. 435 and 447. Also, "Do not be afraid, Jacob, poor worm, Israel, puny mite. I will help you—it is Yahweh who speaks—the Holy One of Israel is your Redeemer" (ibid., 14) is cited in *Writings,* pp. 436 and 447.

118.1 Cf. Isa. 48:10–11: "And now I have put you in the fire (but not) like silver, I have tested you in the furnace of distress. For my sake and my sake only have I acted—is my name to be profaned? Never will I yield my glory to another" (*Autob. Documents* III and VII; *Writings,* pp. 436, 448). Isa. 49:3: "He said to me, 'You are my servant (Israel) in whom I shall be glorified'" (*Autob. Document,* III; *Writings,* p. 436).

119.1 Cf. Luke 2:48–49: "And his mother said to him, 'My child, why have you done this to us? See how worried your father and I have been, looking for you.' 'Why were you looking for me?' he replied, 'Did you not know that I must be busy with my Father's affairs?'" Luke 9: 58: "Foxes have holes and the birds of the air have nests, but the Son of Man has nowhere to lay his head."

120.1 On June 30, 1839, Dr. Casadevall accepted his resignation.

120.2 He had intended to gather together a group of priests dedicated to preaching missions, but Father Bach dissuaded him for the time being because of the civil war. Since Claret felt urgently called to preach, yet was unable to do so in his own country without being unfaithful to his own particular calling, he wished to offer himself to be sent on mission by the Pope.

Chapter II

121.1 At that time, Osseja had 1085 inhabitants. They made their living on the border traffic. The certificate that accompanied the pass for the interior is dated September 13, 1839 (Archives of the Spanish Embassy to the Holy See, Nineteenth Century, *Passports*).

122.1 Since he had been unable to obtain a visa, he followed the shortcut used by smugglers and fugitives, as far as Osseja. In Perpignan he rejoined the normal route between Barcelona and Rome. The stops and time-distances of his whole trip can be reconstructed from, Anonymous, *Guide to Arrival and Departure Roads for the Principal Towns between Spain and Rome* (Manresa, 1843), p. 47.

123.1 His name was Fr. Raymond Raurell, and he was pastor of Castellar de Nuch from 1834 to 1848.

Chapter III

128.1 The "person" in question could have been an aide of Fr. Henry Margalhan Ferrant, pastor of St. Martha's, who used to attend to the needs of priests persecuted by the Spanish revolution as they passed through Marseilles. Nevertheless Claret clearly insinuates that there was something extraordinary about this "person."

Chapter IV

129.1 Probably the pact of Vergara, signed by Maroto on August 30, 1839, wherein he lay down his arms and abandoned the Pretender, Don Carlos.

136.1 The trip from Civitavecchia to Rome took seven hours. They made it on the same day they landed, as Claret says in a note: "In '39, Feast of Rosary, arrived Civitavecchia and Rome" (*Writings*, p. 464). They followed the Via Aurelia to the horsegate near Bernini's colonnade. This explains why the first religious house they came to was the Transpontina.

Chapter V

137.1 The Transpontina was built in 1563 and is located halfway along the Via della Conciliazione, which was called the Via Alessandrina in those days. It is still a Carmelite priory.

137.2 Fr. Edward Comas (1788–1865), Carmelite (1806), Apostolic Commissioner for the Spanish Carmelites (1839–64), pastor of the Transpontina (1841), Beneficiary of Bethlehem Church, Barcelona (1850), professor of philosophy (1854).

137.3 San Basilio is located on the street of that name, between the Piazza Barberini and the Via V. L. Bissolati.

138.1 Fr. Francis Vilardell, a Franciscan missionary for twenty years in Palestine, was Commissioner General of the curia for Franciscan missions. He was named titular Archbishop of Pilippi, Vicar Apostolic of Aleppo, and Apostolic Delegate to Lebanon on March 8, 1839.

138.2 Giacomo, Cardinal Franzoni (1775–1856), created Cardinal (1826), Prefect of *Propaganda Fide* (1834–56).

139.1 The "professed house" was the Gesù. The only Spanish priest in that community was Fr. Bernard Hernandez, a native of Santiago de Compostela (1802–47), who was one of the directors of the Exercises in the house of San Eusebio—although it has not been established that he was the one who directed the Saint.

140.1 Fr. John Philip Roothaan (1785–1853), twenty-first general of the Company, since June 9, 1826, has been called its second founder because of the impulse he gave to its restoration. The love of Fr. Roothaan for Claret can be seen in his letters to him (Roothaan, *Correspondence* [Rome, 1836–40], Letters 257, 401, 402), as well as in those to Casadevall (Letters 480, 481).

141.1 Fr. Joseph Spedaliere (1791–1872), a Sicilian, was Provincial of the Roman Province.

141.2 "On October 29, 1839, I entered the Company, and on November 13, they gave me the habit" (*Writings,* p. 438). The novitiate of Sant' Andrea de Monte Cavallo, now in Via 20 Settembre, was founded by St. Francis Borgia in 1566. St. Stanislas Kostka died there on August 15, 1568. In Claret's day there were 60 novices, and the novitiate was at its peak. Fr. Roothaan considered it a model.

143.1 Fr. Vincent Maurizi (1780–1865) was novice master and rector.

146.1 Fr. John M. Ratti (1767–1851), a Milanese.

147.1 The novices called the one who passed around the notebook the *portinaro, caporale,* or just *capo.*

151.1 Perhaps Claret was thinking back on these times when he wrote to Fr. Lobo, who had been his vicar general in Cuba and was now a Jesuit novice: "For some time now, the Lord has been bringing me up Jesuit-style, that is, depriving me of whatever I like most and denying me what I desire" (*Correspondence,* Letter 537).

152.1 Ignatian spirituality, organized as it is for the service of a universal mission, struck a responsive chord in the spirit of Claret, the novice, who had come to Rome to be sent out by the Pope on a mission throughout the world. Furthermore, he had been initiated into this spirituality when he was in the seminary at Vich. Throughout his life he had kept this high esteem for Ignatian spirituality. However, he assimilated it in his own personal way, according to his own vocational needs, psychological conditioning, and family background, keeping his own originality intact. The *Caritas Christi urget nos* of his coat of arms is an expression of the *Ad majorem Dei gloriam* of St. Ignatius (J. Puigdesens, *The Spirit . . . ,* p. 195).

Chapter VI

153.1 These prayers are in the form of a filial and apostolic consecration to the Virgin Mary, paraphrased with all the vehemence and exuberance of a zeal that yearned to reach out and embrace the whole world but could find no outlet at the time except in prayer. The exalted, often oratorical style reflects the romantic tastes of the era. But beneath these appearances lies the sincerity of an intense and universal apostolic love. These prayers really contain the initial outlines of the spirit of both the Founder and his Missionaries.

157.1 Ps. 53:4: "There is not one who does good, not even one."

164.1 Fr. Geminiano Mislei, author of the book, *Mary, Mother of God and of Men,* and of a commentary on the Letters of St. Paul, was also assistant novice master.

Chapter VII

165.1 It was called San Giacomo in Augusta since it was near the mausoleum of Augustus, by the present-day Corso Umberto. There were 300 beds, 200 of which were usually occupied. It was also called the Hospital of the Incurables. (*Guide to Rome,* 1843, vol. 2, p. 619.)

166.1 In his *Witness to the Truth* (*Writings,* p. 456), Claret says that it was a rheumatic pain, brought on by the rain and dampness.

167.1 His actual words were, "I admire and praise the Providence of the Lord, who, having brought you here to master this weapon (the Spiritual Exercises), then took away your health and afterwards returned you to do so much good in your native land" (Roothaan, *Correspondence,* December 8, 1844, p. 625).

167.2 He left the novitiate on March 3, traveling under a papal passport and a letter from the French embassy. (Archives of the Spanish Embassy to the Holy See, Nineteenth Century, *Passports,* March 15, 1840.) On March 19 he sailed from Civitavecchia.

167.3 Fr. Fermin de Alcaraz (1774–1855) was a Capuchin, a missionary in South America, and Bishop of Cuenca (1849).

168.1 Fr. Joseph Vilanova, an exclaustrated Trinitarian.

Chapter VIII

171.1 Jaime Bofill, a noted herbalist in Barcelona, initiated St. Anthony Mary Claret into the knowledge of medicinal herbs.

173.1 John 11:21: "Lord, if you had been here, my brother would not have died."

176.1 (Translator's note) In this chapter and in chapters 12 and 14 of the *Continuation,* some rather quaint and involved accounts, as well as certain other reserved cases that the Saint included for the indoctrination of priests, have been suppressed, both in this edition and in that of the B.A.C. Their omission is indicated by a series of dots. (Cf. *Writings,* p. 178.) The omitted material may be found in the earlier English translation of the *Autobiography* (Trans. Louis J. Moore, C.M.F., Compton, 1945), as well as in the 1916 Spanish edition of the *Autobiography.*

180.1 Mark 16:18: "They will lay their hands on the sick, who will recover." When he began preaching as an apostolic missionary, Claret abandoned physical remedies and healed people only through prayer and the laying on of hands, explaining that his mission was to save souls.

182.1 Ps. 3:9: "Salvation is Yahweh's."

Chapter X

192.1 In chapters 1 to 10 the Saint has dealt with his vocation to, and formation for, the apostolic ministry. He now turns to treat of the ideal missionary's life and activities. These are the most formative chapters in the whole *Autobiography*.

To be a missionary requires a canonical mission (chapter 10). To be an *effective* missionary calls for an upright intention (chapter 11). Next follows a consideration of: the *examples* of some of the saints (chapters 12 to 15); the use of apostolic *means and methods* (chapters 16 to 22); the acquisition of apostolic *virtues* (chapters 23 to 30); an evangelical *mode of travel* (chapter 31). Chapter 32 complements chapters 19 ff.

193.1 He left Viladrau on January 23 to dedicate himself completely to the apostolate of evangelization. He was then 33 years old.

198.1 Before the government of the Regency fell (1843), Claret occasionally met with obstacles to his ministry. On these occasions he would say, "I have given up this preaching assignment because it was the will of my superior (Dr. Casadevall); but if things had been otherwise I would never have held back, even if I knew that they were waiting for me with daggers drawn at the foot of the pulpit" (F. Aguilar, *Life,* p. 61).

Chapter XI

201.1 Cf. Acts 20:24.

206.1 Zeph. 1:17.

207.1 1 Cor. 9:16.

208.1 Cf. Luke 23:24.

210.1 Mark 16:16.

210.2 Bossuet, *Sermons* (Valencia, 1774), vol. 2, p. 184. The Saint's personal copy.

212.1 Blessed Raymond of Capua, *Life of St. Catherine of Siena* (Rome, 1866), Prologue XV, p. 10. Claret's personal copy.

Chapter XII

214.1 In describing the prophets and Apostles, Claret unintentionally leaves us a self-portrait. The traits he describes are the very elements of his own vocation that he discovered with the light of grace and reproduced in his own life and apostolate.

220.1 Sirach 49:10.

223.1 Acts 2:41; 4:4.

223.2 Acts 4:19.

224.1 Many of the traits he sees in St. Paul coincide with his own unintentional self-portrait in the "pen-portrait" (par. 494).

224.2 Gal. 6:14.

226.1 *Confessions,* 1.8., chap. 11.

226.2 He has omitted St. Alphonsus Liguori, who was his inspiration and whom he named a patron of his missionaries.

228.1 Blessed Diego José of Cadiz (1743–1801), a Capuchin, was one of the apostles of Andalucía. Claret has synthesized in this account—which might as well be his own—the *Historical Compendium of the Life of the Very Rev. Fr. Diego José of Cadiz, Apostolic Missionary of the Propaganda Fide,* by Fr. Seraphim de Hordales, León, pp. 97 ff.

229.1 St. John of Avila (1499–1569), a secular priest, was another apostle of Andalucía. He traveled about tirelessly together with a missionary band of priests. Chronologically he was the first of the great spiritual writers of Spain's golden age. Claret used the works of St. John of Avila in the edition of Francisco de Aoiz (Madrid, 1759, 9 vols.). He probably acquired them as a seminarian, at a cost of 167 reals. They are much underlined and marked with slips of paper containing extracts from the work. Interestingly, both saints were mechanically inclined. Claret invented a system for steering balloons; Avila, four engines for pumping water.

231.1 Avila, op. cit., vol. 1, p. 50.

232.1 Ibid., p. 49.

Chapter XIII

235.1 St. Catherine had a great influence on the spirit of St. Anthony Mary Claret. He wrote to a friend: "I am sending you the *Life of St. Catherine of Siena,* who is my teacher and guide. Whenever I read her life, I am so moved that I have to have the book in one hand and a handkerchief in the other, to dry the tears it causes me" (*Correspondence,* Letter 25). From St. Catherine he derived the practice of the "interior cell," in order to keep the presence of God in the midst of his apostolate, as he explains in his pamphlet *Temple and Palace of the Lord, Our God* (Barcelona, 1866). He chose the saint as a copatron of his missionaries.

235.2 Fr. L. Gisbert, *Life of St. Catherine of Siena of the Third Order of Preachers* (Valencia: Peleguer, 1784), p. 9.

236.1 Ibid., p. 14.

236.2 Ibid., p. 66.

237.1 Ibid., p. 75.

238.1 Ibid., p. 174.

239.1 P. Ribadeneira, S.J., *Flos Sanctorum* (Madrid, 1761), vol. 2, p. 643. Claret's personal copy.

Chapter XIV

242.1 In 1864 the Lord granted Claret some profound insights while reading St. Teresa's works (cf. par. 797) and again in 1869, while reading the Fifth Mansion. The last resolutions he made in his life were based on the *Counsels* of the saint. There are 16 autograph pages of Claret's excerpts from the writings of St. Teresa. Claret chose her as a copatron of the Congregation of Missionaries.

242.2 *Life of St. Teresa,* chap. 7, par. 7.

243.1 Ibid., chap. 23, par. 5.

245.1 Ibid., chap. 27, pars. 14–15.

252.1 Ibid., chap. 30, pars. 1–7.

253.1 Ibid., chap. 38, par. 3.

254.1 Ibid., chap. 40, par. 1.

258.1 *Way of Perfection,* chap. 1, pars. 2–5.

Chapter XV

259.1 John Baptist de Lezena, *Life of the Prodigious and Ecstatic Virgin, St. Mary Magdalen de Pazzi* (Madrid, 1754), pp. 301 ff.

Chapter XVI

265.1 He means the Carmelite Sisters of Charity (founded by St. Joaquina de Vedruna in Vich in 1826), whose direction he undertook at the behest of Bishop Casadevall, from 1843 until his election as Archbishop of Cuba in 1850.

265.2 In a certain sense it could be said that all of his listeners formed a great association of mutual prayers, because wherever he went he requested prayers for his intentions and his request was so well received that it became a custom with his listeners to pray for him.

266.1 To spread devotion to the rosary, he published several pamphlets and the following booklets: *Devotion to the Holy Rosary* (1859); *The Holy Rosary* (1864), and *Remedies against the Evils of the Present Day* (1870).

266.2 Claret, *Meditations on the Seven Dolors of Mary for the Seven Days of the Week* (Vich, 1848). In Catalonia he also propagated this devotion in his *Camino Recto* (The Straight Path).

268.1 Devotion to St. Michael was always one of the Saint's favorites. He placed the Religious Library, the Congregation of Missionaries, and, above all, the Academy of St. Michael, under his protection. He wrote a booklet called *Excellences and Novena of the Glorious Prince, St. Michael* (Barcelona, 1859).

269.1 He published them in his booklet *The Two Standards* (Barcelona, 1870), written during the first Vatican Council.

270.1 This prayer is a synthesis of the spirit of St. Anthony Mary Claret: a *Son* of Mary, formed in the furnace of her love—her heart; a minister and *envoy* of Mary, the arrow of her might turned against the world, the flesh, and the devil. Claret refers here to the words he heard on the day of his ordination to the diaconate, which enabled him to understand the total meaning of the vision he had during his second year of philosophy (pars. 95-98).

270.2 1 Kings 16:31.

271.1 Eph. 6:12.

271.2 Heb. 4:12.

273.1 Testimonies given at the processes for beatification and canonization tell how the devil opposed the Saint's apostolic endeavors ferociously, going so far as to attack him personally. (Cf. Fernandez, *The Blessed . . .*, vol. 1, pp. 287 ff.)

Chapter XVII

275.1 St. Gregory Nazianzen, Or. 1: PG 35,395. Some of these considerations are taken from Bishop Corcuera's *Pastoral Declaration* (Vich, 1830) for the establishment of the CCD. Claret's copy of this document is heavily underlined and marked with arrows, dating from Claret's days as a seminarian.

277.1 St. Jerome, Epistle 128, to Gaudentius: PL 22,1095.

279.1 Gerson or Jean Charlier (1363-1429) dedicated himself to catechizing children mainly during the last ten years of his life. The words cited by Claret are from the prologue of Gerson's treatise, *On Bringing the Little Ones to Christ.*

280.1 John of Avila, *Works* (Madrid, 1759), vol. 1, p. 150. Claret's personal copy.

282.1 César de Bus (1544-1675), a secular priest, founded the Congregation of Secular Priests of Christian Doctrine and that of the Daughters of Christian Doctrine.

282.2 Cf. *Correspondence,* Letter 1418, where Claret tells Fr. Xifré, "I believe that at present they are doing more good than anyone else for the Church and are among those from whom we can expect the most."

283.1 Fr. Ignatius Martins (1530-98), a Jesuit (1547).

283.2 Isa. 33:18. Vulgate edition.

283.3 Fr. Edmond Auger, S.J. (1530–1619), entered the novitiate in Rome during the lifetime of St. Ignatius. He published a catechism and a summary of the Christian religion (Lyons).

284.1 He even taught catechism during the first Vatican Council. He wrote essential questions in Italian on a paper small enough to hold in his hand.

285.1 He actually composed 12 catechisms and edited various others. The catechisms he refers to here are: *Devotions for Little People* (Barcelona, 1858); *Manna for Christians,* an elementary summary of the catechism (Vich, 1850); *Compendium of Doctrine* (Barcelona, 1848); *Amplified Catechism* (Barcelona, 1848). At the time he was writing the *Autobiography,* he was working on a complete catechism, the *Catecismo único.*

Chapter XVIII

288.1 Some of these are preserved in the Claretian Archives in Rome.

291.1 Luke 20:20.

293.1 *Selva,* pt. 3, chap. 6, p. 303.

Chapter XIX

298.1 A Catalan expression equivalent to "That's some pill you expect us to swallow!"

298.2 Catalan for "You're right."

300.1 We still have copies of works by the following authors from the Saint's library: St. John Chrysostom, *Complete Works* (Venice, 1870); St. Alphonsus M. Liguori, *Sermons* (Bassano, 1829), *Selva* (Bassano, 1833), and his works on moral theology; Siniscalcqui, *Lent* (Venice, 1773); Barcia, *Lent* (Barcelona, 1686), *The Christian Awakener, Doctrinal Sermons* (Barcelona, 1687), *Christian Eucharistic Awakener* (Barcelona, 1690); St. John of Avila, *Works* (Madrid, 1759).

301.1 Jer. 2:12.

305.1 In the process for Claret's beatification, doctors attributed the Saint's health, in the midst of all his apostolic labors, to supernatural causes. (Cf. *Apostolic Process,* Vich, session 47.) His voyage to the Canary Islands took place in 1848, not 1847. (Cf. pars. 478 ff.)

Chapter XX

306.1 Cf. pars. 92 and 107.

307.1 Preserved in the Claretian Archives, Rome. Heavily marked and underlined.

309.1 *Spiritual Exercises of St. Ignatius, Explained by His Excellency, Bishop Anthony Mary* (sic), *Archbishop of Santiago, Cuba* (Madrid, D. F. Aguado, 1859). (Cf. *Writings,* p. 279, note 126.)

Chapter XXI

311.1 Cf. Matt. 15:19; Luke 7:21.

311.2 Ps. 14:1; 53:1.

317.1 In Catalonia this prayer became as popular as the "Salve Regina." It resembles the consecration popularized in Italy by Fr. Zuchi but has some entirely original traits of its own. It reads: "O Virgin and Mother of God, I surrender myself to you as your child, and in honor and glory of your purity I offer you my soul and body, my mind and senses, and ask that you obtain me the grace to avoid all sin. Amen." (Then, three times:) "Mother, behold your son!" (Continuing:) "I have placed my trust in you, good Mother, and I shall never be confounded. Amen." (Cf. Ramos, *An Apostle of Mary,* pp. 315 ff.) In par. 830 of the *Autobiography,* Claret mentions an extraordinary conversion attributed to saying this prayer.

317.2 Emmanuele Conciencia, *Life of St. Philip Neri,* 2 vols. (Madrid, 1760), vol. 1, p. 277.

322.1 This took place in 1850. (Cf. Fernández, *The Blessed,* vol. 1, p. 583.)

Chapter XXII

323.1 *The Straight Path* (El Camino recto) has been the most popular devotional book ever published in Spain. Nevertheless, it is not, as its title might suggest, just a collection of devotions but a manual of training in Christian life and piety. It is complete, understandable by everyone, and full of artless unction. An estimated two million copies have been printed.

326.1 Madrid, 1860 and 1861. The first volume deals with the overall training of a seminarian. The second is an ascetical commentary of the ordination ritual, as well as an ascetical and pastoral directory for administering the sacraments.

327.1 *The Art of Ecclesiastical Chant and Book of Chants for the Use of Seminarians* (Madrid, 1861). "Arrangements for this book cost me more trouble than any other because of the diversity of opinions in the field of chant" (*Correspondence,* Letter 952).

329.1 Founded in Barcelona in 1848.

329.2 Bishop Joseph Caixal Estrade (1803–79) was one of Claret's close friends and collaborators. Formerly canon of Tarragona, he became one of the cofounders of the Religious Library, Bishop of Urgel, and one of the Fathers of Vatican I (1870). He was imprisoned by General Martínez Campos (1876) and died in exile in Rome.

329.3 Doctor Anthony Palau y Termens (1806–62), canon of Tarragona and founder and director of *Revista Católica,* became Bishop of Vich (1853) and of Barcelona (1858).

332.1 The Academy of St. Michael was approved in 1859. (Cf. par. 581.)

334.1 He probably read the story in Rodríguez's *Practice of Perfection,* pt. 3, tr. 1, chap. 3.

336.1 2 Cor. 2:15.

336.2 Matt. 21:19.

336.3 Luke 24:32.

336.4 "When worldly people see that we think and talk only about God, they are highly edified and deeply moved to love Him" (Claret, *Memoir of the Academy of St. Michael* [Madrid, 1863]).

339.1 *Origin of the Devotion to the Blue Scapular* (Madrid, 1863).

Chapter XXIII

340.1 An idea he found, substantially, in his copy of Cicero's *De oratore* (Paris, 1740), par. 6, p. 135.

340.2 Acts 1:1.

340.3 1 Cor. 11:1. One of the cardinal points in Claret's spirituality is the idea that the missionary must be conformed to Christ, the chief and model of missionaries. All the virtues Claret treats of here are derived from a consideration of the style of life actually followed by Jesus in his preaching of the Kingdom of God.

341.1 Claret's treatment of humility is, characteristically, Christ-centered (par. 356). *Motives* for humility: because it is essential to the Christian apostolate (par. 341) and because it is pleasing to Jesus (par. 356). *Nature* of humility: a practical knowledge of one's own nothingness and a delight in being dependent on God (par. 347). *Acts* of humility: not taking pride in oneself (par. 348); not looking down on others; being constantly aware of one's own nothingness, even in moments of the greatest exaltation (par. 350); inner illuminations on this virtue (pars. 343, 344); an infused sense (par. 353); humiliations, especially those arising in the exercise of the ministry (pars. 342, 352); meditation and reading (pars. 343, 350); particular examen (par. 351).

341.2 Ps. 119:71.

342.1 This instance is typical of the Saint's spirituality. God's initiative first thrusts his heart into the furnace of love and places it on the anvil of humiliation; the Saint corresponds with all his might and means. But even then, he knows that his corresponding is itself a grace.

343.1 St. Augustine, *Soliloquies,* PL 32.885. Cf. St. Alphonsus Liguori's anthology of sermon topics, *Selva* (Bassano, 1833), vol. 1, p. 183. Claret's personal copy.

343.2 An expansion of an idea taken from St. Catherine of Siena. In Claret's copy of Ribadeneira's *Flos sanctorum* (Madrid, 1761, vol. 1, p. 665), he has underlined the following passage: "Do you know, my daughter, who I am and who you are? Blessed shall you be if you know it. I am who am, you are she who is not."

350.1 Claret annotated the following works on humility: St. John of Avila, *Audi Filia,* chaps. 57–65; Rodríguez, *Practice of Perfection,* Treatise on Humility, II, tr. 5, chaps. 6–7; Scaramelli, *Ascetical Directory,* tr. 3, art. 11, chaps. 1–4.

351.1 The full title was *Résumé of the Main Teachings Needed by Souls Aspiring to Perfection. Written under the Symbol of a Dove* (Barcelona, 1847). It was issued first as a leaflet and a year later as a booklet.

351.2 From 1847 to 1862.

354.1 Isa. 42:8.

355.1 St. Benedict, *Rule,* chap. 7. St. Thomas inverts the order of this rule. Claret studied St. Thomas's treatise on the virtues (cf. note on par. 105) and follows the text of the *Summa* closely.

356.1 Matt. 11:29.

Chapter XXIV

357.1 Claret looked upon poverty as an essential for following Christ, the Preacher (pars. 362, 370; 130–135). Among those texts in which he discovered the elements of his vocation, he stressed some that relate directly to poverty (e.g., Luke 9:59, Isa. 48:10 in the Vulgate edition). There are no reservations in his acceptance of poverty: "I had nothing, wanted nothing, refused everything" (par. 359). This poverty in the ministry of preaching recalls the practice of St. Dominic and all the great apostolic preachers.

357.2 John 2:16.

358.1 Exod. 22:4 ff.

359.1 This norm of conduct was inspired by Jesus' recommendations to his apostles before He sent them out on their first missionary journey (Matt. 9:35–42).

362.1 Matt. 5:3; Mark 19:21; Luke 14:23.

363.1 "As regards holy poverty, I am well aware of what the holy canons of the Church and the laws of the kingdom declare; but this, though it is good, is but our common task. But ours is an exceptional case. God wants us to give public witness in support of poverty, since in our day, unfortunately, more trust is put in money than in God" (*Correspondence,* Letter 946).

365.1 The two towns were ten-and-a-half hours walking distance apart. The Saint would have been walking for five hours before he reached the Inn of San Quirico. The year was 1843.

366.1 It was a ten-and-a-half-hour walk from Igualada to the King's Mill and a three-hour walk from there to Barcelona. This episode also took place in 1843.

367.1 It was July 2, 1845. It was a twelve-hour walk from Baga to San

Lorenzo. This was in the Pyrenees and the Saint had to cross at least five rivers: the Bastereny, the Saldes, the Aguade, the Valls, and the Cardener.

369.1 For a native of Sallent, "the other side of Manresa" means the west. The river he refers to is most likely the Riera de Rajadell.

370.1 Matt. 4:2; Mark 2:23; John 6:9.

Chapter XXV

372.1 Christ announced the reign of God in meekness and humility, not power and violence. (Cf. pars. 372–375.) The missionary is a man of zeal—vehement love—and needs to be held in check by prudence and kindness (par. 381). Meekness is so necessary that it is a sign of a call to the ministry (par. 374). Claret made a particular examen of meekness from 1862 to 1864.

372.2 Matt. 11:29.

372.3 Matt. 5:4.

374.1 Isa. 42:3.

374.2 Isa. 53:7.

374.3 The Isaian "Servant Songs" had a great influence on Claret's vocation, and one of the Servant's traits is meekness.

375.1 James 3:13–15.

378.1 Ps. 119:163.

379.1 2 Cor. 11:2.

379.2 1 Cor. 15:31.

379.3 2 Cor. 11:29.

380.1 St. Augustine, *Commentary on Ps. 58,* PL 36,692.

382.1 2 Sam. 18:5.

Chapter XXVI

384.1 1 Cor. 4:9. Although the missionary is a "spectacle," it is Christ that should show through in his attitudes and actions (par. 387). A missionary must be virtuous "in everyone's eyes" if he is going to enjoy a fruitful apostolate.

385.1 Claret's norms on modesty are practically identical with those of St. Ignatius' *Rule,* which may be traced back historically to the *Rule* of St. Basil.

386.1 Rom. 12:18.

386.2 Sir. 21:20. The notion that Jesus was never seen laughing appears first in St. Basil's *Exposition of the Rule* (PG 31,961, q. 17). From then on, with the authority of St. Basil to back it up, it passes into the commonplaces of the ascetical tradition. Claret, always eager to grasp at any trait of Christ's, presents it here and in Part II of *The Well-Instructed Seminarian.* He read it in Scaramelli, tr. II, art. 3, chap. 4. Cf. Claret, *Writings,* p. 670.

387.1 1 Cor. 11:1.

388.1 Acts 1:1.

389.1 Phil. 4:5.

389.2 Col. 3:12.

Chapter XXVII

390.1 For St. Anthony Mary Claret, mortification is above all a fundamental attitude vis-à-vis God. "I used to abstain from that pleasure *to give pleasure to God*" (par. 391). Mortification is a condition for giving witness (pars. 390, 392) and involves all the senses (pars. 401–411). It makes for an effective apostolate, for growth in holiness and in prayer (pars. 411–413). Cf. *Writings,* "Imitation of the Suffering Christ," pp. 679 ff.

391.1 Pleasing God in everything, with unhesitating ease and joy, is the height of ascetic heroism. It is impossible without the special enlightenment and guidance of the Holy Spirit, moving the person to give his preference to God.

393.1 P. G. Bacci, *Life of St. Philip Neri* (Rome, n.d.), vol. 2, chap. 5.

394.1 Cf. par. 98.

397.1 Claret read this in St. Alphonsus Liguori's *Selva, or Anthology of Sermon Topics* (Bassano, 1833), pt. 3, p. 399. Claret's personal copy. St. Alphonsus calls this preacher "a holy man, now deceased." The handwriting in Claret's copy resembles that of his earliest days as a missionary.

398.1 Six times: (1) Matt. 11:19, Mark 6:41, Luke 9:16; (2) Mark 7:34; (3) Luke 6:20; (4) John 6:5; (5) John 11:41; (6) John 17:1.

400.1 This resolution dates from 1844. The Saint renewed it in 1852, 1854, 1855, and 1858.

409.1 The Saint once told some nuns from Vich, who had asked how he managed to pass the time at banquets, "I attend as few as I can. I always have soup. I take a little *puchero* (a common vegetable dish), too, and as it always has garbanzos in it, I amuse myself by pushing them around the plate" (cf. *Writings,* note 292, p. 306).

410.1 Cf. par. 29.

412.1 St. John of the Cross, *Letters,* par. 20.

413.1 1 Cor. 9:27.

413.2 Rodríguez, *Practice of Perfection* (Barcelona, 1861), vol. 1, p. 343.

Chapter XXVIII

420.1 Luke 21:18.

421.1 Thomas of Jesus, O.E.S.A., *The Labors of Jesus* (Barcelona, 1726), vol. 2, pp. 603, 619. Claret's personal copy. He included these paragraphs in his resolutions for 1864, a year in which he was sorely persecuted.

425.1 Ps. 22:7.

427.1 Claret accommodates the text of St. Paul (Gal. 6:14) to express his own love for and conformity with Christ. Here mortification is more than just a virtue that makes one a good apostle; it is the culmination of the apostolate through incorporation into the Lord's own sacrifice.

Chapter XXIX

429.1 An allusion to the legend of the single tunic of Jesus, which He wore all his life and which grew along with Him. Claret read of it in Mary of Agreda's *Mystical City of God,* pt. II, bk. 4, chap. 29.

430.1 Mark 2:23.

430.2 John 19:29.

431.1 Matt. 8:20.

432.1 Matt. 21:5.

433.1 Matt. 17:26.

434.1 Luke 6:12.

436.1 John 8:50.

Chapter XXX

438.1 This is one of the most stirring chapters in the *Autobiography* and one in which the apostolic personality of the Saint is best portrayed: "A man who is afire with love and kindles that fire wherever he goes."

439.1 Acts 2:41; 4:4.

440.1 Avila, *Works* (Madrid, 1759), vol. 1, p. 45. Claret's personal copy.

441.1 "You are missionaries: you must be sent and impelled. You must be able to say, 'Charitas Christi urget nos'" (Claret, *Spiritual Exercises,* 1865).

441.2 1 Cor. 13:1. "Many who heard him (Claret) used to say, 'How does he know so much?' 'How he loves,' we always said and always will, when speaking of Fr. Claret. Charity is the soul and the powerful driving-force behind all the Archbishop's activities. He takes the sacred fire that always burns in his heart and spreads it everywhere, and this is the mysterious secret that allows him to multiply his moments, himself, and his many works of zeal" (Vincent de Manterola, *Basque-Navarre Catholic Weekly,* September 15, 1866).

442.1 For Claret, keeping the commandments assures a habit of charity; the practice of the evangelical counsels removes the obstacles to acts of charity; and prayer converts charity into the fire of zeal.

443.1 "On April 27, 1859, the Lord promised me the love of God" (par. 683). In 1863 Claret asks, "May I be a lover, as the Son is." In 1869 the Lord gave him the infused gift of love for his enemies. In the year of his death he said that he wanted to go to heaven because one beholder loves more than a thousand wayfarers.

443.2 Luke 11:13.

447.1 "Mother of Divine Love" was the common title for pictures of the Heart of Mary. "In Mary's Heart we must consider two aspects: the physical heart and the spiritual heart—her love and will. The physical heart of Mary is the organ, sense, and instrument of her love and will. Just as we see through the eye, we love through the heart" (Claret, *Correspondence,* Letter 1459).

449.1 Sabunde, *Great Treatise on Man* (Barcelona, 1854), p. 179. The sentence that follows, continuing to the word "ravages" in par. 452, is from a passage in the works of Donoso Cortés ("Letter to María Cristina," *Works* [Madrid, 1946], vol. 2, p. 559).

449.2 Claret has introduced this allusion to the transforming and creative Word into the passage by Donoso Cortés.

450.1 Mark 16:15.

450.2 2 Tim. 4:2.

Chapter XXXI

454.1 This enumeration does not list all the towns he preached in. He seems to have written them down as they came to mind, for they follow neither a chronological, geographical, nor alphabetical order.

458.1 Joaquín Manzano (1805–67) fought for Isabel II in Catalonia (1840–43). As General, he opposed the Carlist insurrection in Catalonia (1847). He was Field Marshal and Commander General of Tarragona and Gerona (1849). He was in Cuba until 1852. Once again in Cuba in

1854, he was second in command of the military establishment of the island.

460.1 Living up to his resolution to travel on foot out of fidelity to the Gospel often carried Claret to heroic lengths. Only a special help from God can explain how he kept up his health or physical resistance during these years.

461.1 He finished the mission in Bañolas on December 7, 1845. The river he refers to is the Fluvia en Esponella.

462.1 In the autumn of 1844.

462.2 The date was December 20, 1846.

463.1 One of these afflictions was a horrible wound in the side, which exposed several ribs. It was cured suddenly when he invoked the Blessed Virgin. The doctors delivered testimony to this effect. (*Informative Process*, Vich, session 79; *Apostolic Process*, sessions 15, 16, 140.)

466.1 Antonio Fernández de Echanove y Zaldívar (1768–1854). Ordained priest (1792), Abbot of the Chapter at La Granja (1818), Titular Bishop of Leukosia (1819) and of Tarragona (1825). Energetic defender of the Church. Expelled from his diocese in 1835 when a mob burned his palace. Returned from exile in 1845. In 1846 he published a circular letter refuting various calumnies that had been spread about Claret.

466.2 Cf. Phil. 1:21. He probably means the persecutions that took place during the second missionary campaign through the archdiocese of Tarragona in September, 1846, which culminated in an attempt at Torredembarra to shoot Claret.

Chapter XXXII

468.1 Cf. pars. 295–296, where he speaks of the distribution of sermon topics.

473.1 The retraction is dated February 20, 1847. Cf. Fernández, *The Blessed*, vol. 1, pp. 265 ff.

Chapter XXXIII

477.1 Partisans of Don Carlos. This group of about 3,000 men, by using guerrilla tactics, managed to keep 40,000 of the queen's troops in check for over a year.

478.1 Bishop Bonaventure Codina (1783–1857) was born in Hostal-Vich (Gerona). He entered the Vincentians when he was 29. He became a missionary and was appointed Visitator of the Daughters of Charity in Spain. He was made Bishop of Palma in 1847.

479.1 José María Ramírez y Cortés (1789–1855) was ordained in 1813 and became rector of the Italian Church in Madrid. A pious and charitable man, he initiated the Forty Hours Devotion in the capital. He was the uncle of St. Micaela of the Blessed Sacrament, whom Claret met on this occasion and encouraged in her apostolate of a school for the underprivileged.

479.2 Founded by Philip II and moved to Atocha Street in 1748.

480.1 The bishop's consecration took place on February 20. On February 23 they left Madrid for Córdoba and Seville, where they stayed a few days. After a stopover in Jérez, they sailed from Cádiz on March 6, 1848.

480.2 He is a month off. In fact they didn't arrive in Santa Cruz until March 11. Here the Saint preached on Sunday, March 12, and embarked for Grand Canary the next day, where they arrived on March 14. On March 20 he began preaching in the cathedral of Las Palmas.

483.1 Once again, the formative aim of the *Autobiography* appears: "so that the missionaries may learn from it." For a more thorough picture of Claret's apostolate in the Canary Islands, see F. Gutierrez, *St. Anthony M. Claret, Apostle of the Canary Islands* (Madrid, Coculsa, 1969).

484.1 Fr. Salvador Codina (1785–1864) was born in Barcelona. He became a Capuchin in 1802 but was expelled from the monastery of Valls by the decree of the government against religious orders. He accompanied his brother to the Canary Islands and became a canon of Las Palmas (1860). He died in Barcelona.

486.1 So ends a remarkable apostolate whose effects have lasted to this day. Pius XII named St. Anthony Claret Patron of these islands, together with the Virgin of the Pines.

487.1 "It seems that God took me from Catalonia, where I couldn't do any missionary work because of the disorders there, and placed me where I could reap an abundant harvest. Blessed obedience! Through it, God guided me and I thank Him for it continually" (*Correspondence*, Letter 84).

487.2 Cf. Ps. 89:2.

Chapter XXXIV
488.1 May 11, 1849.

488.2 Dr. Jaime Soler, canon of Vich, Capitular Secretary and rector of the seminary, became Bishop of Teruel in 1849, consecrated at the same ceremony as Claret. He died in 1851.

488.3 Dr. Jaime Passarell, secretary of the Vicar Capitular of Vich and professor of theology. He later became canon.

488.4 After experimenting with a number of titles, he decided to form this association of priests living in common and dedicated totally to the ministry of the Word of God. His choice of the title, "Sons of the Immaculate Heart of Mary," can be explained from the influence on his life and apostolate from 1847 on, of the Archconfraternity of the Heart of Mary that had been established at the church of Notre Dame des Victoires in Paris. *Heart of Mary:* the center of Mary's whole being—Mother of the whole Christ through her love. *Immaculate:* for Claret, an apostolic title, manifesting God's plan to conquer the offspring of the Serpent through the Offspring of the Woman. The prophecy in Genesis and the Apocalypse are the panorama in which Claret's apostolic activity is set. *Sons:* the most Christian and theological attitude vis-à-vis the Blessed Virgin.

489.1 The Monastery of Our Lady of Mercy was at that time the city jail and had been a barracks earlier, ever since the Mercedarians had been evicted by the government.

489.2 *Stephen Sala* (1810–58) succeeded the Founder in governing the Congregation. The Saint thought highly of him, "as being one in spirit with me" (*Correspondence,* Letter 584).
    Joseph Xifré (1817–99) was the third Superior General, and under him the Congregation spread to France, Africa, and the Americas.
    Dominic Fábregas (1817–95) dedicated his whole life to preaching parish missions and retreats.
    Manuel Vilaró (1816–52) accompanied the Founder to Cuba as his secretary.
    Jaime Clotet (1822–98): his cause for beatification has been introduced. He was very devoted to Claret and was his second biographer.

489.3 Claret waited on tables for his confreres from the opening day of the Spiritual Exercises. He also acted as infirmarian to Fr. Fábregas and Don Mariano Aguilar, attending to the needs of the latter even after he had been elected archbishop.

490.1 The manuscript of the outline of this first talk, as well as that of all the Exercises, has been preserved. (Cf. J. M. Lozano, *Constitutions and Texts* [Barcelona, 1972], pp. 563 ff.)

490.2 The Vulgate text begins, "Virga tua et baculus tuus," hence Claret's play on the words "virga" and "virgo," which St. Alphonsus Liguori had connected with the rod of Jesse in Isa. 11:1. (Cf. Liguori, *The Glories of Mary*, vol. 1, chap. 2, par. 3.)

490.3 Fathers Vilaró and Sala had died.

494.1 This paragraph is a synthesis of the apostolic spirit of Claret. It is generally known as the "pen-portrait of a missionary." In a letter to Fr. Xifré, the Saint remarked, "I would like each one of the missionaries to copy it and carry it with him." The same letter contains another text of the pen-portrait, with slight variations, written in the hand of the Saint, entitled, "A Reminder that Anthony Claret Frequently Repeats to Himself." The rest of the text follows: "A Son of the Immaculate Heart of Mary is a man who sets fire wherever he goes. He desires mightily and strives by all means possible to set the whole world ablaze with the fire of God's love. Nothing or nobody daunts him: he delights in privations, welcomes work, embraces sacrifices, smiles amid whatever calumnies may arise, rejoices in the torments and sorrows he may suffer, and glories in the Cross of Jesus Christ. His only concern is how he may follow Jesus Christ more nearly and imitate him in prayer, work, suffering, and in striving constantly and single-mindedly for the greater glory of God and the good of souls." (Cf. *Writings*, p. 328, note 259.)

Chapter XXXV

495.1 In his letter to the Nuncio, Claret gives another reason, which affords us a glimpse of his spirit: "If I accepted, I would be tied down and limited to a single archdiocese, whereas my spirit goes out to the whole world. And even on this little dot on the map, I would not be able to preach as much as I would like to, for I have seen with my own two eyes how many business matters an archbishop has to attend to" (*Correspondence*, Letter 95).

495.2 Msgr. Giovanni Brunelli (1795–1861) was Nuncio to Madrid (1847), Cardinal (1853), Prefect of the Congregation of Studies, and Member of the Papal Secretariat of State (1853–61).

495.3 Lorenzo Arrazola (1797–1873), head of the moderate party, was seven times Attorney General (and hence in charge of church-state relations), and three times head of the government.

495.4 The bishop's letter, dated October 1, 1849, states, "Having consulted the Virgin of Montserrat in prayer, I command you to accept the aforesaid Archbishopric."

497.1 This mission lasted from April 5 to 16.

498.1 During these days he had to deal with matters of the utmost responsibility: the consolidation of his missionaries, the Religious Library, the final draft of the Constitutions of the Carmelite Sisters of Charity, and the organization of his future apostolate in Cuba. (Cf. *Correspondence*, Letter 120.)

498.2 In September he preached the Spiritual Exercises for the clergy of Vich. Among the participants was Canon Soler, who was preparing for his own consecration together with Claret. It must have been during this time that he drew up his plan of life. (Cf. *Writings*, p. 537.)

Madrid,
Palacio Nacional

PART THREE

Archbishop

Chapter I

CONSECRATION, VOYAGE, ARRIVAL, AND FIRST MINISTRIES

499 October 6, 1850—the feast of St. Bruno, founder of the Carthusian order I had once wished to join[1]—was also the first Sunday in October and the Feast of the Most Holy Rosary, which has always been one of my favorite devotions. On this day I was consecrated Archbishop, together with Don Jaime Soler, Bishop of Teruel, in the cathedral of Vich.[2] The local ordinary, Don Luciano Casadevall, was the consecrating bishop, assisted by their Excellencies, Bishops Dominic Costa y Borrás[3] and Fulgencio Lorente,[4] of Barcelona and Gerona, respectively.

500 On Tuesday, the eighth, I left Vich for Barcelona and Madrid, where the Papal Nuncio, Msgr. Brunelli, invested me with the pallium on the thirteenth. I was presented to Her Majesty and the Ministers of State.[1] During the time it took to arrange all my credentials, I busied myself preaching and hearing confessions in Madrid.[2] When all was in order I returned to Catalonia. I arrived in Igualada on October 31 and preached there for All Saints' Day. The following day I visited Montserrat, where I also preached.[3] Next I went to Manresa, where Father Mach was conducting an All Souls' Novena.[4] I preached there in the evening, and on the following morning gave Holy Communion to a large crowd who had heard that I would be there and so had prepared for it.

501 That afternoon I went to my home town, Sallent, where everyone came out to meet me. In the evening I preached to them from a balcony overlooking the town square because the church wasn't large enough to hold the crowd. Next day we celebrated a Solemn High Mass, and in the afternoon I left for Sanmartí. The following morning I traveled to the shrine of Our Lady of Fussimanya, the scene of my great childhood devotion. I said Mass in the shrine and preached on devotion to Mary. From there I went on to Artés, where I also preached,

as I did at Calders, as well. I ate at Moyá and preached there that night. The following morning I was off to Collsuspina, where I preached; then I went on to Vich where I had dinner and preached that night. Next I went to Barcelona, where I preached every day in various churches and convents[1] until December 28, when we sailed on the frigate *La Nueva Teresa Cubana,* under the command of Captain Manuel Bolívar.

502 My traveling companions were my Vicar General, Father John Lobo, with a young man named Telésforo Hernández; Fathers Manuel Vilaró, Anthony Barjau, Lorenzo San Martí, Manuel Subirana, Francisco Coca, Philip Rovira, Paladio Currius, and John Pladebella; and Mr. Ignacio Bertríu and young Philip Vila and Gregory Bonet.[1]

503 Among the other passengers sailing with us were eighteen Daughters of Charity who were also bound for Havana, together with their chaplain, Father Peter Planas, a Vincentian. There were numerous others aboard as well.

504 We were all well and happy as we set sail from Barcelona for Cuba, but on reaching the Rock of Gibraltar we had to wait for a change of weather before we could pass through the straits. The sea got worse, and so the captain had to turn back to Málaga, where we had to wait three days for better weather. Meanwhile, some work was found for me and I preached 15 sermons in the cathedral, the seminary, schools and convents, etc.[1]

505 At last we set sail under fair skies for the Canary Islands, where we hoped to land and visit with my beloved islanders. They were looking forward to it and so were we, but the sea was so choppy that we couldn't dock there, much to our mutual regret.

506 We continued our voyage to Cuba in high spirits and excellent order. The ship's cabin space was divided into two parts: I and my companions were quartered in the space between the main mast and the poop; the nuns were quartered all to themselves in the space between the main mast and the bow, and separated from the rest of us by shuttered doors.

My group got up every day on schedule,[1] washed, and made a half-hour's meditation together. The nuns did the same in their quarters. After meditation I celebrated Mass in our quarters, where an altar had been set up. I said Mass every day of our voyage. It was attended by all in my group as well as by the sisters, who heard it from their own quarters by pushing back the shuttered doors that formed the dividing line between them and us. The sisters and priests all received Communion, except for one of the priests who celebrated a second Mass, during which we made our thanksgiving. There was a system of rotation for the priest who said the second Mass, so that every day we had two Masses—one said by me, the other by the priest whose turn it was that day.

507 After our first set of devotions, we went up on deck to take tea, during which each of us studied what he wished. We met again at eight in our quarters, recited the minor Hours in common, and held a conference on moral theology until ten, when we went to take lunch. Afterwards we were free to rest and study until three, when we gathered to recite Vespers, Compline, Matins, and Lauds. Then we had another conference lasting until five, when we went to dinner.[1] At eight we assembled again to say the rosary and other devotions. We had a conference on ascetical theology and finally, after taking a cup of tea, all retired to their berths.[2]

508 This was our schedule on all working days. But on holy days of obligation the second Mass was said when it was most convenient for the ship's crew to attend. On holy days we also had a sermon in the evening, each priest preaching in turn, starting with me, then the Vicar General, etc.

509 On reaching the Gulf of Damas, I began conducting a mission on deck.[1] Everyone on board attended it, passengers and crew, from captain to cabin boy, and everyone went to confession and received Communion at a general Communion service. We were on friendly terms with the crew, and on every voyage they would make to Cuba they used to come and visit us. We landed on February 16, 1851, in good spirits, and were received with demonstrations of joy and good will. On the day following our arrival, we made our official entry

into the capital city, in accordance with the established local custom.[2]

5 1 0 Fifteen days after our arrival we went to visit the Shrine of Our Lady of Charity at El Cobre, four leagues away from the capital, a center of devotion for all the inhabitants of the island. The picture of the Virgin is enshrined in a chapel that has been very richly adorned through the continual offerings brought there from far and near.[1]

5 1 1 On my return to Santiago, the capital city of the diocese, I began a mission that lasted until March 25, when a general Communion service was held. There was an unbelievably large crowd, both for the sermons and for the general Communion service. While I was giving one mission in the cathedral, Father Vilaró was giving another in the church of St. Francis, the next largest church in the city after the cathedral, and on the Sunday following the Feast of the Annunciation I went to give Communion in the church of St. Francis.[1]

5 1 2 I also conducted the Spiritual Exercises for the entire clergy: canons, pastors, beneficiaries, etc. This was my yearly practice as long as I was on the island.[1] For the greater convenience of all concerned, however, I also had them held in the principal cities of the diocese.

5 1 3 I and the members of my household also made our own retreat each year, before the others did. We remained in the palace during this time, keeping strictest silence. No letters or calls were received. Absolutely no business was conducted during that period of ten days, and since everyone had been so informed we were left in peace throughout.

5 1 4 When the missions were over and the Holy Week and Easter services completed, I divided my companions into three groups. I sent Fathers Manuel Subirana and Francisco Coca to the city of El Cobre, and Fathers Paladio Currius and Stephen Adoain, a Capuchin, to the town of Caney, two leagues from Santiago. The latter presented himself to me on my arrival and was very helpful to me, as I shall tell later.[1] I distributed the third group as follows: Father John Lobo in

the chancery as vicar general and ecclesiastical governor in my absence; Fathers Philip Rovira and John Pladebella in the seminary, to teach Latin grammar and moral theology, respectively; and Fathers Lorenzo San Martí and Anthony Barjau to the city of Puerto Príncipe to teach catechism until I arrived there.

515 I remained in the capital, where I inaugurated the pastoral visitation, starting in the cathedral and then going through the parishes.[1] Every day I administered the Sacrament of Confirmation. There were a great many to be confirmed, and so, to avoid confusion, I had some forms printed and distributed the right quantity of them to the rectories the day before confirmations. These forms were then filled in with such data as the names of those to be confirmed, their parents, and their sponsors. This helped avoid confusion and crowding and made it easier to record the data later with greater accuracy and leisure. I always followed this procedure, and it worked quite well with all those I confirmed—and that came to no less than 300,000 persons during my stay of six years and two months on the island.

516 Besides the visitation and confirmations, I preached on all Sundays and holy days of obligation. I never failed to preach, no matter what part of the diocese I happened to be in at the time.[1] Toward the beginning of June I left the city and went to Caney, to conclude the mission that Father Stephen and Father Currius had started and were very successfully carrying on. After confirming everyone, I preached the closing service of the mission.

517 After this I went to the city of El Cobre, where Fathers Manuel Subirana and Francisco Coca were giving the mission, as I have said. They had worked very hard, with excellent results. Suffice it to say that when they got there only eight couples were properly married; and by the time the mission was over, 400 couples who had been living together illicitly were married. I stayed there several days, administering the Sacrament of Confirmation, putting the finishing touches on the mission, and legitimizing some unions, in virtue of the faculties granted me by the Holy See.

Chapter II

PERSECUTIONS IN EL COBRE
AND EVENTS AT PUERTO PRÍNCIPE

518 It was in the city of El Cobre that the unpleasantness and persecutions began. Naturally, the devil could hardly have been expected to look on indifferently at the multitude of souls who were daily being converted to the Lord. Moreover, God was right in letting us feel some tribulation for the great satisfaction we took in seeing everything going so well.

This is how the troubles began: I had not yet left town and there were still some couples who wanted to get married because they hadn't been able to before. I wanted to be sure of my cases, and so I called on the major in charge of the town and said to him, "You know the people of this town better than anyone else. Could you tell me which of the people on this list of couples living together can contract a good marriage, or whether they have some legal impediment of race? I want to make sure, and not do something that would eventually cause trouble."

519 The major came to my house every day and informed me about the petitioners, and the parish priest made public inquiries to ascertain whether the marriages in question would be licit. One day a European came to see me. A native of Cádiz, he had been living out of wedlock with a woman of mixed blood who had borne him nine children. I didn't speak with him personally, but he told my secretary that he had to see me because he wanted by all means to marry the woman and do right by the children she had borne him. The secretary said he would talk to me about the case and that the man should come back later because the major wasn't present and we ourselves knew nothing of the man's background. And that was the long and the short of it.

520 That very night the major brought charges against the parish priest, to the effect that he had been performing illicit marriages between racial classes—referring to the case of the man from Cádiz whom I mentioned. The parish priest in turn

191

reported this to me, very much to my surprise. I summoned the major and told him that in acting as he did he was taking steps not against the parish priest, but against me, and that his charges were both untrue and unfounded. I made it clear to him that on my part I had been extremely careful not to announce the banns of anyone's marriage without first consulting him, to avoid any unpleasant surprises; whereas he had now started spreading this slanderous misstatement. In the notice he had served on the parish priest, he had stated that he was going to prefer charges against him to the Governor General of Cuba. In an effort to nip this rumor in the bud, I asked him whether he had done so or not. He lied to me again by telling me that he had not yet done so. Lo and behold, the Governor General, acting on nothing more than the allegation of the major at El Cobre and the bad advice of the secretary of government, instigated a series of wild investigations that only resulted in arguments and trouble.[1]

5 2 1 Notwithstanding all these difficulties, with God's help in every way imaginable a great deal of good was accomplished. While I was still working in El Cobre, General Gemery, the major general in charge of the central district of Cuba, wrote me from his residence in Puerto Príncipe urging me to come there at once, to dampen the mounting fires of revolution. At the same time I received another letter from the captain general of Havana, Don José de la Concha,[1] advising me not to go there because any petition for clemency on my part would prevent him from dealing out justice and making a public example of the rebels. I informed him of the urgings of the major general of the central district, after which he told me to proceed as planned.

5 2 2 I went to Puerto Príncipe[1] toward the end of July of that year. As the whole city was deeply involved in the revolution of Narciso López[2] or with the anti-European insurgents of the north, a great many precautionary measures surrounded my arrival. At the start of the mission many people came to see whether or not I was going to talk about the political upheavals taking place all over the island of Cuba, and especially those at Puerto Príncipe. When they observed that I didn't breathe a word about politics either from the

pulpit or in the confessional, publicly or privately, they were greatly impressed and I won their confidence.

523 Just at this time, the troops had captured four revolutionaries who were citizens of the town. They were carrying firearms at the time of their capture, and so they had been sentenced to death. The guilty men and their relatives had such confidence in me that they asked me to come to the prison to hear their confessions, which I did.[1] Their confidence in me grew to the extent that they asked me to act as their intermediary with the general. I was to tell him that all those who were implicated in carrying firearms would, if they were pardoned, lay down their arms and return home secretly, without saying a word about the event or revealing the names of those involved. I obtained the general's agreement to these terms, with the result that the whole band was dissolved, all their guns, ammunition, and money were dispersed, and everything returned to peace. Two years later some North Americans made another attempt, but it failed to achieve the same response as before. Later another effort was made, but it failed utterly.

524 Thus there were three attempts to overthrow Cuba during my stay there: the first was very powerful but disappeared completely with the Lord's help; the second was not so strong; the third was totally ineffective. Because of this, the enemies of Spain could hardly stand the sight of me. They said that the Archbishop of Santiago did them more harm than the whole army. They were sure that as long as I remained on the island their plans would fail, and so they began plotting to kill me.[1]

Chapter III

MISSIONS IN PUERTO PRINCIPE, MANZANILLO, SAN FRUCTUOSO, AND BAYAMO

525 The first thing I did on arriving in Puerto Príncipe was to lead the local clergy in the Spiritual Exercises. So as not to

leave the parishes unattended, I gave the Exercises in two different shifts. I rented a house big enough for all of us to live in. Then I organized one group of 20 and another of 19. We ate together and lived under the same roof day and night. Our schedule included lectures, meditations, recitation of the Divine Office, and the talks I gave. Everyone made a general confession, drew up a plan of life, and everything was put in order.[1]

526 After focusing on the clergy, I turned my attention to the laity. Because the city was more than a league long, I had three missions held simultaneously for the convenience of the people. I assigned Fathers Lorenzo San Martí and Anthony Barjau to preach the mission at the church of Our Lady of Charity, at one end of town, and Father Manuel Vilaró to preach the mission at St. Anne's, at the other end of town. I myself preached the mission at Our Lady of Mercy, the largest church in town, located in the center. The mission lasted two months, August and September, and with God's help it did incalculable good. I also visited the six parishes and other churches of the town.

527 From Puerto Príncipe I pushed on to Nuevitas,[1] where we also gave a mission, and from there we went on to Baga, San Miguel, and San Jerónimo, returning to Puerto Príncipe to celebrate Christmas. We chanted Matins and celebrated a Solemn High Midnight Mass in the Church of Our Lady of Solitude. At this time Father Barjau fell ill with yellow fever. His condition became quite serious, but he recovered perfectly, thank God.[2] After this we continued giving missions, administering Confirmation, visiting parishes, and working our way, parish by parish, until we reached Santiago for Holy Week. We performed all the ceremonies of Holy Week with great solemnity because well in advance of this we had instructed all the priests who were to take part in the Mass of Chrism, and other services, in the proper observance of the rubrics.

528 Toward the end of April I left Santiago and headed for Manzanillo, together with two of my priests, while the rest of my missionary band went off to different locations. At Man-

zanillo I began preaching for the month of May; I preached several times daily. Without realizing it, I let slip some remarks about great earthquakes that would be coming soon.[1]

From Manzanillo we pushed on to the parish of San Fructuoso, and wherever we went we followed the same routine: hearing confessions, preaching, confirming, and performing marriages. From here we went to Bayamo, where I started the mission and did as elsewhere. I gave the Spiritual Exercises to the clergy, preached every day, and kept on confirming people until August 20, 1852. That day, at ten in the morning, as I was standing in the chapel of the Blessed Sacrament of Our Lady of Sorrows, I felt the first of a series of earthquakes that were to be repeated for several days.[2]

Chapter IV

THE EARTHQUAKES IN SANTIAGO

529 The havoc wrought by the Cuban earthquakes was truly dreadful. The people were terrified, and my vicar general sent for me to come to Santiago as I was needed there. I left the mission at Bayamo and went to Santiago,[1] where I was appalled at the sight of the ruins; one could hardly move through the streets, for all the wreckage and debris. The cathedral was a total disaster. To give some idea of the power of the tremors that hit that great church, I will describe just one detail. At the ends of the cathedral's facade there were two matching towers, each of which had four corners topped by macelike finials. One of these finials was dislodged and thrown through one of the bell tower windows. Imagine the arc that finial had to describe to break through one of those windows. The episcopal palace was a wreck, and so were all the other churches, more or less. Public squares were converted into chapels where Mass was said, the sacraments distributed, and sermons preached. Nearly all the houses in town were in a state of greater or lesser disrepair.

530 No one who hasn't experienced a major earthquake can have the slightest idea of what it's like. It's not just the moving or heaving of the earth and the sight of utensils and furni-

ture sliding from one end of the room to the other. If that were all there was to it, then anyone who has sailed on rough seas has seen the like happen on a ship. But there is a great deal more to an earthquake than that.

531 Horses and other four-footed animals are the first to sense the quake; it's awful to see them freeze in their tracks, their legs braced like table-legs, so that all the beating and goading in the world couldn't budge them. Then all the birds —chickens, turkeys, doves, parrots, parakeets, etc.—begin cackling, shrieking, crying, thrashing about, and flailing their wings. Next there is a deep, subterranean rumbling, and everything begins to sway, and you can hear the creaking of timbers, doors, and walls and the sound of pieces falling from buildings. This is accompanied by a change in the electrical field that throws compass needles completely off.

532 Moreover, everyone feels—and sees the same in everyone else—as if he were at the scene of an explosion. The air is filled with terrifying cries of "Mercy!" and, driven by their instinct for self-preservation, people start running for the nearest square, patio, or street, for nobody feels safe in his own home. Then, after running a while, they stop and suddenly grow silent. They look at each other foolishly and tears come to their eyes. What is happening is beyond explanation. In the midst of all these terrors, one touch of incongruous humor stands out: all the sick in private homes and in civilian and military hospitals—all of them wrapped in their bedsheets —arise and leave their sickbeds. Not one of them but says that he is quite well and that nothing could induce him to return to bed.

533 So much was destroyed; yet we hardly had time to lament our personal losses. A great number of people were praising the wonders of God's mercy for preserving them from all bodily harm when their houses were utterly destroyed. The ruins were extensive and repairs were costly. Repairs on the cathedral cost me 24,000 duros, on the seminary 7,000 duros, and on the episcopal palace, 5,000.

Chapter V

THE CHOLERA EPIDEMIC IN CUBA

5 3 4 The quakes lasted from August 20 to the end of December, with a few brief interruptions—although there were days on which there were as many as five tremors. We offered prayers of supplication, and all the canons and other priests went in procession to the esplanade along the seashore where an outdoor chapel, made of posts covered by a large awning, had been set up. In the morning everyone gathered here, the authorities as well as the townspeople, to sing the litany and a votive Mass of supplication.

5 3 5 I preached a mission, exhorting all to penance, telling them that God had treated some of them as a mother treats a sleepy-headed child of a morning. She shakes his cot to awaken him and make him get up. If this fails, she has to nudge him bodily. This, I told them, was what God was doing with his children who were oversleeping in their sins. He had shaken their cots, beds, and houses. If they still weren't awake, He would strike their bodies with a plague of cholera, for God our Lord had given me to understand that this is what He would do. Some of my listeners resented this and grumbled about me, but in scarcely a month's time a frightful epidemic of cholera broke out. There were streets in which everyone died within two days.[1]

5 3 6 Many who had not gone to confession during the mission did so because of the earthquakes and the plague. How true it is that some sinners are like walnut trees; the only way they will yield their fruit is by being beaten with sticks. Withal I could only bless the Lord and thank Him continuously for visiting this plague upon us in due season; for I saw quite clearly that this was an act of his adorable mercy. I know that many who confessed on their deathbed had not gone to confession during the mission and that others who had confessed and been converted at the mission had already fallen back into their former sins. God used that plague to take them to Himself, and this very day they are with Him in heaven. If it

197

had not been for this plague, they would have fallen back again into their sins and, dying in them, would have been condemned. Blessed and praised be God, our good Father, the God of kindness and of all consolation!

537 During the cholera epidemic, all the clergy acquitted themselves admirably, day and night. I and all the priests were among the sick constantly, caring for their spiritual and corporal needs. Only one priest, the pastor of El Cobre, died and he was a victim of charity. He began to feel some slight symptoms of the disease, but he took his medicine and there was some hope of his being cured. He was in bed recuperating when word came that one of the victims needed to see a priest. At this, the pastor said, "I know that if I go I'll die because it will only worsen my condition; but because there is no other priest available, I'll go. I'd rather die than fail this sick man who is calling for me." He went and on his return took to his bed and died.[1]

Chapter VI

JOURNEY TO BARACOA, MAYARÍ, AND SANTIAGO. OUTCOME OF MY FIRST PASTORAL VISIT

538 During the first two years, despite the earthquakes and the cholera epidemic, we managed to visit all the parishes in the archdiocese. In every one of them a mission was led either by myself or my companions, and in rural parishes with a very large territory, several missions were given. Every two or three leagues we would hold a mission in one of the many large tobacco sheds. We would set up an altar, a pulpit, and a confessional with the help of some chairs and gratings we brought along for that purpose.

539 Throughout those first two years it rained a great deal. On one occasion it rained for nine months without skipping a day; and there were days when it rained through the night as well. This made traveling difficult, but I and my companions kept on going and the people kept on coming. We were

all happy and in good spirits, although we sometimes lacked even the necessities of life.

540 I remember that in my second year on the island I wanted to go overland to Baracoa because the sea wasn't fit, and I took off with my companions.[1] We took along a cook, both because the places we were going to were few and far between and because the inhabitants of the few outlying houses had abandoned them in their flight from the cholera epidemic. Our good cook fell behind because his pack-mule couldn't walk; so the rest of us went on ahead, arriving very late that night at a house where we could find nothing to eat but a small and really tough piece of hardtack, which we broke into four pieces, one for each priest. Next morning we had to start out, fasting, on the worst road I've ever traveled in my whole life.

541 We had to cross the river Jojó 35 times because it zigzags between two high mountain ridges, and the traveler has no course open to him other than to cross it. After we made it past the river, we had to climb a stretch of mountains called the Knives of Baracoa. The name fits them perfectly because they really are like a row of knives. A road runs along the crest of the mountains, and there are stretches of it as tortuous as a chambered nautilus. These are divided, so that anyone descending can avoid ascending traffic. Otherwise, if two horses confronted each other, one would have to back up because the road is too narrow to turn around in. The mountains run along the spine of the island for about four leagues, and they are so high that you can see the ocean on both sides. We had to climb and cross these mountains fasting, and the road is so steep that on the way down I slipped and fell twice, although I wasn't badly hurt, thank God.

542 Around noon we arrived at a farmhouse where we were able to get something to eat, and that evening we reached the city of Baracoa, where the explorer Columbus first set foot on Cuban soil. They still have the cross he planted on landing. Well, now, it had been 60 years since a bishop had visited this city, which meant that the sacrament of Confirmation had not been administered there in all those years.[1] When I ar-

rived, two of my mission band had already been there and given a mission; nevertheless, I preached there every day during my stay. I confirmed and visited everyone and then passed on first to the parish of Guantánamo and then to Mayarí. Some of my mission band had given a mission in both of these parishes, and all that I did at Baracoa I did here, too.

543 From Mayarí I traveled to Santiago, the capital, a distance of 40 leagues. We set out on the Monday of Holy Week. Since the route we were to travel was very isolated, we had to take along some provisions, which consisted of an earthenware pot containing a stew made of codfish, garbanzos, and potatoes. After we had been walking for a long stretch of road, my companions said that we needed to eat; so we stopped, took out the pot, lit a fire, and huddled behind the trunk of a large mahogany tree to shield ourselves from the wind. We all took turns gathering wood and the fire got so hot that the pot broke. We got a piece of palm-bark (it peels off the palm tree like a large piece of cowhide) and poured what we could salvage of the stew into it. We didn't have any spoons or forks; so we hunted up a gourd and ate our mess of pottage with it. We were thirsty and got another piece of palm-bark, tied both ends of it together like a bucket, filled it with water, and enjoyed a refreshing drink. We were all so happy and content that it was a wonder to behold. The following day we arrived in Santiago to celebrate Holy Week services, as I did every year.

544 As I said, we had the earthquakes and cholera epidemic during the first two years; and yet, between me and my companions, we managed to give missions in every parish in the archdiocese. I made my pastoral visit to each of them and administered the sacrament of Confirmation, remaining as long as it took to confirm everyone.[1] Everywhere we went, we distributed books, holy cards, medals, and rosaries, with the result that everyone was as pleased with us as we were with them.

545 During that first round of visits and missions we took the trouble to keep a count of all the articles we distributed

and found that we had given away 98,217 books, either gratis or in exchange for the bad books that people brought in and we destroyed—and there were very many of these bad books. We also gave away 89,500 holy cards, 20,663 rosaries, and 8,931 religious medals. After the first visit we no longer kept track of these things because we ordered such large quantities from Spain, France, and elsewhere that we distributed them throughout the diocese and beyond. May it all redound to God's greater glory and the good of the souls redeemed by Jesus Christ.

546 From the opening to the closing days of my tenure in office, I wrote a number of circular letters; but I had no desire to write a properly pastoral letter until I had finished my first pastoral visitation of the whole archdiocese, so that my words would apply to the real situation and not be just so much idle talk.

547 My first pastoral letter, written and signed on September 20, 1852, was addressed to the clergy. This letter was reprinted and expanded to include declarations on the following: (1) clerical dress, (2) duties of vicars forane, (3) duties of pastors and other priests, (4) arrangements for pastors and assistants, (5) style of life, (6) chaplains, (7) marriage regulations, (8) marriage dispensations.[1]

548 To these points I added seven appendices on: (1) church furnishings and parochial books, (2) cemeteries, (3) stipends, (4) the distribution of allowances for repairs, (5) conferences, (6) the Confraternity of Christian Doctrine, (7) the method of removing scandals.[1]

549 My second pastoral letter of March 25, 1853 was addressed to the laity, reminding them of what we had taught them in the missions and pastoral visits we had just completed.[1] The third pastoral was in protest against a shipment of evil books brought in by boat.[2] The fourth was an invitation to prayer and other pious works in order to obtain the declaration of the dogma of Mary's Immaculate Conception.[3] The fifth was written on the occasion of the declaration of the dogma of the Immaculate Conception. This was published in

Cuba, Barcelona, and Paris. May it all be for the greater glory of God and Mary Most Holy, and for the good of souls, as this has always been my intention.[4]

Chapter VII

VARIOUS ARRANGEMENTS I MADE FOR THE GOOD OF THE DIOCESE

550 Despite the fact that I had visited and given missions in all the parishes of the diocese during those first two years, I kept on doing so even afterwards. The Council of Trent demands that the pastoral visitation be made every one or two years; during my six years and two months in office, I visited every parish in the diocese four times.[1]

551 During my time the salaries of the cathedral and parochial clergy were adjusted and raised; my own salary was cut. Previously the Archbishop of Cuba had received a salary of 30,000 duros, plus parochial stole fees of 6,000 duros; in my time I had it reduced to 18,000 duros, minus all stole fees.

552 Curates were earning a mere pittance. Those of Santiago were receiving only 33 duros, plus votive offerings, half of which went to the bishop and a so-called sacristan, who did nothing. During my stay in office, curates received 700 duros on commencing, 1,200 on promotion, and 2,000 on termination. They also received 200, 400, and 700 duros, respectively, for church expenses on these occasions.

I also raised the salaries of canons and provided them with a very well appointed and well endowed chapel. I brought in good musicians and organists from Spain, and some magnificent services were held.

553 I insisted that canons, pastors, and other priests make a ten-day retreat each year. I also insisted that they always wear the cassock and imposed a fine of ten duros for noncompliance. Only one failed to comply. I had him appear in lay garb and made him pay the fine.

554 I established clergy conferences to meet three times a week in all towns of the diocese; one of them was on rubrics, the other two on moral theology. I always presided over those in the capital. The first conference each month was a day of retreat, consisting of reading, prayer, and a talk.

555 I undertook the restoration of the diocesan seminary. More then 30 years had passed without seeing the ordination of a single resident seminarian. At the beginning of their studies they all said they had a vocation and were educated at the seminary's expense; but toward the end of their studies they would say that they didn't want to be priests, after which they were graduated and became lawyers. And so it came about that Santiago had a swarm of lawyers, all fed and educated at the seminary's expense, while the few priests there were outsiders.

556 With God's help this situation was completely changed. I appointed Father Anthony Barjau, a priest whom heaven had endowed with a gift for educating young men and boys, as rector of the seminary. This good churchman by his winning ways put them back on course again, bringing them to practice their religion and apply themselves to their studies. Thus they finally began to show some progress, both in virtue and learning, and many of them have been ordained or soon will be.

557 Since the need for priests was pressing and the seminary could provide none for a long time, I hit upon the plan of writing to several Catalonian seminarians who were nearing the end of their studies and inviting them to come to Santiago to finish them. I ordained 36 of them with title to the benefice of a sacristy and the right to apply later for a parish of their own.

558 With the help of the Vicar General I got rid of many grave abuses in chaplaincies. I saw to it that those chaplaincies I could dispose of were awarded to native sons of good character who were resident seminarians and showed some expectations of eventually becoming good pastors.

559 I increased the number of parishes and saw to it that pastors taught Christian doctrine and either preached or read to the people every Sunday.

560 I established the Confraternity of Christian Doctrine[1] and, from the very outset of my stay in Cuba, insisted that seminarians be sent about to all the churches of the diocese to teach Christian doctrine. Every Sunday we had a children's procession, which used to stop in the courtyard of the church, where two tables had been set up, facing each other. A child would get up on each of these tables and in their clear, high voices ask each other their catechism questions. The first two would be followed by two others, and so on. The people who crowded around just for the novelty of it would also learn some sorely needed Christian doctrine in the process.

561 I also established a convent of nuns dedicated to teaching girls, and I bought them a house that cost me about 12,000 duros.[1]

562 With the Lord's help, I saw to the needs of the poor. Every Monday of the year, as long as I was in Cuba, I gathered together the poor of whatever town I happened to be in and gave each person there a peseta; but since they were often poorer in spirit than in the flesh, I first instructed them personally in Christian doctrine. After teaching them catechism I always gave them a talk and urged them to receive the sacraments of Penance and the Eucharist. Many of them did go to confession to me, because they knew I loved them—for the Lord has indeed given me a heartfelt love of the poor.[1]

563 I bought a ranch for the poor of Puerto Príncipe. By the time I left Cuba I had spent 25,000 duros of my savings on it. Father Paladio Currius oversaw the construction work on the house I was building there, for the Lord had gifted him with a good head for that sort of work. He ate and slept with the workers at the ranch, to keep an eye on them and direct the work.

564 My object in starting this ranch was to gather together poor boys and girls, many of whom were wandering the

streets begging. At the ranch they were fed, clothed, and taught their religion, as well as reading, writing, and whatever art or trade they wanted to learn. One hour—and only one hour—a day they had to work on the ranch. This provided enough food to make the ranch self-supporting. Whatever else they might earn had to be put in a savings account. In this way, when they left the ranch they had had some formal education, learned a trade, and earned some money for their efforts.

565 The building itself was divided into two major sections, a boys' wing and a girls' wing, with a chapel between them. At church services the boys sat in the body of the chapel, while the girls had their own section in the upper galleries that connected with their wing, so that both sections were completely separated. The building had two stories; shops and classrooms were on the first floor, dormitories on the second.

566 The front part of the boys' wing housed a physics and chemistry laboratory, some agricultural equipment, and a library. The library was open to the public for two hours in the morning and two in the afternoon. The class in agriculture, which met three times a week, was open to all who wished to attend. All the other classes were for resident students only.

567 I had the whole ranch walled and enclosed and later divided into plots. Around and along the dividing lines of these plots, I had a sort of botanical garden of trees planted, some native to the island, others foreign but adaptable and useful in that climate. The trees were numbered and listed by number in a catalog that explained their type, source, use, propagation, improvements, etc. I myself planted more than 400 orange trees with my own hands, and they were doing just fine when I left. I also had a yard sectioned off for animals, some native to the island, others imported for purposes of breeding and improving the various strains.

568 While the ranch was still being built, I wrote a little work called *The Delights of the Country,* which contained a sketch in embryo of the foundation I had started. This little book has been very helpful in Cuba, and ranch owners give

copies of it to their foremen and tell them to follow it.[1] The Generals of Havana and Santiago, whose duty it is to provide for the welfare of the country, were among the work's chief backers. General Vargas,[2] who was then in Santiago but now is stationed in Puerto Rico, has had this book reprinted there for Puerto Rico and Santo Domingo.

569 I also set up a licensed *credit union* in the diocese, for the use and benefit of the poor. For I saw that when the poor have proper direction and are given a decent means to earn a living, they are upright citizens; it is only otherwise that they become debased. Hence my eagerness to help them was as much spiritual as it was material. With the Lord's help it has worked out very well. May it all be for God's greater glory.[1]

570 I also visited prisoners in jail, catechizing them and preaching to them frequently. After my visits I would give each of them a peseta, and so they were happy to listen attentively to what I had to say.

571 I was equally regular in visiting poor patients in the hospital and also gave them some help, especially those who were leaving as convalescents. I was president of the League of Friends of the Country. We met at my residence, and all of us took an active interest in any advances on the island. We procured a workshop for poor boys, and we saw to it that prisoners in jail were taught reading, writing, religion, and a trade of some sort. With this in mind we had workshops set up in jail; for experience had shown us that many men turn to crime because they have no trade and don't know how to make an honest living.

572 I made it easier for the poor to straighten out their marriages and baptismal records so that they could escape the evils of concubinage. I did what I could to combat crimes of rape, and I opposed marriages between close relatives, granting dispensations for the latter only when there was no alternative, because I had seen the results of such unions.

Chapter VIII

HOW I WAS WOUNDED
AND EVENTS SURROUNDING
MY CURE

5 7 3   I was in Puerto Príncipe making my fourth pastoral visit since my arrival in Cuba five years before.[1] After I had finished visiting the parishes of that town, I headed for Gibara, visiting Nuevitas in passing. From the seaport of Gibara I moved on to Holguín. For several days I had been feeling very fervent and full of longing to die for Jesus Christ. The love of God seemed to be the only thing I knew how or chanced to talk about, both to the members of my household and to outsiders who came to visit me. I had a great hunger and thirst to suffer trials and shed my blood for Jesus' and Mary's sake. Even in the pulpit I would remark that I desired to seal the truths I was preaching with the very blood of my veins.[2]

5 7 4   On February 10, 1856, after arriving in Holguín, I opened the pastoral visitation. Because it was the eve of the Purification of the Blessed Virgin Mary, I preached to the people on this adorable mystery, making them see the great love the Blessed Virgin showed for us in offering up her most holy Son to suffer and die for us. I have no idea what I said or how I said it, but people remarked that I was happier than ever before. The sermon lasted an hour and a half.

5 7 5   I came down from the pulpit filled with the greatest fervor, and at the end of the service we left the church to go to my lodgings. I was accompanied by four priests, my attendant, Ignacio, and a sacristan who carried a lantern to light our way, since it was 8:30 in the evening and it had already grown dark. We had left the church and were walking down the broad and spacious main street. On both sides of the avenue there were large crowds, and all were greeting me. A man stepped forward, as if to kiss my ring, when suddenly his arm flew back and he brought the razor he was holding down upon me with all his might. I had my head down and was touching a handkerchief to my mouth with my right hand, and so,

207

instead of slitting my throat as he had intended, he slashed my face across the left cheek, from the ear to the chin. The razor also caught and wounded my right arm in passing because I was holding it up to my mouth, as I said.

576 The razor had cut clean through the flesh and sliced into the bone of the upper and lower jaw. Blood was gushing both outside and inside my mouth. I immediately pressed my right hand to my cheek to stop the torrent of blood, and my left hand to the wound in my right arm. We happened to be standing in front of an apothecary shop, and so I said, "Let's go in here; they'll have the medicines we need." Because all the civilian and military doctors had attended the sermon and had left the church at the same time we did, word soon got around and they were there in a moment. They were shocked at the sight of a bishop, vested in his mantle and pectoral, all bathed in blood—especially a bishop who was also a friend they all loved and revered. In fact, they were so overcome at the sight of me that I had to cheer them up and tell them what to do for me, since I myself was very tranquil and serene. Later the doctors said I must have lost no less than four-and-a-half pints of blood. With the loss of blood I felt somewhat faint, but I came to as soon as they gave me a little vinegar to smell.

577 After this first-aid treatment, I was carried to my lodgings on a stretcher. I can't describe the pleasure, delight, and joy I felt in my soul on realizing that I had reached the long-desired goal of shedding my blood for the love of Jesus and Mary and of sealing the truths of the Gospel with the very blood of my veins. My spirits soared at the thought that this was but a promise of what I might achieve in time—to shed my blood completely, in the ultimate sacrifice of death. These wounds reminded me of the circumcision of Jesus; in time they might lead me to the incomparable good fortune of dying on the cross of some gallows, of some assassin's dagger, or the like.

578 This joy and delight lasted throughout the time I had to stay in bed and was itself a source of joy to all who came to visit me. It gradually left me as my wounds began to heal.[1]

579 The healing of these wounds was attended by three remarkable phenomena that I shall briefly describe here. The first was the instant healing of a fistula that the doctors had said would be permanent. The razor had completely severed the ducts of the salivary glands, so that the saliva was draining through a small opening in the scar on my cheek, just in front of the ear. The doctors were planning a painful operation of doubtful value, for the following day. I commended myself to the Blessed Virgin Mary in prayer, offering and resigning myself to God's will, when I was suddenly healed. Next day, when the doctors examined the wound, they were astonished to see the results of this remarkable healing.

580 The second phenomenon concerned the wound on my right arm. As it healed, it formed a raised image of Our Lady of Sorrows in profile. Not only was it raised in relief, but it was colored white and purple, as well. For the next two years it was perfectly recognizable, so that friends who saw it marveled at it. Afterwards it began to disappear gradually and is scarcely visible today.

581 The third striking phenomenon was the master plan for the Academy of St. Michael, which came to me during those first few days I was in bed. As soon as I could get up, I started designing its emblem and drafting its bylaws, which have since been approved by royal charter and have received the blessing and good wishes of His Holiness, Pope Pius IX.

582 The queen and king were the first to be enrolled. Since then, numerous branches have been formed and are doing an incalculable amount of good.[1]

583 The would-be assassin was caught in the act and sent to jail. He was tried and sentenced to death by the judge, notwithstanding the deposition I had made, stating that I forgave him as a Christian, a priest, and an archbishop. When this was brought to the attention of the Captain General of Havana, Don José de la Concha, he made a trip expressly to see me on this matter. I begged him to grant the man a pardon and remove him from the island because I feared that the people would try to lynch him for his attack on me, which had been

the occasion both of general sorrow and indignation as well as of public humiliation at the thought that one of the country's prelates had actually been wounded.

584 I offered to pay the expenses of my assailant's deportation to his birthplace, the island of Tenerife in the Canaries. His name was Antonio Pérez,[1] the very man whom a year earlier, unknown to me, I had caused to be freed from prison. His parents had appealed to me on his behalf, and, solely on the strength of their request, I had petitioned the authorities for their son's release. They complied with my request and freed him, and the very next year he did me the favor of wounding me. I say "favor" because I regard it as a great favor from heaven, which has brought me the greatest joy and for which I thank God and the Blessed Virgin Mary continually.

Chapter IX

HOW I WAS SUMMONED TO MADRID

585 Jesus told the men who came to seize him in the garden, "This is your hour—the triumph of darkness."[1] I might well have said the same, because for me that was the hour when God had allowed the wicked and the demons to wound me. For when my assailant wounded me, I saw the demon himself helping him and giving him the strength to strike. It made me think of those words in the formulas of anathema, "If anyone, the devil persuading...." I thought to myself, "This poor man, 'the devil cooperating,' planned to lay violent hands on your miserable self. And though it's true you are a poor sinner and an unworthy priest, still, you are a priest and a prelate of the Church, a minister of Jesus Christ." My Father, forgive him, for he knew not what he was doing!

586 I was restored to the Church to give thanks to God, and once more I began conferring the sacrament of Confirmation on all who were prepared for it. After this I returned to Santiago, administering Confirmation in all the parishes we passed along the way. We spent the night at Santo Domingo Ranch.

The opposition, thinking that we were staying at Altagracia Ranch, burned it to the ground that night.[1] We arrived in Santiago by nightfall of the following day, and the whole town came out to meet us amid signs of great joy at seeing me, since they had thought I was dead. The day after my arrival was Friday, the feast of Our Lady of Sorrows, and I went to the church of Our Lady of Sorrows in thanksgiving. I celebrated Mass, distributed Holy Communion to a large crowd, and attended a solemn High Mass with sermon. Later I performed the Palm Sunday blessing and all the ceremonies of Holy Week and Easter.

587 As a result of the wound, my face was considerably disfigured, my voice was not very clear, and my speech was somewhat slurred; so, for the first few months after I got back to Santiago, I had to abandon my accustomed round of preaching engagements. I devoted my spare time, after confessions and my other ministerial duties, to private talks. But at the end of a few months I was back at work as usual, and during Lent of that year I started giving a mission in the church at San Francisco, Cuba. I was a few days into the mission when I received a royal summons to Madrid. The Archbishop of Toledo,[1] who was confessor to the queen, had died, and Her Majesty had chosen me as her new confessor.

588 I received the royal summons on March 18 and on the twenty-second left Santiago for Havana, where I boarded a packet boat bound for Cádiz. All the people came to see me off at the port and bid me a sad farewell. My departure signaled the dispersal of my staff; nevertheless, I begged Don Dionisio González, whom I had left as administrator of the diocese, to continue in his post until further advised. I also asked Father Anthony Barjau and Father Galdácano to stay at their posts in the seminary until my successor arrived so as not to abandon the field.

589 From the day I arrived in Havana until April 12, the day I left, I preached daily and heard the confessions of the most prominent citizens of the town.[1] At one ceremony I gave First Communion to the Captain General's daughter and to his wife.

590 En route we were in great danger of shipwreck a number of times, but the Lord looked to our welfare and delivered us.[1] We stopped at the Portuguese Islands of Terceiras and were treated very well there; but we suffered the unfortunate loss of two artillerymen who were killed in an explosion that took place as they were answering the salute of the city of Zayal. We all went ashore for their burial, after which we resumed our voyage and arrived at the end of May in Cádiz.

Chapter X

BIOGRAPHICAL SKETCH OF MY CO-WORKERS

591 *Father John Nepomucene Lobo:* I first met this priest as I was passing through the court on my way to the Canary Islands and was pleasantly impressed by his wisdom and virtue. When I became archbishop, I offered him the post of vicar general and, after commending the matter to God in prayer, he accepted. I also made him treasurer and, later, dean, so that he could watch over the cathedral chapter for me, which he did very well. In addition to his satisfactory fulfillment of the duties of vicar general, he also acted as administrator in my absence. He is a very virtuous, wise, and zealous priest and was a great help to me. Later he renounced all his possessions and entered the Jesuits.[1] I appointed Dr. Dionisio González to replace him and he, too, met with my satisfaction.[2] When Dr. González had to return to Spain for reasons of health, I designated him vice-president of the Escorial.

592 *Father Manuel Vilaró:* This priest accompanied and assisted me in the missions I was giving in the diocese of Tarragona. He was one of the original members of the Congregation of the Sons of the Immaculate Heart of Mary, and when I left for Cuba he was kind enough to accompany me. For this reason I made him my secretary and he fulfilled this job very well. Besides acting as my secretary, he also preached and heard confessions frequently. He was well educated, virtuous, zealous, and a hard worker. He fell ill and, because the doc-

tors in Cuba could do nothing for him, they ordered him back to Spain, where he died in his hometown of Vich.[1]

593 *Father Manuel Subirana:* A native of Manresa, he was a schoolmate of mine. We were ordained together, although to different orders. He was a very virtuous and wise man and a zealous worker in Catalonia and later in Cuba. He later went to Guatemala and Honduras, where he still is, working wonders and going from town to town preaching, as he did in my diocese.

594 *Father Francis Coca:* A native of Capellades in the diocese of Barcelona. I met this priest when I went to preach the Month of May devotions at Villanueva, where he was an assistant pastor. When he learned of my nomination he offered me his services; I accepted and he came along with me. He was a very kind priest, as simple as a child and very zealous and fervent. He always worked with Father Subirana as a teammate, and there was a great bond of sympathy between them. They were very zealous and fervent, always on the move from one village to another, giving missions. Both had very pleasing voices, and everyone used to go to the mission just to hear them sing; of course, after the songs came the sermon, and so they were caught. There's no telling the amount of good they did. Later on Father Coca went to Guatemala, entered the Company of Jesus, and died a Jesuit.[1]

595 *Father Stephen Adoain, Capuchin:* On my arrival in Santiago, this good friar offered me his services. He had come to get away from Havana, where he was being persecuted for his tireless preaching. He stayed in my palace and went out with another priest as a mission team. The first priest to accompany him was Father Paladio Curríus; the second was Father Lorenzo San Martí. This good Capuchin was most zealous and eminently practical in giving missions. Later on he went to a Capuchin monastery in Guatemala.[1]

596 *Father Philip Rovira:* On arriving in Cuba, I placed him in the seminary to teach Latin because that is what he had been doing when he joined me to go to America. I made him secretary after Father Manuel Vilaró left. He accompanied

me on visitations and missions and returned with me to Madrid. Afterward he went to Puerto Rico with the new bishop, His Excellency Dr. Benigno Carrión. He was very zealous and a hard worker.

597 *Father John Pladebella:* A priest of the diocese of Gerona and a good theologian. I placed him in the seminary as professor of moral theology, and he did an admirable job of it. He was very virtuous and diligent. He died of yellow fever, although the doctors didn't know he had it until after his death, when he turned yellow as happens to those who die of this disease.[1]

598 *Father Paladio Currius:* A native of Ridaura in the diocese of Gerona, a pious and zealous priest. He started going out on missions with Father Stephen, but he fell ill and was brought to the palace, more dead than alive. As soon as he recovered I sent him to the seminary as moral theology teacher, to replace the late Father Pladebella. After this I sent him to the model ranch I was building at Puerto Príncipe. He remained in Santiago as secretary when Father Philip Rovira returned to Spain with me. At length I recalled him to Madrid, where he helped me with my projects for the hospital and church of Montserrat. Finally I assigned him to the monastery of the Escorial.[1]

599 *Father Lorenzo San Martí:* Born at La Curríu, in the diocese of Solsona. He started giving missions with Father Anthony Barjau, then with Father Stephen Adoain. Later I stationed him in Puerto Príncipe as vicar forane, a task he performed very well. He was always very fervent and utterly detached. He eventually joined the Jesuits and is presently working in Fernando Poo.[1]

600 *Father Anthony Barjau:* A native of Manresa in the diocese of Vich, he began giving missions with Father Lorenzo San Martí. As he was exceptionally gifted for teaching and instructing boys, I made him rector of the seminary, a task he performed very well, remaining at his post until the arrival of my successor. He then returned to Spain, where I made him rector of the royal monastery of the Escorial. He is a priest

who is detached from all earthly things and very zealous for the glory of God and the salvation of souls.[1]

601 *Father Anthony de Galdácano, a Basque Capuchin:* This priest joined my company after two years in Cuba. A religious exclaustrated by the Revolution, he went first to the United States and later to Puerto Rico as a pastor. As he found Puerto Rico unsuitable to him, he came to Cuba, where he did better. He is a very well educated and zealous religious and has accompanied me on numerous mission campaigns, helping with confessions. I gave him a teaching position in the seminary and, after the arrival of my successor, brought him to Spain, where I appointed him to the chair of theology in the seminary of the Escorial.[1]

602 *Mister Telesforo Hernández:* He came, as I have said, with Father John Lobo, who employed him as a secretary in the chancery. He died of yellow fever.

603 *The cook, Gregory Bonet:* The climate did not agree with him. He was a wounded veteran and the heat irritated his wounds. He had to return to his birthplace in Mallorca.

604 *Mister Philip Vila:* Born in Vich. I took him along as house boy. He took very good care of the sick and the poor, distributing alms to them, teaching them Christian doctrine, and exhorting them to virtue. His instructions were so timely and forceful that the native clergy, who sometimes listened to them, began telling him he should give up service and study for the priesthood. He decided to follow their advice. I told him to forget about it because I knew that God didn't want him to become a priest, for all his winning ways. Despite my advice he began his studies, but in a short time he developed chest pains and had to return to Europe, where he died.

605 *Mister Ignacio Betríu:* Born at Herus in the diocese of La Seo. He was most dependable, very well mannered, kind to the poor, and zealous. He also taught Christian doctrine to the poor and, during the missions, to others. He distributed books, medals, holy cards, and rosaries from the supply I or-

dered him to bring along with us. He returned from America with me and is still in my service to this day.

606 These were the helpers who accompanied me in my apostolic labors amid the thorns and thistles of my diocese. I owe God endless thanks for providing me such good companions. The conduct of all of them was above reproach. They never caused me a moment's pain; on the contrary, they were all a great comfort to me. All had good dispositions and solid virtue, and they were so detached from worldly cares that they never once spoke or thought of self-interest or honors. Their only concern was for God's greater glory and the conversion of souls.

607 I had something to learn from all of them because they gave me such a good example in all virtues, especially humility, obedience, fervor, and a constant readiness to work. They gladly set themselves to do whatever I asked, whether it was my commonest request—to go on missions—or something like taking charge of a parish or deanery. It was all the same to them, no matter what I asked them. They never asked for or refused anything or any task whatever.

608 Thus our residence was the admiration of all outsiders who came to visit with us. I mention this because I had given orders that any outside priests who came to town were to be guests in my residence, whether I was there or not, for as long as they cared to stay. A canon from Santo Domingo was forced to resign his post because of a revolution. He came to Cuba and stayed at my residence, where he was a guest at my table for three years. Clergy from the United States and other countries came to visit us, and all of them found bed and board at my residence. It seemed that God Himself brought them just to witness such an agreeable sight. They couldn't help noticing that our house was like a beehive, with everyone coming and going at my request, and all of them quite content and happy. Outsiders were always amazed at the sight of it and praised God for it.

609 I often wondered how it was possible for so much peace, joy, and harmony to reign for so long a time among such a

large group. I always ended up saying the same thing, "This is the finger of God."[1] This is a singular grace God has given us in his infinite mercy and kindness. I knew that God was blessing the efforts we were putting forth when He gave us such a special grace. The following were some of those efforts:

610 (1) We got up every day on schedule and together made a half-hour's mental prayer, which no one ever missed. We all had lunch and dinner together, during which we all took turns reading at table. After lunch and dinner we all took a bit of recreation, which gave us all a chance to see and talk with each other. We rounded out our day by saying the rosary and other devotions.[1]

611 (2) Every year at a stated time we gathered in the palace to make a ten-day retreat, during which we never broke silence nor received visitors, letters, or business calls. Every day each of us would take turns waiting on tables, while another read, beginning with me. They always asked me to preach each day of the retreat. At the closing exercise I kissed the feet of everyone present, and they in turn asked to kiss my feet and those of all the rest. This was a very moving, imposing, and most profitable gesture.

612 (3) The third thing we did was to avoid exclusive friendships; everyone showed an equal liking for everyone else. Moreover, we maintained no friendships outside the house. All that we had, we had in the residence, and so we didn't go out on social calls and we didn't receive social calls from outsiders. We had all learned by experience that this was an effective and even essential means for keeping peace and avoiding unpleasantness, jealousy, envy, suspicion, grumbling, and other very serious evils.

613 (4) The fourth thing that I forbade them to do with all the power of my authority, and begged them not to do with all the love of my heart, was to read anonymous accusations. These were four of the main practices we adhered to, and God deigned to bless them so that all went well for us. May the Lord be blessed in all things forever.

217

Chapter XI

HOW I DISLIKED LIVING IN MADRID

The Saint now introduces us to a new stage in his life. He was immersed in this new world as he was writing these lines, and so he lacks the proper distance required to see it all in a more detached perspective. In these chapters we can see something of the tension he felt in his spirit "which goes out to the whole world," and how living in court hedged him in. Despite this, his fidelity to his missionary vocation, his apostolic activities, and his interior life shine through.

614 At the beginning of June, 1857, we arrived in Madrid, where I was presented to Her Majesty, the Queen. On the fifth of that month the royal decree of my appointment as the queen's confessor was approved and published.[1] A few days later the queen told me that one of my duties would be to attend to the religious instruction of the Infanta Isabel, then five years old.[2] I always took personal charge of her lessons and on April 11, 1862, when she was ten years old, she made her First Holy Communion, in the company of her mother. I had been hearing her confession since she was seven. Presently, in addition to her instructions, she has made a ten-day retreat.

615 The queen made the Spiritual Exercises that first year and has made them annually ever since. She always leaves them with a great sense of contentment and has asked others to make them. She especially likes the text of them that I published, and she has asked me to bring her copies so that she can have the pleasure of giving them as gifts; and she counsels the recipients to at least read them.

616 All the ladies of the court have a copy of both *The Straight Path* and the *Spiritual Exercises*. Their Majesties both enjoyed *The Straight Path* so much that I had a deluxe edition brought out for them by Aguado Printers in Madrid. At present, both Their Majesties and the ladies of the court lead very edifying lives: they hear Mass, read the lives of the

saints daily, recite the Holy Rosary, and frequent the Sacraments. The queen and the infanta, as well as many ladies of the court, come to me for confession. They all keep busy all the time.

617 The queen, besides attending to her devotions and affairs of state, as well as receiving many people in audience, busies herself with various sorts of handiwork such as painting, embroidery, etc. Her commonest pastime is embroidering. Last year[1] she embroidered a beautiful flowered cushion for my prie-dieu. She also makes lace ruffles from time to time.

618 The Infanta Isabel also keeps busy all the time. Besides her devotions and spiritual reading, she spends a great deal of time at her lessons. At recreation she prefers boys' toys to girls', so much so that in the five years I have known her I have never seen her with a girls' toy. Her favorite trinkets are an embroidered sombrero and a sword. She also busies herself from time to time with wire and pliers, making rosaries. She embroiders and sews very well.

619 The chambermaids of the queen and the infantas are also continuously busy, either with their duties, or reading good books, doing needlepoint, etc.

620 Although I am pleased to see how well Her Majesty lives and how well she practices piety, charity, and the other virtues, so that others in the court follow her good example, still I can't settle down or become accustomed to staying in Madrid. I have no inclination or disposition to be a courtier or palace retainer; hence, living at court and being constantly in the palace is a continuous martyrdom for me.

621 I have sometimes remarked that God sent me to this job as a kind of purgatory where I am supposed to pay for the sins of my past. I have also said that in all my life I have never suffered as much as I do here at court. I am always sighing to get away from it all. I'm like a caged bird that keeps looking through the bars of its cage for a way to escape, and I keep dreaming up ways to get out. I would almost have been glad if a revolution had come along and they had thrown me out.

622 I sometimes ask myself, "What cause have you to be so upset? Everyone in the palace respects you; the whole royal family appreciates you and values your presence; Her Majesty the Queen loves you and dotes on you. Well, then, what makes you have such violent feelings on the subject?" In truth, I have none. I can't come up with any good reason for it. My only answer to the enigma is that the repugnance I feel is a grace God has sent me to prevent me from becoming attached to the prestige, honors, and riches of this world. For I can see clearly that this constant feeling of disgust for the court and my desire to escape from it have kept me from envy and from setting my heart on the things the world holds dear.

623 I can see that what the Lord is doing in me is like what I observe going on in the motion of the planets: they are pulled by two forces, one centrifugal, the other centripetal. Centrifugal force pulls them to escape their orbits; centripetal force draws them toward their center. The balance of these two forces holds them in their orbits. That's just how I see myself. I feel one force within me, which I'll call centrifugal, telling me to get out of Madrid and the court; but I also feel a counterforce, the will of God, telling me to stay in court for the time being, until I am free to leave. This will of God is the centripetal force that keeps me chained here like a dog on his leash. The mixture of these two forces, namely, the desire to leave and my love for doing God's will, keeps me running around in my circle.

624 Every day at prayer I have to make acts of resignation to God's will. Day and night I have to offer up the sacrifice of staying in Madrid, but I thank God for the repugnance I feel. I know that it is a great favor. How awful it would be if the court or the world pleased me! The only thing that pleases me is that nothing pleases me. May you be blessed, God my Father, for taking such good care of me. Lord, just as you make the ocean salty and bitter to keep it pure, so have you given me the salt of dislike and the bitterness of boredom for the court, to keep me clean of this world. Lord, I give you thanks, many thanks, for doing so.

Chapter XII

HOW I HAVE NEVER SOUGHT POSITIONS OR MEDDLED IN POLITICS

625 Because the queen likes me and thinks so much of me, I know that she would be pleased if I asked any favors of her; but so far I haven't asked her for a single thing and I have no desire to do so in the future. What's that I've just said? No, I didn't put it quite right. There is one favor I have, indeed, asked of her many times and with great insistence: to let me withdraw from Madrid and the court. And it is just this favor, the only one I have ever asked for, that I have so far been unable to obtain. The worst of it is that, although I have some hope of getting it, I can see no way of getting it quickly.

626 All those who hunger and thirst not after justice or any personal merit, but simply for the favor of some job, post, or dignity, besiege my house every day and pester me with their ambitions and pretensions. I have to tell them all that it cuts me to the quick not to be able to please them, but that I have made it a rule never to meddle in these matters. Nevertheless, after five years in Madrid, during which I have never budged from this position, they still haven't given up, and we're still at it every day. The greater part of those who come to see me during my daily audience from 11:00 to noon are looking for jobs, positions, or preferments (not to mention the pile of letters I receive daily, asking for the same). What would have become of me if I'd ever allowed myself to get involved in that briar patch!

627 Furthermore, I see that those who are pushing, striving, and begging for these jobs, positions, and preferments, without sparing bribes and other such wiles, are usually the very ones who least deserve them. May God deliver me from ever cooperating in a business that has such evil consequences: all the jobs ill-done, all the deserving and virtuous people passed over, all the pedantry, vice, and immorality enthroned—and all of it by the wicked hand of favor. Yes, I say it, and I say it

loudly and clearly, hoping that everyone will take notice and leave me in peace: *I have no interest in such things.*

628 Despite all the precautions I have taken in treading on this terrain, I have not escaped the malice of wagging tongues. Some have murmured against me for refusing to be the tool of their baseless ambitions, others out of envy; some for fear of losing what they have, others out of malice. Still others, out of ignorance or mere hearsay, have invented all sorts of rogueries about me and started the ugliest rumors. But I have remained silent and rejoiced in the Lord, because He has given me a sip from the chalice of his sufferings. As for my detractors, I have prayed to God for them, after forgiving and loving them with all my heart.

629 I have never wanted to get mixed up in politics, not even when I was a simple priest, let alone nowadays, although I have certainly been pressed in that direction. One of our leading politicians once asked me to recommend a certain policy to Her Majesty. "My dear sir," I answered, "you may as well know that I look upon present-day Spain as a gambling table; the players are the two political parties. Now, just as it would be utterly reprehensible for a mere onlooker to give the slightest help to one of the players in the game, it would be equally reprehensible for me, a mere spectator, to make any recommendation favoring one or the other political party to Her Majesty. In the long run, all political parties are nothing more than players who are out to win the pool, so that they can lord it over the others, or simply to fatten their own wallets. The real motive in politics and political parties is often no more than ambition, pride, and greed."

630 One matter that I have been deeply involved in at the queen's insistence is in arranging a system for electing bishops. I should like to say something about the progress that has been made in this business so far. The Attorney General asks each and every bishop whether or not he knows of any priest in his diocese with proper qualifications to be a bishop, should the need for one arise. The bishop in question answers yes or no. If he knows of one, he gives whatever information he can about him, such as his age, educational background, virtue,

experience, and other data. The Attorney General collects and files all these data, and when a see falls vacant, he sends the dossiers to Her Majesty, who reads them and asks God's guidance in helping her choose the right one. After this, she draws up a list of three, makes inquiries about the three men, commends herself to God, and finally makes her choice, basing it solely on the greater glory of God and the good of the Church. I can stand surety for the fact that, if any priest ever so much as hinted that he wanted the position, it would be more than enough to bar him from being considered eligible for nomination. The queen once told me, "It will go badly for anyone who asks for or strives to obtain a bishopric." There is perhaps no matter in Spain that is handled more equitably and justly than the nomination of bishops, but neither is there any matter that is looked into more carefully.[1]

631 The matter of canonries is not so carefully scrutinized. I'm not suggesting that Her Majesty or the Attorney General have themselves ever been implicated in simony, but God knows whether or not office-hunters have made deals with or offered presents to some members of the circle that surrounds them, and surely these could not pass God's scrutiny. For this reason I have never meddled in this business of soliciting canonries. Would to God that all priests sought to be the last and the least among their brothers, as our Divine Master taught us. The best canonry is to love God deeply and save souls, so as to obtain a place of distinction in the glory of heaven. There can be no doubt that it will stand a priest in better stead to have been a missionary than not to have been a canon. Let him choose now what he would prefer to have chosen at the hour of his death.

Chapter XIII

MY CONDUCT HAS NEVER BEEN SELF-SERVING

This chapter parallels chapter 24 in Part Two, on apostolic poverty. Claret sees this virtue as essential to his vocation and shows here how he endeavored to practice it under this new set of circumstances.

632 There is a popular saying that contains a great lesson: "The little doggy wags his tail, not for thee, but for thy meal." Every day I see ladies and gentlemen feting, fawning, and doing who knows what else for the king and queen, not so much for Their Majesties themselves as for what they hope to gain by their efforts. Well, I have no wish or pretension, except to get out of the court. Someone may say, "Yes, but you have been decorated with the two Great Crosses." True, indeed, but how did I get them? I didn't ask for the Great Cross of Isabel the Catholic, and I didn't want to take it when it was offered me. But I was told that, as I was going to Cuba, I would have to have the title of Excellency because I was to be primate of that Church and act as possible substitute for the General of the island.[1]

633 As for the Cross of Charles III, I neither sought it nor wanted it; it was conferred upon me against my will, as I shall relate. After the birth of the Prince of Asturias,[1] on the very day Their Majesties were leaving for Atocha, I was summoned to the palace. As soon as I arrived, the queen and king came out of the room in which they had been waiting, and without a word of warning both of them pinned the cross and ribbon on me. Because the two of them were there and I did not have the same confidence in the king that I now have—we are now good friends—I held my peace and said nothing, although inwardly it caused me a great deal of suffering.[2] At a later date, when I was alone with the queen, I told her that the least I could do was to thank her for her good intentions in bestowing the Cross of Charles III on me but that it had caused me great pain and suffering. To prove my point, I re-

fused to wear any decorations whatsoever for a long time. Even now I wear them only on occasions when court etiquette dictates that full dress is *de rigueur.*

634 As far as anything else is concerned, I have nothing. There is no other bishop in the whole of Spain who has not received a pectoral cross, a chalice, or something else from Her Majesty on the occasion of a baptism, a visit to their cathedral, etc., but I neither have nor want anything. When I baptized the Infanta Concepción,[1] they were obliged by custom to offer me something, but I begged and beseeched them not to, and to spare my feelings they did as I asked. When I retired from the palace, I had the great satisfaction of being able to say that I had nothing from Her Majesty, not even a pin.

635 Their Majesties are surrounded by self-serving men who are always hunting and grasping after titles, honors, greater salaries, and sums of money; but I, as I have said, have gained nothing; rather, I have lost much. Her Majesty wanted me by all means to accept the office of Guardian of Montserrat—the church, hospital, etc.—but I declined. Both she and the Commissioner General asked me many times to take the post, and when I learned that the buildings had already been advertised for sale in the *Official Bulletin,* I finally accepted, just to save them. And what did I gain by it all? I had to pay 5,000 duros out of my own pocket for repairs on the church and the hospital.[1]

636 I can say much the same of the royal monastery of the Escorial, which neither is nor has ever been a source of profit to me; rather, it has brought me nothing but troubles and pains, and it has been the occasion of persecutions, slanders, and bills.[1] Three times I tried to resign from its presidency, but failed. Well, God be praised for it all: if the Lord wants me to carry this cross, all I can do is submit to his will. My God, I want nothing of this world, nothing but your grace, your holy love and heavenly glory.

225

Chapter XIV

ORDINARY AND EXTRAORDINARY OCCUPATIONS

637 Every day in winter I ordinarily rise at 3:00, sometimes earlier, because I always get up when I can't go to sleep and am never in bed unless sleeping.[1] Then I begin the Divine Office, reciting Matins and Lauds, after which I say the Trisagion, read Scripture, prepare for Mass, celebrate Mass, make my thanksgiving,[2] and remain in the confessional until 11:00, when I go to hold audience for anyone who wishes to speak with me. The hour from 11:00 to 12:00 is the most burdensome of my day, since it is then that I receive all those requests that I can't grant, such as petitions for jobs, appointments, and things of that sort. From 12:00 to 12:15 I make my particular examen. At 12:15 we eat, after which I say the Minor Hours, Vespers, and Compline. Later in the evening or at night, I visit the sick, prisoners, or other charitable institutions, preach to nuns and sisters, study, or write books and pamphlets.

638 Besides these ordinary daily occupations, there have been others such as giving retreats to the clergy, to the men and women of the St. Vincent de Paul Society, to nuns and sisters, not to mention missions to the laity.[1] But this is not enough work to satisfy me; what I would really like to do would be to walk through towns and villages, giving missions. This is my great dream. I have a holy envy of those missionaries who are lucky enough to be able to go from town to town preaching the Holy Gospel.

639 I have had some consolation in the midst of my sufferings. When I go on tour with Their Majesties and Highnesses, I get to preach to the people in the morning, before Their Majesties leave the house.[1] Afterward I go around preaching in convents to nuns, sisters, priests, seminarians, members of the St. Vincent de Paul Society, etc., so that my whole day is spent in preaching, except for the exact period of time I have to spend in the palace with the royal family.

640 One of the things that has kept me most occupied since I've been in Madrid has been writing books and pamphlets, having them printed, and buying these and other books for circulation by the Academy of St. Michael: in confessionals, institutions, schools, and on the streets.[1]

641 My God, I wish that I could prevent anyone from offending you; rather, I wish that I could make you known, loved, and served by all creation. This is my only desire; the rest is not worth bothering about. My God, how good you are! I love you with all the strength of my heart.

Chapter XV

THE PLAN OF LIFE AND RESOLUTIONS I WILL STRIVE TO KEEP WITH GOD'S HELP

This plan of life and resolutions are basically the same as those he made at his episcopal consecration, with certain variants, either in the direction of greater strictness or on the basis of the different occupations imposed by his new post. Comparing all the lists of resolutions he made during this period, the present list might have been used as a general outline for all of them.

642 (1) Jesus and Mary are my only support and guide, the models I propose to follow and imitate. Furthermore, I take the glorious St. Francis de Sales, St. Charles Borromeo, St. Thomas of Villanova, and St. Martin as my patrons and exemplars.

643 (2) I will bear in mind the Apostle's words to Timothy (1 Tim. 4:16): "Watch yourself and watch your teaching." As Cornelius says, "These are the two duties of bishops; those who neglect them are of no use to themselves or others."[1]

644 (3) Every year I will make the Spiritual Exercises.
(4) Every month I will make a day of retreat.
(5) Every week I will go to confession at least once.
(6) Three days a week I will take the discipline, and on

the other days I will wear the cilice or do some equivalent penance.

(7) Every Friday of the year and on the vigils of feasts of our Lord and the Blessed Virgin, I will fast.

645   (8) Every day I will get up at 3:00 or earlier, if I can't sleep. After rising I will recite Matins and Lauds and read the Holy Bible until time for meditation.

(9) I will meditate for an hour.

(10) I will celebrate Holy Mass and afterwards spend a half hour in thanksgiving and in asking graces for myself and others.

646   (11) Then I will go to the confessional until 8:00, when I will go and take a cup of chocolate, after which I will return to the confessional. If there is no one there, I will do something else until 11:00, when I hold audience for an hour. At 12:00 I will recite the Angelus and make my examen.[1]

(12) At 12:15 I will have lunch with spiritual reading.

(13) I will rest until 1:30.

(14) I will work until 8:30, when I will recite the rosary and my other devotions.

(15) At 9:00 I will have dinner and at 10:00 I will retire.

647   (16) I resolve never to lose a moment's time, and hence I will always keep busy either studying, praying, preaching, conferring the sacraments, etc.

648   (17) I resolve always to walk in God's presence, referring all things to Him, never seeking my own praise, but only greater grace to imitate Jesus. I will always try to ask myself how Jesus would have acted under similar circumstances.

649   (18) I resolve to do well the ordinary things that I do. If there is a choice of two good things, I will try to select the better, even though it might cost me the sacrifice of my own will. I will likewise choose whatever is poorest, meanest, and most painful.

650   (19) I resolve to keep an even temper and disposition,

never allowing myself to be carried away by anger, impatience, sadness, or exaggerated joy, always remembering the example of Jesus, Mary, and Joseph, who also had their trials, and far greater ones than mine. I will think that God has arranged things this way for my own good, and so I will not complain. Rather, I will say, "Thy will be done." I will remember what Augustine says, "Either do what God wills or suffer what you would not." I will also recall what God told Mary Magdalen de Pazzi: to maintain the same unchanging pleasant mood with every sort of person, yet never let slip one word of flattery.[1] Of St. Martin we read that he seemed never to be upset or sad or laughing, but always in an even mood of heavenly joy. So great was his patience that although they knew he was their prelate, even the least of his clergy could rest assured that if they offended him, he would not chastise them.[2]

Selected Maxims

651 Perfection consists in loving God very much and despising oneself (St. Mary Magdalen de Pazzi).

To despise oneself and despise no one; to despise the world and despise being despised (St. Louis Bertrand).

Do your duty and let come what may.

It is a thing of great courage to suffer without complaining and a thing of great wisdom to listen with patience.

In quiet and in trust your strength lies (Isa. 30:115).

652 The strong man should fear nothing, not even death, when it comes to doing his duty.

We should hold the post God has assigned us, fighting to the death without fear of the consequences. The only thing we should fear is acting unjustly.

653 If you want to achieve high virtue, do not be lifted up in self-esteem. Believe that you are doing nothing and you will do all (St. John Chrysostom).

Abstine et sustine: forbear and bear, abstain and endure.

Abstain from gluttony, luxury, and every pleasure, even if it be licit.

Endure work, illness, persecution, and slander.

229

The Holy Spirit teaches us to speak little and discreetly, to do all things fervently, and to praise God constantly.

Chapter XVI

SOME PARTICULAR DEVOTIONS

The greater part of this chapter is written in Latin in the original.

654 *Litany*[1]

Holy Mary
St. Joseph
St. Joachim
St. Anne
St. Anthony
All ye holy Seraphim
All ye holy Cherubim
All ye holy Thrones
All ye holy Dominations
All ye holy Virtues
All ye holy Powers
All ye holy Principalities
All ye holy Archangels
All ye holy Angels
All ye holy Patriarchs
and Prophets
St. John the Baptist
St. Peter
St. Paul
St. James
St. John
All ye holy Apostles
and Evangelists
St. Francis de Sales
St. Charles Borromeo
St. Thomas of Villanova
St. Antoninus
St. John Chrysostom
St. Ambrose
St. Augustine
St. Gregory
St. Athanasius
St. Jerome
St. Paulinus
St. Martin
St. Julian
St. Lawrence Justinian
St. Ildephonsus
St. Alphonsus Liguori
St. Bernard Calvó[2]
St. Bernard, Doctor
St. Francis Xavier
St. Francis of Assisi
St. Francis Borgia
St. Thomas Aquinas
St. Dominic
St. Stephen
St. Lawrence
St. Vincent
St. Sebastian Martyr
St. Sebastian Bishop
St. Philip Neri
St. Ignatius Martyr
St. Ignatius Loyola
St. Eligius
St. Teresa
St. Catherine Martyr
St. Catherine Virgin
St. Mary Magdalene
St. Mary Magdalen de
Pazzi

St. Thecla   All ye men and women
St. Agnes   Saints of God.
St. Philomena

655 *Petitions for Myself*
  I believe, Lord, but let me believe more firmly.
  I hope, Lord, but let me hope more surely.
  I love, Lord, but let me love more warmly.
  I repent, Lord, but let me repent more deeply.

656 O Lord, I am your servant, the son of your handmaid
(Ps. 116:16).
  Behold your servant, may your will be done in me.
What would you have me do?
  Teach me to do your will, for you are my God (Ps.
143:10).
  Give your servant, therefore, an understanding heart
to judge your people and to distinguish right from wrong
(1 Kings 3:9).

657 Father, give me humility, meekness, chastity, patience,
and charity.
  Father, teach me goodness, knowledge, and discipline.
  Father, give me your love together with your grace and
I will be rich enough.
  My God, my Jesus, and my all!

658 On the cross I have lived and on the cross I wish to die;
from the cross I hope to come down, not by my own hands,
but at the hands of others, after I have finished my sacrifice.
  God forbid that I should glory save in the cross of Our
Lord Jesus Christ, through whom the world is crucified to me
and I to the world (Gal. 6:14).

659 *Petitions for the People*
  Father, look upon the face of your Christ.
  Father, look upon the face of your handmaid.
  Father, look toward me and have pity on me, for I am
alone and afflicted (Ps. 25:16).
  Turn toward me and have pity on me; give your

strength to your servant, and save the son of your handmaid (Ps. 86:16).

O Lord, I am your servant; I am your servant, the son of your handmaid (Ps. 116:16).

660 Spare, O Lord, spare your people, through the humility and patience of Jesus Christ, our Lord, and the Blessed Virgin Mary.

Spare, O Lord, spare your people, through the love and merits of Jesus Christ, our Lord, and the Blessed Virgin Mary.

Spare us, O Lord; Jesus, Son of David, have pity on us.

661 Come then, Lord, sustain your people, bought with the price of your own blood.

Save your people, Lord, and bless your inheritance; govern them and lift them up unto eternity.

Deign, O Lord, to keep us from sin this day.

Have mercy on us, Lord, have mercy on us.

Let your mercy come upon us, Lord, as we have hoped in you.

In you, O Lord, I have trusted; I shall never be put to shame.

662 My God, I would never want you to say of me what you said of the priests of Israel: "You did not step into the breach, nor did you build a wall of prayer about the house of Israel that would stand firm against attack on the day of the Lord" (Ezek. 13:5).

You have said, my God: "I have searched among them for someone who would build a wall or stand in the breach to keep me by his prayers from destroying the land; but I found no one" (Ezek. 22:30).

663 I am nothing, Lord, yet like Moses I want to pray: "Pardon, then, the wickedness of this people, in keeping with your great kindness" (Num. 14:19).

Father, I ask you this through the merits of Jesus Christ, your Son and our Redeemer, and through the merits of Blessed Mary, the Mother of your most holy Son and our Mother. Yes, I, the first and foremost sinner of all, ask you this in the name of all you wish us to ask and know that we need the most.

Chapter XVII

SOME HOMELY ANIMALS THAT HAVE SERVED ME AS EXAMPLES OF VIRTUE

The following paragraphs are copied from another of Claret's manuscripts, entitled Domestici Dei, *based on a phrase from Ephesians: "members of the household of God" (2:19). One of the characteristics of the gift of piety is that it gives its possessor the ability to see the whole world as a gift of God. Throughout Scripture, Claret sees symbols of apostolic virtues in various animals. The naive quality of some of his expressions only serves to heighten the Franciscan flavor of this chapter. St. Micaela of the Blessed Sacrament made her own copy, which is included in* Notes Compiled from the Writings of our Blessed Mother Foundress, *p. 27.*

664 The Holy Spirit tells me, "Go to the ant, O sluggard, study her ways and learn wisdom."[1] And learn I shall, not only from the ant, but from the cock, the donkey, and the dog as well.

"Who gives the cock its understanding?" (Job 38:36).

"At that moment a cock crowed."[2]

(1) The cock crows for me, and I, like Peter, should recall my sins and weep.

(2) The cock crows out the hours of day and night. I, too, should praise God every hour of the day and night, and urge others to do so.

(3) Day and night the cock watches over his brood; day and night I, too, should watch over the souls that the Lord has entrusted to my care.

(4) At the slightest sound or sense of danger the cock crows out an alarm; I, too, should do the same, by warning souls of the slightest danger of sin.

655 (5) The cock defends his brood against the attacks of hawks and other birds of prey; I, too, should defend the souls

the Lord has entrusted to my care against the hawks of error, sin, and vice.

(6) The cock is very generous; as soon as he sees a bit of food, he fasts himself, but calls the hens to eat. I should forego pleasures and conveniences so that I may be generous and charitable toward the poor and needy.

(7) Before he crows, the cock first beats his wings; I, before preaching, should move and beat the wings of study and prayer.

(8) The cock is most prolific; so must I be spiritually, so that I can say with the Apostle, "It was I who begot you in Christ Jesus through my preaching of the Gospel."[1]

The Donkey

666 "I was like a brute beast in your presence. Yet with you I shall always be."[1]

(1) The donkey is by nature the humblest of beasts. His name is an insult; his place is the lowest in the yard; his food is poor and so are his trappings. I, too, should see to it that my room, food, and clothing are poor, so as to win for myself humiliation and the scorn of men. This will help me to acquire the virtue of humility because in my fallen nature I am vain and proud.

667 (2) The donkey is a very patient beast; he carries men and their burdens and suffers beatings without complaint. I, too, must be very patient in bearing the burden of my duties and in suffering meekly all the pains, trials, persecutions, and slanders I am subject to.

668 (3) The Blessed Virgin Mary rode upon a donkey, both when she went to Bethlehem to give birth to Jesus, her Son, and when she fled with Him into Egypt to deliver Him from Herod. I, too, offer myself to Mary, to be the joyful bearer of devotion to her, to preach about her glories, joys, and sorrows, and to meditate day and night upon these adorable mysteries.

669 (4) Jesus rode upon a donkey when He entered Jerusalem in triumph. I, too, gladly offer myself to Jesus to make

use of me in his triumphant march over his enemies, the world, the flesh, and the devil, as He makes his way into the souls and towns of those who are converted to Him. I will, of course, know that the honors and praises I hear will not be for me, the donkey, but for Jesus, whose dignity I, though unworthy, bear.

The Dog

670 "They are all dumb dogs, they cannot bark."[1]

(1) The dog is so faithful an animal and so constant a companion to his master that neither misery, poverty, hardship, nor anything else can separate them. I should be the same: so faithful and constant in serving and loving God that I might say with the Apostle that neither death nor life nor anything else can ever separate me from Him.

671 (2) The dog is more loyal than a son, more obedient than a servant, and more docile than a child. Not only does he willingly do what his master orders, but he scans his master's face to tell from his looks what he wants, so that he can do it without being told to, with the greatest alacrity and joy. He even shares his master's affections, becoming a friend of his friends and an enemy of his enemies. I should practice all these beautiful traits in serving God, my beloved Master. Yes, I shall gladly do what He commands me, and I shall study to know and do his will without waiting for a command. I shall promptly and gladly do all that He disposes through his representatives, my superiors. I shall be a friend of the friends of God, and I shall treat his enemies as He tells me, barking out against their wickedness to make them leave it.

672 (3) The dog watches by day and redoubles his vigilance by night. He guards the person and the property of his master. He barks at and bites all those he knows or suspects are planning to harm his master or his master's interests. I should strive to be always vigilant, and denounce vices, faults, and sins, and cry out against the enemies of the soul.

673 (4) The dog's greatest joy is to be in his master's presence and walk along beside him. I shall strive always to walk

joyfully in the presence of God, my dear Master. Thus I will never sin and will become perfect, according to his word: "Walk in my presence and be blameless."[1]

Chapter XVIII

SOME NOTEWORTHY THINGS THAT GOD AND THE BLESSED VIRGIN MARY HAVE MADE ME UNDERSTAND

From 1856 on, St. Anthony Mary Claret was ordered by his confessor, Fr. Paladio Currius (and later, Fr. Xifré), to note down any inner enlightenments he received concerning either his personal spirituality or his apostolate. Some of these notes entered the Autobiography; *others were written after it. (Cf.* Claret, Writings, *pp. 621 ff.)*

674 *1855.* On July 12, 1855 at 5:30 in the afternoon, after I had just finished my pastoral letter on the Immaculate Conception, I knelt down before a picture of Mary to thank her for helping me write the letter. Suddenly I was surprised to hear a clear and distinct voice issuing from the picture, saying *"Bene scripsisti."*[1] These words made a deep impression on me and filled me with a strong desire to be perfect.

675 *1857.* On January 15, 1857, at 5:00 in the afternoon, while I was meditating on Jesus, I said, "What do you want me to do, Lord?" Jesus answered, "You'll have work to do, Anthony; your hour has not yet come."

For several days since this happened I have been feeling many spiritual consolations, especially during Mass and meditation.

676 *1857.* On October 8, 1857 at half-past noon, the Blessed Virgin told me what I would have to do to become very good: "You already know what to do; repent the faults of your past life and be watchful for what is to come. Do you hear me, Anthony?" she repeated. "Watchful for what is to come. Yes, yes, I tell you so."

677 On the ninth of the same month, at 4:00 in the morning, the Blessed Virgin Mary repeated several times what she had told me on other occasions—that I was to be the "Dominic of these times in spreading devotion to the rosary."

678 On December 21 that same year, I was advised on four points: (1) more prayer, (2) writing books, (3) directing souls, (4) more tranquillity at being in Madrid. God wants me here.

679 On December 25 God infused in me a love of being persecuted and slandered. The Lord even favored me with a dream the following night. I dreamed that I had been jailed on a charge I was innocent of. Because I considered it a gift from heaven to be treated like Jesus, I was silent, as He had been. Nearly all my friends had abandoned me, as had the friends of Jesus, too. One of my friends wanted to defend me, as Peter had wanted to defend Jesus, but I said to him, "Don't you want me to drink the chalice my Father has prepared for me?"[1]

680 *1859.* January 6, 1859. The Lord made me understand that I am like the earth; in fact, I am earth. The earth is trampled on and is silent; I should be trampled on and be silent. The earth is raked; I should be mortified. Finally, the earth needs to be watered if it is to be productive; I need grace if I am to produce good works.

681 March 21. While meditating on Christ's words to the Samaritan woman, "I am he who speak with you,"[1] I understood some great, very great things. He gave the woman faith and she believed; He gave her sorrow for her sins and she repented; He gave her grace and she preached Jesus. He has done the same in my case, giving me faith, sorrow, and a mission to preach Him.

682 The Lord told Moses, *"Ego sum,"*[1] and sent him into Egypt. Jesus, walking on the Sea of Galilee, told his terrified Apostles, *"Ego sum,"*[2] and they took heart. Jesus told Saul, *"Ego sum,"*[3] and he was converted and became a great preacher. Well, then....

683 On April 27, He promised me the love of God and called me "my little Anthony."

684 On September 4, at 4:25 in the morning, Jesus Christ told me, "You have to teach your Missionaries mortification, Anthony." A few minutes later, the Blessed Virgin told me, "If you do, the results will be great, Anthony."

685 On September 23, at 7:30 in the morning, the Lord told me, "You shall fly throughout the world or walk with great speed and preach of the great punishments that are approaching." The Lord gave me a deep understanding of those words of the Apocalypse (8:13): "As my vision continued, I heard an eagle flying in mid-heaven cry out in a loud voice, 'Woe, woe, and again woe to the inhabitants of the earth,' because of the three great chastisements that are to come." These chastisements are:
    (1) Protestantism, communism. . . .
    (2) The four archdemons that will make fearful inroads: the love of pleasure, the love of money, independence of the mind, independence of the will.
    (3) The great wars and their consequences.

686 On September 24, the feast of Our Lady of Mercy, at 11:30 in the morning, the Lord gave me an understanding of another passage in the Apocalypse (10:1): "Then I saw another mighty angel come down from heaven wrapped in a cloud, with a rainbow about his head; his face shone like the sun and his legs like pillars of fire. In his hand he held a little scroll that had been opened. He placed his right foot on the sea and his left foot on the land [first in his diocese of Cuba and later in other dioceses], and then he gave a loud cry like the roar of a lion. When he cried out, the seven thunders raised their voices too." Here come the sons of the Congregation of the Immaculate Heart of Mary. It says seven, but seven is an indefinite number here, meaning all. They are called thunders because they will shout like thunder and make their voices heard. They are also called thunders because of their love and zeal, like that of Sts. James and John, who were called the sons of thunder. And the Lord wants me

and my companions to imitate the Apostles James and John in zeal, chastity, and love for Jesus and Mary.

687 The Lord told me both for myself and for all these missionary companions of mine, "You yourselves will not be the speakers; the Spirit of your Father (and of your Mother) will be speaking in you."[1] So true is this that each one of us will be able to say, "The spirit of the Lord is upon me; therefore he has anointed me. He has sent me to bring glad tidings to the poor, to heal the brokenhearted."[2]

688 On October 15, 1859, the feast of St. Teresa, there was a plot to assassinate me. The would-be assassin entered the church of St. Joseph on Alcalá Street in Madrid. With evil intent he had entered the church just to pass the time, and he was converted through the intercession of St. Joseph, as the Lord let me know. The assassin came to talk with me and told me he was a member of a secret lodge that was backing him. It had fallen to his lot to kill me, and if he didn't succeed within 40 days, he would be killed, just as he himself had killed others who failed to carry out their orders. The man who was supposed to kill me cried, embraced, and kissed me and then went into hiding so as not to be killed for not having fulfilled his orders.

689 I have endured great sufferings, slanders, and persecutions; all hell has conspired against me.

690 On June 7, 1860, at 11:30 in the morning of the feast of Corpus Christi, after saying Mass and just before I was to lead the procession, I was in prayer before the Blessed Sacrament. I was filled with fervor and devotion. Suddenly, to my surprise, Jesus said to me, "It's good. I like the book you've written." The "book" was the first volume of *The Well-Instructed Seminarian,* which I had just finished the day before, and I knew quite clearly that this was the book He was telling me about. When I finished the second volume, He was also good enough to give me his approval for it too.

691 On November 22, 1860 I was feeling very low at the prospect of having to take over the whole project of the

Escorial. The burden of it robbed me of rest by day and of sleep by night. Because I couldn't sleep, I got up, dressed, prayed, and laid all my burden before God. In the spirit I heard the clear, intelligible voice of the Lord telling me, "Courage! Don't lose heart; I'll help you."

692 *1861.* On March 2, 1861 Jesus Christ condescended to give me his approval for the leaflet I had written on his Passion.

693 On April 6, 1861 I was counseled not to be in such a rush, and that I should perform the task at hand as if I had nothing else in the world to do so as not to lose the spirit of meekness.

On June 15, 1861 Jesus told me, "Be patient, you'll be working soon enough!"

694 On August 26, 1861, at 7:00 in the evening while I was at prayer in the church of the Rosary at La Granja, the Lord granted me the great grace of keeping the sacramental species intact within me and of having the Blessed Sacrament always present, day and night, in my breast. Because of this I must always be very recollected and inwardly devout. Furthermore I must pray and confront all the evils of Spain, as the Lord has told me. To help me do this, I have engraved in my memory a number of things, such as that without any merit, talent, or personal recommendation, He has lifted me up from the lowest of the low to the highest post, at the side of the kings of this earth. And now He has put me at the side of the King of Heaven. "Glorify God and bear him about in your body" (1 Cor. 6:20).[1]

695 On August 27, 1861 in the same church, during Benediction of the Blessed Sacrament that I was conducting after Mass, the Lord let me know the three great evils that were menacing Spain: (1) Protestantism, or rather, the loss of the Catholic spirit; (2) the Republic; (3) communism. To combat these three evils, He showed me that three devotions should be practiced: the Trisagion, the Blessed Sacrament, and the rosary.

696 The Trisagion should be said every day. The Blessed Sacrament should be honored by hearing Mass, receiving Communion frequently, visiting the Blessed Sacrament, and making spiritual communions. The rosary should be said daily, all three parts or at least one part. We should meditate on the mysteries, applying them to the circumstances of our own lives.

697 On the feast of the Conversion of St. Peter, the Lord helped me understand what happened in that event. Peter failed and denied Jesus. The cock crew, but Peter was not converted. The cock crew again and Peter was converted, because Jesus looked at him—Jesus, "who looks upon the earth and makes it tremble."[1] I knew that I would have to preach again and again and at the same time pray that the Lord would turn his kind and merciful eyes on worldly men that they might tremble, shudder, and be converted.

698 *1862*. On May 11, 1862, at 6:30 in the evening, while I was in the Chapel of the Blessed Sacrament at the palace of Aranjuez, I offered myself to Jesus and Mary to preach, exhort, labor, and suffer even death itself, and the Lord accepted my offering.

699 Faced with a choice of two goods, each of which would give God equal glory, I feel called to choose the poorer, the humbler, and the more painful.

700 On the morning of May 16, 1862, at 4:15 while I was at prayer, I thought of what I had written down the day before concerning my experience of the Blessed Sacrament the previous August 26. I had been thinking of erasing it and was still thinking of it today, but the Blessed Virgin told me not to erase it. Afterward, while I was saying Mass, Jesus Christ told me that He had indeed granted me this grace of remaining within me sacramentally.

241

Chapter XIX

701 THE MOST NOTABLE DATES IN MY LIFE

NOTES TO PART THREE

Chapter I

499.1 Cf. pars. 77–78, 88–90.

499.2 A journalist of the time offers the following details of the service: "Bishop Claret's sponsor was a venerable priest of this church, Don Fortián Bres, who has been his protector and like a father to him. Occupying a place of honor were Bishop Claret's father, one sister, and an older brother, who, although they are all as humble and simple as the Bishop himself, were beside themselves with joy and were the envy of all, especially his father, now somewhat elderly, in his simple workingman's suit. It seemed as if Bishop Claret had been a bishop all his life, judging from his calm and confident behavior during the blessing, chanting, and performance of the rubrics. Nothing seems able to ruffle this apostolic man, so full of charity and yet so apparently unmoved." The writer goes on to note that Bishop Soler, on the other hand, was visibly shaken. (*Daily of Barcelona,* October 8, 1850.)

499.3 Bishop Dominic Costa y Borrás (1805–64) was Bishop of Lérida (1848) and of Barcelona (1850). Exiled in 1855, he returned to Spain to become Archbishop of Tarragona (1857) and Senator of the Realm (1858). He founded the Conceptionist Sisters and published several books. Claret had his *Complete Works* in his library.

499.4 Bishop Fulgencio Lorente (1797–1862), Bishop of Gerona (1847).

500.1 More likely he arrived in Madrid October 16 and received the pallium from the Nuncio on October 20 in the palace chapel. He had an appointment for a royal audience on October 27, at which he arrived late from a preaching engagement in the Italian Church.

500.2 One preaching engagement was at the Hospital of St. John of God, where St. Micaela of the Blessed Sacrament was senior nun and Fr. Lobo was spiritual director.

500.3 Claret, ever the missionary, turned this journey into a mission, preaching everywhere. Among the saints who have been pilgrims to the shrine of Our Lady of Montserrat, only of Claret is it recorded that he preached there. St. Ignatius offered the Virgin his sword of knighthood, Anthony that of the Word of God.

500.4 Fr. Joseph Mach, S.J. (1810–65), famous Jesuit preacher and admirer of Claret, wrote numerous devotional works: *The Anchor of Salvation* (Barcelona, 1854); *The Priest's Thesaurus* (1861).

501.1 He was in Barcelona from November 16 to December 28, preaching seven to ten sermons daily and seeing several books through the press. When someone asked him how he was able to do so much work, he answered, "Fall in love with Jesus Christ and souls and you'll understand it all and do much more than I do."

502.1 Claret gives a sketch of each in pars. 591–605.

504.1 "The people of Málaga were very pleased with me, as I was with them. What a harvest of souls I was offered!" (Claret, *Correspondence*, Letter 160.)

506.1 At 6:00 A.M.

507.1 Between Compline and Matins they read a chapter from the Gospels.

507.2 The Archbishop always led the rosary, which concluded with the singing of "Holy God" and some verses on the rosary, which Fr. Barjau accompanied on the accordion.

509.1 The mission lasted from January 27 to February 10.

509.2 The capital of the archdiocese was Santiago, with a population of 26,668 in 1851. It was a difficult field of apostolate: a far-flung diocese, with a poor communications system and a very hot climate. It had been without a bishop for 14 years (some important cities had not seen a bishop for 60 years). Socially, it was plagued by slavery, and the political climate was restless, with a growing separatist faction.

510.1 The visit to the shrine at El Cobre took place on March 3. Earlier, when Claret's ship had sailed into the Bay of Santiago, the captain had turned it toward the mountain of El Cobre and fired a five-gun salute, while all on board sang a prayer to the Virgin. On the day of his installation Claret placed his episcopate under the protection of the Virgin: "The Blessed Virgin will always be the Prelate here; and my administration will be of the kind she inspires me to."

511.1 The mission began on Ash Wednesday, March 5. Although the general Communion service took place on March 25, the closing had to be deferred until April 6.

512.1 This clergy retreat lasted from February 4 to March 1.

514.1 Cf. par. 595.

515.1 The first pastoral visitation began on April 2 and was interrupted by Holy Week services. Claret confirmed 500 of the faithful each morning of the visit.

516.1 "Preaching has always been considered the principal obligation of bishops. Woe to those bishops who neglect this essential obligation. They will be treated as dogs who were silent when they should have barked. Woe to them!" (Claret, *Notes on Government* [Barcelona, 1865], p. 54.)

Chapter II

520.1 A royal decree of October 16, 1805 required that the Governor's permission be obtained before any white man of noble blood might marry a colored woman. The terms of this decree had been falsely amplified to apply to any white man whatsoever. The practical outcome of this distortion was a huge increase in concubinage.

This marriage question was drawn out until 1854, when the Marquis of la Pezuela revoked the erroneous interpretation. With Espartero's rise to power, however, it was reinstated. Meanwhile, Claret had regularized more than 10,000 marriages and legitimated more than 40,000 illegitimate children.

521.1 Don José Concha (1809–95), Captain General of Cuba (1850–52; 1854–59). In 1868 the queen made him president of the Council of Ministers, but the revolution forced him into exile in France.

522.1 Present-day Camagüey, capital of the province of Camagüey, was government headquarters of the central district of Cuba. It was notorious for political unrest and was the port of entry for revolutionaries.

522.2 Narciso López (1798–1851), a native of Venezuela, fought against the Carlists. Appointed governor of Valencia (1839) and General (1840), he was sent to Cuba where he fell into disfavor. In 1848 he joined the guerrilla movement for independence and organized two landings. Captured in 1851, he was executed on September 1 of that year.

523.1 The four prisoners were Joaquín Aguirre, Miguel Benavides, Tomás Betancourt, and Francisco Zayas. Claret wrote two petitions to General Concha requesting their release.

524.1 "Not knowing how to get rid of me in any other way, they tried to poison me. They would have carried it off, too, if the culprits had not been overcome by remorse and told me of the plot. I forgave them with all my heart" (Claret, *Correspondence,* Letter 198, to General Concha).

Chapter III

525.1 These Exercises lasted from July 27 to August 2.

527.1 November 15, 1851.

527.2 The Saint nursed him devotedly, watching by his bedside day and night. He had already lost Telesforo Hernández, on September 21, and Fr. Juan Pladebella on October 6.

528.1 "Around the middle of May, God gave me to understand that great calamities were approaching and first of all, earthquakes" (Claret, *Correspondence,* Letter 247).

528.2 On August 31 he interrupted his sermon abruptly and said, "Let us pray God for our brethren living in Santiago, for they are in great tribulation. We will go tomorrow to console them. (*Informative Process,* Vich, session 23).

Chapter IV

529.1 He arrived in Santiago on September 3.

Chapter V

535.1 The Saint received a supernatural message of all this toward the middle of May. (Cf. *Correspondence,* Letter 247.) Within three months, 2,734 persons died of cholera.

537.1 Once more, the Saint had to interrupt the mission at Bayamo. "I have come to this city, breaking off my visitation, to care for the plague victims. No one has died without the sacraments. The priests have acted with the greatest heroism" (*Correspondence,* Letter 257).

Chapter VI

540.1 On January 22, 1853, Claret recommended the pastoral visitation that had been interrupted by the outbreak of the cholera epidemic. On February 21 he began the ascent of the Knives of Baracoa. This was without doubt the most heroic journey of his life.

542.1 Bishop Felíu had made the last pastoral visit to Baracoa in 1791. Archbishop Claret confirmed 4,620 people, 62 marriages were performed, and 3,000 Communions were distributed.

544.1 According to the testimony of some of his collaborators, 8,517 common-law marriages were rectified and 210 divorced couples were reunited. Confirmations numbered 90,070. (Curríus, *Apostolic Process,* Tarragona, session 6.)

547.1 This pastoral was published in Santiago in 1852. It consists of 83 pages on the holiness, learning, and zeal appropriate to priests. It was reprinted in Barcelona by the Religious Library in 1855.

548.1 These 70 pages of appendices were published in 1853 and incorporated into the reprint of the first pastoral in 1855.

549.1 Published in Santiago, Cuba, 116 pages. It is a synthesis of Claret's mission catechesis. Reprinted by the Religious Library, Barcelona, 1853.

549.2 Santiago, Cuba, 1854. A ten-page exhortation to beware of Protestant propaganda and to read the Bible in Catholic editions.

549.3 November 20, 1854. It is, rather, a two-page circular organizing the celebration of the Feast of the Immaculate Conception.

549.4 Santiago, 1855, 38 pages. It is in two parts, one dogmatic, the other pastoral. The Barcelona edition is dated 1855, while the Paris edition is undated. It was reprinted in Madrid in 1954.

Chapter VII

550.1 Council of Trent, session 24, *De Ref.* chap. 3. The first pastoral visit lasted from February 2, 1851 to March 23, 1853. The second lasted from July 8, 1853 to September 25, 1854. The third lasted from November 12, 1854 to Holy Week, 1855. The fourth, which started in August, 1855, was interrupted by the attempt on his life at Holguín, February 1, 1856. As Claret was preparing to resume this visit, he was called to Spain by Isabel II.

560.1 Founded July 9, 1851, under the patronage of the Immaculate Heart of Mary.

561.1 This convent was the birthplace of the Institute of the Teaching Sisters of Mary Immaculate. The foundress was Mother Antonia Paris de San Pedro. The school opened on August 25, 1855 in Santiago.

562.1 He gave the surplus income of the diocese, to the amount of 20,000 pesos, to the poor. He also distributed 200,000 free books.

568.1 *The Delights of the Country* (Barcelona, 1856, pp. 311). Out of concern for the people of his diocese, he wrote *Reflections on Agriculture* (Barcelona, 1854, pp. 22), the first of a series of publications aimed at introducing the latest techniques in agriculture to supplant the outmoded methods then in use.

568.2 Carlos de Vargas y Cerveto (1817–76), a Carlist general, took refuge in France after the treaty of Vergara (1839). On his return to Spain, he was sent to Cuba (1849). He was Captain General of Santo Domingo (1863) and of the Basque country (1867). He accompanied the queen into exile (1868).

569.1 Its charter was approved in 1854. In granting loans, preference was given to those interested in farm work or in some mechanical trade. Liquid profits were distributed to deserving widows and to provide dowries for poor girls.

Chapter VIII

573.1 He was in Puerto Príncipe from October 29, 1855 until the end of the following January.

573.2 The attempt upon his life that the Saint is about to describe was not an isolated instance but rather the culmination of a campaign of persecutions on many fronts. It was also a culminating point in his spirituality, the spirit of witness carried to its fullest expression: martyrdom. It seems that the Lord was preparing him for this moment by means of these desires and presentiments.

578.1 Throughout the rest of his life these wounds were a visible sign of his consecration to Christ in the apostolate. (Cf. *Correspondence,* Letter 451, to Pius IX.) In this, he resembled St. Paul, whose exclamation, "I bear the brand marks of Jesus in my body" (Gal. 6:17), he repeated during Vatican Council I.

582.1 Cf. par. 332.

584.1 The name that appears in the trial records is Antonio Abad Torres. On receipt of the pardon that the Saint had petitioned, he was sent to the fortress at Ceuta.

Chapter IX
585.1 Luke 22:53.

586.1 They also burned Santo Domingo Ranch after Claret had left. "I was looking at a picture of the Blessed Virgin, when she told me, 'Your enemies have burnt this house as they burnt the other at Altagracia. They will do the same to any house you are a guest in. Anthony, get out of here'" (Claret, *Manuscript*).

587.1 Cardinal John Joseph Bonel y Orbe (1782–1857) had been the queen's confessor since 1847. He had been Bishop, successively, of Ibiza, Málaga, and Córdoba.

589.1 He arrived in Havana on March 28. The following day he preached to two houses of the Daughters of Charity; on March 30, to the Ursulines and at the military hospital; on March 31, at a hospital and to the Sisters of St. Clare; April 1, to the Carmelite nuns, to the College of St. Francis Xavier, and the Seminary; on April 2, to the Sisters of St. Catherine; on April 3, to the Brothers of St. John of God and at the Cathedral; on April 4, at the Church of Guadalupe. He spent Holy Week with the Jesuits. Their local chronicle records the acts of humility practiced by the holy archbishop.

590.1 One of these dangers occurred when they struck a reef near Cayo Sal on April 13.

Chapter X
591.1 Fr. J. N. Lobo, S.J. (1816–82), was a native of Madrid. He became Claret's vicar general (1850), a Jesuit (1856), and the Jesuit Provincial of Castile (1872–76).

591.2 Dr. Dionisio González de Mendoza (1815–87), born at Barrio-suso (Palencia), Doctor of Theology, Licentiate in Law and Attorney of the Realm, Secretary of the Bishop of Puerto Rico (1847), and capitular (1848). Persecuted by the government, he sought refuge in Cuba, where he became vicar general (1856) and administrator of the diocese of Santiago (1857). Director of the Escorial (1860–68). Auditor of the ecclesiastical court of Madrid (1868). He was one of the Saint's most faithful collaborators.

592.1 Cf. par. 489.

594.1 Fr. Francis Coca (1820–58), Jesuit (1856), died while still in the novitiate.

595.1 Fr. Stephen de Adoain (1808–80), Capuchin (1828), missionary in Venezuela (1839), in Cuba (1849), in Central America (1856), and in Spain (1873). The cause for his beatification has been introduced.

597.1 He was ordained in 1844 and died in 1852.

598.1 Fr. Paladio Currius (1818–93). Stayed in Cuba until 1859, Madrid (1859–61), Escorial (1861–68). Chaplain to the Teaching Sisters of Reus (1868–75) and of the Carmelites of Valls. He spent his last years with the Claretians at La Selva, reminiscing about their Founder, whose confidant he had always been.

599.1 Fr. Lorenzo San Martí (1821–64) became a Jesuit (1857). He remained in Fernando Poo for five years, until illness forced him to return to Spain where, on the feast of the Assumption, 1863, he died in the arms of Fr. Lobo, a member of the same religious house in Puerta Santa María.

600.1 He remained at the Escorial for three years but had to retire to Manresa because of illness. A canon of Santiago, Cuba, from which he was exiled because of the integrity of his conduct.

601.1 Fr. Anthony de Galdácano (1811–63), Capuchin (1825), Venezuela, United States, Puerto Rico (1842–52), Cuba (1852–57), Escorial (1857–63).

609.1 Exod. 8:19.

610.1 Fr. Currius notes that the Saint attended all community acts, including recreation. They rose at 4 A.M. and retired at 10 P.M. "The rest weren't sure when the Venerable rose or retired, but I had observed that he retired later and sometimes not at all. When he did retire, he got up at 2 or, at the latest, 3 A.M. (*Apostolic Process,* Tarragona, session 6).

Chapter XI

614.1 Isabel II (1830–1902). Queen at five years of age, first under the regency of her mother, María Cristina (1835–41), and then under General Espartero (1841–43), she came into her majority at 14. Two years later she married her cousin, Francisco de Asís, from whom she separated, only to be reunited in 1858. Of a lively and spontaneous disposition, she felt the loneliness and bitterness of being the pawn of opposing political parties. She poured out her heart to a few intimates, among them St. Micaela of the Blessed Sacrament, Sor Patrocinio the Nun of the Wounds, and later, Claret.

614.2 Isabel de Borbón, eldest daughter of Isabel II (1851–1931).

617.1 1861.

Chapter XII

630.1 Claret's involvement in the process of episcopal nominations was one of the greatest services he rendered the Church in Spain. "Evil doctrines have not infiltrated there (Spain), because all the bishops, without exception, stand on firm ground. Among all of them I know, there is not one who has abandoned solid doctrine" (Pius IX).

Chapter XIII

632.1 Granted by royal decree, October 22, 1850.

633.1 Alfonso XII, born November 28, 1857.

633.2 Don Francisco de Asís de Borbón (1822–1902), nephew of Ferdinand VII, married his cousin, Isabel II, in 1846. He enjoyed the titles of King and Captain General of the Armada.

634.1 The Infanta Concepción was born in 1859 and died two years later.

635.1 The hospital of Montserrat was founded in 1616 for the poor of the kingdom of Aragon. Claret was appointed its guardian on March 28, 1859. As such, he was the queen's representative and the highest authority in the establishment. He made the church one of the best attended centers of worship in the country, and the hospital a model of its kind.

In 1866 he brought in the Carmelite Sisters of Charity to care for the sick.

636.1 The celebrated monastery of the Escorial, founded by Philip II as a pantheon of the kings of Spain, had been in a ruinous state since the expulsion of its guardians, the Monks of St. Jerome, in 1837. The Saint took official charge of it on August 5, 1859. He was concerned not only with its material restoration, but with its restoration as an institution. He formed a group of chaplains to take the place of the monks in worship. He also made it into a national seminary and a college for laymen. He would have liked to make it a national and international center for missions and spiritual exercises (cf. par. 869). The queen accepted the Saint's resignation on June 24, 1868.

Chapter XIV

637.1 For further remarks on these early morning hours, see pars. 757–758.

637.2 He spent an hour preparing for Mass and a half hour in thanksgiving.

638.1 "He is a truly tireless apostle. It is a blessing of God for Madrid that this outstanding archbishop has come here. He has been the means of reviving the Catholic spirit. Priests who want to fulfill their obligations have a master and guide in him. The word of God is bearing fruit and converting unbelievers and the corrupt" (Letter from Msgr. Barilli to Cardinal Antonelli).

639.1 Speaking of these journeys, the Saint remarked, "The queen attracts the people and I preach to them." His confessor, Fr. Carmelo Sala, wrote, "Curiosity once led me to take note of the number of sermons Fr. Claret preached each day: it came to 12 or more. One day I asked him how he could survive such a constant ordeal. He answered, 'I'm just a horn; someone else does the blowing.'" By the time the Saint wrote this chapter, he had accompanied the royal family on the following excursions: Levante (May 24–June 5, 1858); Asturias, Galicia, and León (July 21–September 21, 1858); the Balearic Islands, Catalonia, and Aragon (September 9–October 16, 1860); Palencia, Santander, and Burgos (July 15–August 19, 1861).

640.1 Cf. par. 678. He felt a special heavenly inspiration to write just now, and he corresponded with this grace so thoroughly that this became the most active literary period in his life.

Chapter XV

643.1 Cornelius à Lapide, *Commentary on the Letters of St. Paul* (Antwerp, 1679), vol. 15, p. 739.

646.1 Throughout his life, the Saint always kept this quarter of an hour before lunch as a period of examen.

650.1 J. Croisset, S.J., *The Christian Year* (Barcelona, May 25, 1853), p. 481.

650.2 Cornelius à Lapide, op. cit.; Rodríguez, *Practice of Perfection* (Barcelona, 1861), I, tr. 8, chap. 8, p. 377. The Saint's personal copy.

Chapter XVI

654.1 This litany is a copy of another in the Saint's handwriting that may go back to his earliest days as an archbishop. He may have recited it during his thanksgiving after Mass, according to resolution 10 of par. 645.

654.2 St. Bernard Calvó (1180–1234) was born in Reus (Tarragona), became a Cistercian monk at Santes Creus, and Bishop of Vich (1223), where he is buried in the cathedral.

Chapter XVII

664.1 Prov. 6:6.

664.2 Mark 14:68.

665.1 1 Cor. 4:15.

666.1 Ps. 73:22, 23.

670.1 Isa. 56:10.

673.1 Gen. 17:1.

Chapter XVIII

674.1 "You have written well."

679.1 Matt. 26:63; Mark 15:34, 14:47; John 18:11.

681.1 John 4:26.

682.1 "I am," or "It is I." Exod. 3:14.

682.2 John 6:20.

682.3 Acts 9:5.

687.1 Cf. Matt. 10:20. Claret adds a Marian nuance of meaning, in accordance with the distinctive perspective with which his Sons are to interpret their apostolic mission.

687.2 Isa. 61:1; cf. Luke 4:18.

694.1 On the meaning and implications of this grace and what he says of it in pars. 695 and 700, see *Writings,* Introduction to the section "Lights and Graces," pp. 621 ff.

697.1 Ps. 104:32.

· *Vich,*
Claret's reliquary

PART FOUR

Continuation
of the Autobiography

Chapter I

ON TOUR WITH THEIR MAJESTIES
AND HIGHNESSES IN ANDALUCIA

702 On September 12, 1862, I left the court at Madrid in the company of Their Majesties and Highnesses for Mudela. On the thirteenth we went to Andújar, on the fourteenth to Córdoba, where we stayed for the fifteenth and sixteenth; on the seventeenth we arrived in Seville; from the eighteenth to the twenty-fifth inclusive, we stayed in that city; on the twenty-sixth we headed for Cádiz, where we stayed until October 2. On the third we returned to Seville; on the fifth we went to Córdoba; on the sixth to Bailén; on the seventh to Jaén; on the ninth to Granada; on the fourteenth to Loja; on the fifteenth to Antequera; on the sixteenth to Málaga; on the nineteenth to Almería; on the twentieth to Cartagena; on the twenty-third to Murcia; on the twenty-fifth to Orijuela; on the twenty-seventh to Novelda; on the twenty-eighth to Aranjuez, and on the twenty-ninth, at 5:00 in the evening, we entered Madrid.

703 May the Lord be blessed for stooping to use such a miserable person as myself to do such great things. May God's be the glory and mine the confusion I deserve. Everything I have I owe to God; He has given me health, energy, words, and all the rest besides. I have always known that the Lord was my fuel; but on this trip all the rest knew it too. They could see that I hardly ate or drank anything all day, except a potato and a glass of water. I never ate meat, fish, or eggs, or drank wine. I was always happy and they never saw me tired, despite the fact that some days I preached as many as 12 sermons.[1]

704 I cannot tell the number of sermons God has preached through me, his unworthy minister and useless servant, in the course of the 48 days of this tour. One member of our company was curious enough to list them, and he says that they came to 205: 16 to the clergy, 9 to seminarians, 95 to nuns,

28 to the Sisters of Charity, 35 to the poor in charitable institutions, 8 to the men of the St. Vincent de Paul Society, and 14 to the general public in cathedrals and great churches.

705 Besides preaching, we distributed thousands of leaflets, pamphlets, and books. To facilitate this work we had large boxes of printed material sent ahead to each of the towns we were going to stop in. I simply can't describe the enthusiasm with which everyone came to listen to the words of God, the effect it had on them, their eagerness to have some souvenir of it, and the love with which they cherished whatever we gave them, even if it was nothing but a leaflet.

706 There were great conversions, even though time didn't allow me to hear their confessions. Some of those who were converted have written to me and I would like to cite just one of the many letters delivered to me at this court. It goes:

"Most Excellent Sir and Dear Father: The person who is so bold as to be writing your Excellency these lines is a very great sinner who had forgotten the sound principles I had been taught by my parents and teachers in the course of my long years of training in science. With all the madness of my corrupt heart, I threw myself into the revolution of 1834–35 and had not entered a confessional in all that time, despite my awful fears and gnawing remorse of conscience. But, thanks be to God and the Blessed Virgin Mary, I finally came around and yesterday, December 1 of this year 1862, I made a general confession of my life.

707 "My heart is filled with joy. The harm I've done by my pen, especially in my high post, is incalculable. I scorned my Savior and He abandoned me to my passions, and I lived in them until the Lord took pity on me. His first call came to me as follows: I sailed from Barcelona on the same boat with a priest who gave me a holy card of the Immaculate Conception with some Christian maxims printed on it. I took it, and though I attached little importance to it, I put it in my wallet and said a Salve for the priest. Her Majesty came to Andalucia and your Excellency came with her. When I saw you I thought of the picture of the Blessed Virgin. But how did I see her? I saw her asking that justice be done against me! I heard that

your Excellency was going to be preaching and ran to hear you. I left church terrified and went into my house saying, 'It's all over now.'"

708 Let us all praise God and sing his mercies everlastingly and let us, at the same time, encourage one another daily to do more to use these great means God uses to convert sinners: leaflets, books, and preaching. How important it is nowadays to circulate good books to counteract the flood of bad ones!

Chapter II

THINGS DONE FOR THE NUNS OF ANDALUCIA

709 In all the towns we passed through where there were nuns, I went to preach to them, and not to lose time while I was at the convent I sent a priest ahead to have them gather within the enclosure before the main altar. Thus, when I got there I could start giving my talk immediately, and when I had finished I could go directly to another convent without their detaining me as they always liked to do. Although I had a prelate's freedom to enter the cloister, I never wanted to for fear of talking and wasting time, which would be contrary to the silence and diligence I always exhorted them to observe. I used to tell them sometimes that if all nuns were mute they would be holier than they are now.[1]

710 I noticed that in all towns the majority of convents were following an individualistic style of life rather than one truly lived in common. E.g., in Seville, out of the present 20 convents, only 5 practiced common life, whereas 15 followed an individualistic style of life; and the same proportion holds true of the other towns in Andalucia.[1]

711 Those who have dealt with nuns know that in a community in which common life is not observed there can be no real perfection. Instead of describing the resultant sad state of affairs myself, I would like to let a novice in one such con-

vent describe it in her own words as she does in a letter she wrote to me, dated December 18, 1862.

712 "I find myself here in this convent. For the love of God and the blood of our Lord Jesus Christ I beg you to take me out of this hell I'm in. It's not a convent, it's a tenement. There's no peace here; it's just one big maze. There's nothing here to please me. If our bishop knew what goes on in this convent, he would have closed it down long ago. I am about ready to make my profession, and I'll be a nun fit for hell. I can't trust anyone. My only hope is that through you, your Excellency, I will find some remedy and salvation for my soul. Since you are Her Majesty's confessor, you should counsel her to make a royal decree forbidding any novice to make her profession in any convent in which common life is not observed.

"Dear Sir, I'm not telling you the half of it. What a sad life it is! It's like a death: all I can do is suffer and hold my tongue. I hope that your Excellency will be able to remedy it somehow before the day of my profession comes. Everyone who lives in individualistic convents is going through the same thing I am. God only knows what goes on in convents like this. Help me quickly—time is running out; my profession is coming soon and I'll be caught beyond remedy in the deepest compromise."

713 This poor nun is blurting out haphazardly what we already knew in minute detail goes on in such convents. Hence, whenever I have visited any of these individualistic convents, I have preached to them so energetically that they could clearly see that God Himself was inspiring me.

714 I made them see that they needed to seek to be perfect if they were going to be saved, and that just being nuns was not enough to save them; for many of them, like the foolish virgins, will have to hear from the lips of Jesus, their Spouse, the words, "I know you not."[1] I told them how necessary common life is for perfection. I also gave them a series of comparisons between the individualistic and common life, showing them the physical, spiritual, and economic advantages of common life over the other, presenting them with examples

from the life of Jesus, the Apostles, the disciples, and all the communities that have achieved perfection, all of which have observed common life.

715 I also used another argument that made a really strong impression on them, namely, that Her Majesty, in granting all convents an alms of at least 2,000 reals, preferred that it went to convents in which common life was observed. This, I told them, was not her command but only her desire, and that she entrusted the alms of 2,000 reals for each convent to the safe-keeping of the local bishop, obliging him to give it immediately to communities observing common life and to the other communities whenever they adopted it.

716 I also told bishops and communities not to allow novices to enter convents that did not observe common life and, if some had already entered, they should not be allowed to profess until common life was observed. But I added that to fulfill this requirement the whole community need not adapt; that it would suffice if two or three of the present nuns began to do so and all incoming novices were required to do so. Thus, some of the older nuns began observing common life while others were dying off, and the whole community was undergoing a gradual reformation. I told the older nuns that the only thing I asked of them was not to be like those Pharisees whom Jesus scolded because, not entering heaven themselves, they would not let anyone else enter, either.[1]

Chapter III

DANGERS AND ERRORS SPREAD BY PROTESTANTS AND SOCIALISTS IN THE PROVINCES OF ANDALUCIA

717 For some years now, there has been a great deal of apathy in this region, both on the part of the government and that of the clergy, and the socialists and Protestants have been quick to take good advantage of the opportunity. While the one group has slept, the other has sown tares in this lovely

field. Everyone knows about the uprising at Loja and the large numbers that joined it—it had the support of no less than 80 thousand enlisted men.[1] We also know that quelling it involved great bloodshed and exile for many. Thanks to Her Majesty's visit and the general amnesty she proclaimed, many of the latter have been able to return to their families. Official records show that of those indicted in the Loja incident 387 were single, 720 were married, and 76 were widowers—1,183 in all.[2]

718 A great variety of means was used to stir up this trouble, but the main ones were money, books, hate-sheets, and quack propagandists. And the instigators resorted to violence; they persecuted those who refused to join them by preventing them from working and trying to starve them out. During our tour and our stay there, I went to the trouble of jotting down some of the errors that had been spread in the region, a brief summary of which follows:[1]

719 (1) Man should acknowledge no father or mother but the earth, from which men sprout like mushrooms, toadstools, or any other plant, without having to bring in God to explain any of it.

(2) Children owe their parents nothing because they were only amusing themselves, and if their pleasure resulted in a child, perhaps it was against their will. Maybe they had some feelings for it, but who knows whether they hadn't tried an abortion? Language like this was used not only at home but also in the streets, in the public squares, and even in the courtroom.

720 (3) Kings and ministers of states are nothing but tyrants; they have no right to tell other men what to do. We are all equal.

(4) Politics is nothing but a game to get control of the land, honors, financial interests, etc., of the people.

(5) There is no law but the law of the strongest.

721 (6) The earth belongs to no one; all things come from it, and all things are for everyone and belong to everyone.

(7) The rich are scoundrels, thieves, and loafers who do

nothing but loaf, eat, and lust. Just as the rest of the bees in a hive rise up and kill as many drones as they can, so the workers must rise up and finish off these drones of society.

722 (8) Brothers, we are all equal and share the same nature, but the rich treat us as if we were members of a distinct species lower than theirs. Yes, they treat us as if they alone were men and we were beasts of burden. They never work and are always at their ease; they are always off on a round of amusements at cafés, theaters, dances, and outings, while we are constantly working. They won't even let us rest on holidays. They want and get the most comfortable places, cool in summer and warm in winter, while we not only have to wear ourselves out working, but have to put up with the heat, cold, wind, and rain outdoors, or else are cooped up in factories, basements, and mines, breathing in that heavy, polluted air until we die before our time. Every day their tables groan beneath sumptuous dishes, while we can hardly get a piece of bad bread, for which the monopolies they run overcharge us.

723 They wear the prettiest and finest clothes and have the best suits, which they change daily, while we are hard put to it just to have another shirt to change from the pitiful one we work and sweat in every day.

724 They live in magnificent big houses, decked out in oriental luxury, while we live in hovels and basements at rents so high that we can't pay them. We build their houses, clean their rooms, make their clothes, and prepare their meals, but they give us nothing—rather, they rob us of the little we make and suck our blood with their rents, rights, and contributions. How long are we going to put up with their robbery and injustice? Let's all rise against them.

725 (9) So far the rich have enjoyed the land; now it's time for us to enjoy it and divide it among ourselves. A division such as this would be not only fair and just but highly useful and profitable as well because the great landholdings of the thieving rich lie fallow, whereas we would divide them up into small plots and till them with our own hands, to reap an abundant harvest.

726 (10) Moreover, as the socialist leader Pérez del Olmo, the blacksmith of Loja, often said: Once upon a time the hospitals, almshouses, religious orders, chapters, beneficiaries, and that lot had farms, lands, and rents, and those loafers kept it all to themselves and even robbed the people of their property. They gave us none of it. It's only right that we reclaim what's ours. We have as much right to it as they do, and because they won't give us any we're only taking what belongs to us.

Let us all unite, then. Let us arise and set our hands to the task!

727 By means of these and similar seductive and persuasive arguments, coupled with threats and insults for those who refused to give in to them, they made great strides in a short time.

And while they were spreading such evil and destructive teachings, they were promoting immorality, cutting people off from everything good, and leading them to do all sorts of evil. People were no longer receiving the sacraments of Penance, the Eucharist, and Matrimony, or attending Mass on holy days. They worked until noon and then, in the afternoon and at night, they were off gambling, dancing, making the rounds of theaters, cafés, taverns, and outings. Religion got nothing, worldliness got everything. Ministers of religion were sneered at, slandered, and condemned.

728 When I learned of all this in Madrid, it broke my heart and I wanted to go there to preach, but Her Majesty told me to wait and that I could preach when we went there, and so I did. But this is not enough; missionaries must be sent there, and with this in mind, I spoke to the bishops of the region. The papal Nuncio and the queen have both spoken and written requests for missionaries, and I am in hopes that some will respond, but few, I fear, because there is a shortage of available men. Heavenly Father, send missionaries![1]

Chapter IV

THE SLANDERS
MALICIOUS MEN HAVE SPREAD
ABOUT CATHOLIC PRIESTS

729 Protestants, communists, and socialists are well aware that their greatest enemies, the ones that do the most to foil their plans, are Catholic priests. Because the errors of these groups are only darkness, all that Catholic priests have to do is train the light of Catholic teaching on them and the darkness is dispelled. Hence the best fighting tactic of these groups has been to speak ill of Catholic priests. They know full well that what they are saying is a pack of fables, slanders, and lies, but that makes no difference to them: something of what they say remains, something sticks and, once they have discredited the teachers, the light of truth goes out and they remain in undisputed command of the darkness of their errors. There's no telling how much propaganda they've made by both the written and the spoken word. I shall transcribe just one of the many leaflets they have circulated everywhere and put within the reach of all. It reads as follows:

"Religion and Morals"

730 "What would become of the Catholic religion if we had to judge it by the conduct of most of its members, let alone that of all its ministers? Look, if you doubt, at those ministers of religion and you will observe that they are steeped in worldly pleasures and involved in political intrigues. They have become such egotists and hucksters that they have forgotten entirely what their divine Master told them, 'My kingdom is not of this world.'

731 "They neither study nor teach morality, but dedicate themselves to the pursuit of their ambitions and disorderly appetites. They do not preach the Gospel, but are occupied incessantly with the interests of political parties and are the prime movers in the most scandalous intrigues and wickedest schemes.

"Whenever you witness some low intrigue, some atrocious slander, or some base maneuver, you can say without fear of error that this is the work of a Catholic priest.

732 "Priests abuse everything; nothing is sacred to them. They have profaned and debased everything: pulpit, confessional, conscience, family, all of society. They have been the ruin of everything.

"Some of them seem to be austere—but beware! Beneath that cassock they carry an envenomed dagger to kill you with. What is worse, they do not even forgive one another.

"Forgetting Christ's words, 'Give unto Caesar the things that are Caesar's and to God the things that are God's,' which were meant to uphold the separation of Church and state, they meddle in everything, confuse everything, and traffic in everything.

733 "Catholic priests are traitors to themselves, to the Church, and to the state. They call themselves ministers of the God of peace and are the first to start wars, either by word or example.

"They should be the light of the world, but they fill it with darkness by their ignorance. They have made themselves odious throughout the world by their vanity, ambition, and other rogueries.

"In conclusion: Flee them, separate yourselves from them. They are twice-told impostors: voracious wolves instead of good shepherds."

734 Impious men and socialists are doing incalculable harm by such teachings, as well as by their actions and the contempt with which they treat the priesthood, the Mass, the sacraments, and other religious services. To all this they add the mockery and jeers they hurl at those who profess their religion. This is how they swell their ranks daily with new proselytes and quicken the pace of society along the path that leads to perdition.

735 I have often, or rather constantly, wondered what remedy there might be for such an evil. After much thought I have come to the conclusion that the remedy consists, on the

one hand, of training a good, learned, virtuous, zealous, and prayerful clergy and, on the other, of catechizing and preaching to both children and adults and circulating good books and pamphlets. For those who really want to work, there is still faith in Israel and the land is ready to yield of itself. At the sight of the virtue and fortitude of good priests, the irreligious will lose their boldness and daring.

Chapter V

THINGS I HAVE DONE
SINCE MY RETURN FROM ANDALUCIA

736 On arriving here at court I felt as happy and rested from my labors as if I had been loafing all the while, and so I went straight to the Escorial to begin a novena-mission to Our Lady of Perpetual Help. A great crowd attended and much good was done, thank God.[1]

737 After closing the novena, I began to preach the Spiritual Exercises to the community of priests and students at the seminary. Some visiting priests also attended. The results were truly most gratifying.

738 Back in Madrid, I busied myself with giving the Spiritual Exercises to the Sisters of Perpetual Adoration. All of them derived great profit from their retreat, asked to make a general confession, and left the retreat full of fervor.

739 During the Christmas season I gave a retreat to the French Teaching Sisters. They run a school for young girls, and because the girls go home for the holidays, the nuns are free to make their retreat and have done so every year since I have been in Madrid.

740 Resolutions I made during my retreat at the Escorial, from November 10 to 19 inclusive, this present year of 1862:
    (1) Every year I will make the Spiritual Exercises.
    (2) Every month I will keep a day of strict recollection, without speaking to anyone.

(3) Every week I will confess my sins.

(4) Every week I will fast on three days, namely, Monday, Friday, and Saturday, and on some days I will abstain from dessert. On Mondays, Wednesdays, and Fridays, I will take the discipline or something equivalent to it; on Tuesdays, Thursdays, and Saturdays, I will wear the cilice.

741 (5) During my prayers I will think on the mysteries of the rosary and on the sufferings of Jesus Christ. I will avoid rushing, mindful of how St. Catherine of Siena was reprimanded for this.[1]

742 (6) I will continue my particular examen on meekness.[1] I realize that it is better to do less, in a spirit of meekness, than to do more in haste and ungraciously. People are very disedified by the latter, and so I have resolved never to get angry or complain about anything. I will be amiable with everyone, even those who annoy me. I shall frequently make Meditations 20, p. 264, and 28, p. 356, in the *Exercises.*[2]

743 (7) I will ask the Lord continually to let me know Him and make others know Him, to let me love Him and make others love Him, to serve Him and make others serve Him. I will say to Him, "Lord, if you want to use me for the conversion of sinners, here I am."

744 (8) Before meals I will say, "Lord, I am eating to gain the energy I need to serve you better." Before study I will say, "Lord, I am studying to know, love, and serve you and to help my neighbor." Before retiring I will say, "Lord, I am taking this rest to build up the energy I have spent and to serve you better. I am doing this, my Lord and Father, because you have ordered me to."

745 (9) Maxims I have resolved to keep:
1. to eat little and work much
2. to sleep little and pray much
3. to speak little and suffer many sorrows and slanders without complaining or defending myself, but rather rejoicing in them

746   4. exterior and interior mortification
5. spiritual reading from Rodríguez
6. mental prayer from La Puente
7. particular examen on meekness

747   8. I will do everything with an upright intention, with attention, and with a firm will to do each thing well.

748   9. I will always walk in the presence of God and will frequently repeat: "Lord, either to suffer or to die. To suffer not to die. To suffer and be scorned for your sake. God forbid that I should glory in anything except the cross of our Lord Jesus Christ."

Things to Remember

749 (1) I will ask the Blessed Virgin Mary for a burning love, perfect union with God, the most profound humility, and a desire to be held in contempt.

750 (2) I will hold the virtue of everyone else in high esteem, especially that of all my superiors. I will think the best of all they do, and I will reserve my reproofs, censures, and judgments for my own actions. This course of action will benefit me; the opposite would not.

751 (3) I will remember what the Lord told a missionary: that He had saved him from hell in order to save souls. I will think of how He saved me from drowning and other dangers so that I might work for his greater honor and glory and for the salvation of the souls He bought back at so dear a cost.

752 (4) What could Jesus have done for the glory of his Father and the salvation of souls that He did not do? Ah, I can see Him hanging dead upon the cross, scorned by all. For this very reason I, even I, with the help of his grace, am resolved to suffer pains, fatigue, contempt, and mockery, complaints, slanders, persecution—even death. Thank God I am already suffering many of these things, but I am encouraged

to say with the Apostle, "I bear with all of this for the sake of those whom God has chosen, in order that they may obtain salvation."[1]

753 (5) I know that I can offer God no morsel more delicious nor drink more refreshing than the souls that repent before the pulpit or in the confessional. Jesus invites me to his banquet, to eat his flesh and drink his blood, and He wishes me to invite Him to a banquet of converted souls.

I know that this is his favorite food, since He told his Apostles so. The kings of this earth receive the most exquisite fruits, even though they are hard to find. What should I not do for the King of Heaven?

754 During the half hour after Mass, I feel that I am totally annulled. I desire nothing but his holy will. I live by Jesus' own life. In possessing me He possesses nothing, while I possess everything in Him. I tell Him, "Lord, you are my love. You are my honor, my hope, and my refuge. You are my glory and my goal. My love, my happiness, and my preserver. My delight, my reformer, and my master. My Father, Spouse of my life and soul.

755 "Lord, I do not seek or wish to know anything but how to fulfill your holy will. I want nothing but you, and in you and for you alone all other things. You are more than enough for me. I love you, my strength, my refuge, and comfort. You are my Father, my Brother, my Spouse, my Friend, and my All. Make me love you as you love me and as you would have me love you.

756 "My Father, take this poor heart of mine and devour it as I do you, so that I may be changed totally into you. At the words of consecration the substance of bread and wine are changed into the substance of your body and blood. Almighty Lord, consecrate me; speak over me the words that will change me totally into you."

Chapter VI

ACCOUNT OF CONSCIENCE TO MY SPIRITUAL DIRECTOR TOWARD THE END OF 1862

757 Every day, winter or summer, I get up at 3:00 in the morning. While I am dressing, which doesn't take long, I pray. I should very much like permission to sleep fully clothed on a plank and not go to bed because my head feels heavy when I lie in bed.

758 After I get up I take a strong discipline, the harder the better, when I think of my sins and of the scourging of Jesus and of his great love. I seem to hear a voice that says, "Give me blood and I will give you spirit." In accordance with my resolutions, I take the discipline one day and wear the cilice the next. The cilice hurts me more than the discipline, but I never omit it because it is more repugnant to the body.

759[1] My greatest struggle is with eating. My body is like a stubborn mule that often conquers me and mocks me. It is hungry when it sees food on the table. I make it fast three times a week—Wednesday, Friday, and Saturday. Every day of the year I forbid it to eat meat or fish, even on major feast days. But I see to it that these dishes are prepared for the others in the house. They eat them, but I do not. For the body this is the torment of Tantalus. I do the same with regard to wine. I like meat and wine but will not partake of them and I find that this makes me feel better in body and in soul.

760 When it comes to abstaining from meat, fish, and wine, the body conforms, although this takes a little work; it puts up the most resistance in abstaining from other foods. It always wants more than I'm willing to give it, and at best it makes me commit the fault of taking a little more than I'd planned. I have a worse fault than this, namely, I eat faster than I want to and had resolved to. Because I am served first, and take only potatoes and greens, while the others are

served after me and take what they please, it naturally takes
them more time to eat what's on their plates. I want to slow
down my eating so that we finish at the same time, but
there's the rub. Because I am served earlier and have nothing
to carve up, and because I have a hearty appetite besides, I
can't hold back that little mule of a body, and so it breaks
loose and I end up eating faster than I'd planned. During the
day, outside mealtimes, I never take food or drink.

761 I practice abstinence for a good number of reasons: (1)
to mortify my body, (2) to edify my neighbor—as I know we
must nowadays, (3) to be less of a burden to my neighbors as
a guest, (4) to economize so that I'll have more to give away.
There are other reasons especially to imitate Jesus and Mary.

For some time now, God in his infinite goodness has
been favoring me with many telling insights when I am at
prayer and arousing in me many desires to do and suffer for
his greater honor and glory and the good of souls.[1]

762 I have such a deep longing to leave Madrid and go out
into the whole world that I can't tell you how much I suffer
at not being allowed to do so; God only knows. Every day I
have to make acts of resignation to God's will, for I know
that He wills me to stay on here for the present. I resolve to
be silent, but at best I speak and say that I'd like to leave.[1]

763 Seeing that for the time being I have to stay here in this
court, I busy myself hearing confessions every day until 11:00.
Two-thirds of those who come haven't been to confession
with me before, and they come to make general confessions.[1]

764 At 11:00 I receive callers until noon, and this is the
most bothersome hour in my day because people come to ask
me for things in connection with the palace I can't agree to.
I spend the afternoon preaching, studying, writing, or doing
something else. The same holds true of the night, for I strive
never to have an idle moment.

765 At 3:00 in the morning, before meditation, I say the
Trisagion. At noon, before lunch and after my examen, I
make a short Way of the Cross. At night I say the three parts

of the rosary, the seven Our Fathers and Hail Marys of our Lady of Mt. Carmel, another seven for our Lady of Sorrows, ten more for our Lady of the Rosary, and the Chaplet.

766 Vocal prayer suits me better than strictly mental prayer, thank God. At each word of the Our Father, Hail Mary, and Glory, I glimpse an abyss of goodness and mercy. Our Lord has granted me the grace of being very attentive and fervent when I say these prayers. The Lord in his goodness and mercy also grants me many graces during mental prayer, but in vocal prayer I have a deeper awareness.[1]

767 When I am before the Blessed Sacrament, I feel such a lively faith that I can't describe it. Christ in the Eucharist is almost tangible to me; I kiss his wounds continually and embrace Him. When it's time for me to leave, I have to tear myself away from his sacred presence.[1]

Chapter VII

AN ACCOUNT OF MY MISSION TO THE PALACE

768 I hardly know what to say on this topic; God only knows whether or not I have done my duty here. Although it's true that Her Majesty appreciates and sets great store by my advice, her position holds her back from doing all that she knows would be the better thing, especially when it comes to externals. But she is always well disposed to do everything she can when it is a question of herself alone and her inner self. Every day she reads the life of the saint of the day, says the rosary, attends Mass, prays before an image of the Blessed Virgin, and receives the sacraments with great fervor and devotion. Every year she makes the Spiritual Exercises at La Granja[1] because she has more free time there. She never tires of pious things. She is most charitable and gives away a great deal with a right good will. She is very compassionate and the sight of any misfortune touches her heart. Her greatest trials have to do with external conduct, either because of her courtly training or because she hates to clash

with worldly people. She tries to correct external abuses prudently, and although they are not terribly grave, she knows that it would be better if they were otherwise. The following are a few of the most difficult areas she has to deal with:

769 (1) *The theater.* When I arrived in Madrid, she went to the theater every evening and lavished gifts upon the actors and actresses. At present she rarely goes, except on ceremonial occasions, after serving notice that a morally acceptable play be performed. Even at that, as she herself has told me, she gets tired and has to make a supreme effort not to doze off.

770 (2) *Dances.* Formerly there were frequent balls given at the palace. Now there are few and they are very orderly, as I have been told by those who have attended them; for I myself never go and discourage as many as I can from going. However, these balls are less a matter of dancing than a pretext for getting together to discuss politics and other matters, and from this point of view they might be tolerated or even necessary at times.

771 (3) *Banquets.* Formerly there were many banquets; now there are but a few, and these indispensable. This month only three had to be held: one for the birthday of the prince, another for that of the Infanta Paz, and one more for another reason; yet these three were celebrated jointly at one banquet. I prefer that the money be spent as an alms for the poor rather than on banquets, balls, etc.[1]

772 (4) *Receptions.* I have the most trouble with these functions because I want the ladies of the court to wear higher necklines, that is, to cover themselves more than they do. They object that they wear such dresses because etiquette requires it, that they have always dressed like this, and that ladies dress like this in all the courts in the world at such functions, etc. I give my formal opinion, and I say and do what I think is my duty and, although the queen is presently the most decently covered woman in the gathering, I am still not satisfied; and I complain and show my displeasure and my desire to quit the court because of this state of affairs.

Blasphemy punished.[1]

I could relate a number of cases in which blasphemy has been chastised, but I shall cite only two of them here.

773 (1) In the court of Madrid, in Councillor Street, in the year 1862, some repairs were being made on a house and because of them the street was partially blocked. A carter with a loaded cart had to get by, and when his cart got stuck in the debris he began to curse God, beating his mules and blaspheming away, when one of the mules gave him a swift kick in the head and the man fell dead with the blasphemy still on his lips.

774 (2) In this same year of 1862, in Madrid again on del Viento Street, some bricklayers and their helpers were digging up the street to connect the cesspool of a house with the main sewer line in the middle of the street. One of the men was swinging his pickax and cursing, and among other blasphemies he said that he would heap filth on God Himself. But God punished this blasphemer with filth. The wall broke before he could get out of the way, and he was covered with a pile of ordure so foul-smelling that it suffocated him and he drowned in a lake of filthy water, his mouth and body stuffed with offal.

Chapter VIII

ACCOUNT OF CONSCIENCE TO MY SPIRITUAL DIRECTOR FOR THE YEAR 1863

775 This year the royal family has not made a tour but has remained either in Madrid or at the residences of Aranjuez[1] or La Granja. This has allowed me to spend more time preaching, hearing confessions, and writing books and leaflets.

776 As regards my preaching, I gave a retreat to the ladies and gentlemen of the court, and it did a great deal of good. God did it all. I also preached at a novena to St. Joseph on

the occasion of the dedication of a new altar and statue in the church of Montserrat. This novena was well attended and very beneficial. I also preached retreats to the Sisters of Perpetual Adoration, the Piarists, the Tertiaries,[1] to young girls, and to servant girls.

777 I hear confessions every morning in Madrid from 7:00 to 11:00, after which I receive visitors. This is my most bothersome hour because they are always asking me to help them in affairs I never meddle in.

778 This year during our stay at the royal country estates, I have stationed myself in the confessional every day after Mass because I hear the confessions of all the royal maids and servants. As they all frequent the sacraments, there is always someone who wants to go to confession. In Madrid each of them has his own confessor and spiritual director, but in the country they come to me. All of them are very well behaved. They have meditation and spiritual reading every day, both from conviction and because of Her Majesty's good example. She, besides her ordinary daily religious practices, makes the Spiritual Exercises of St. Ignatius yearly at La Granja, whereas the others make them in Madrid.

779 While at Aranjuez I wrote the second volume of *The Well-Instructed Seminarian,* as well as various leaflets. At La Granja I wrote *The Well-Instructed College Girl.* I presented 200 free copies of the former book to every seminary in Spain, as well as 5 Bibles to be given to the most studious seminarians. I have given away many books, holy cards, and rosaries.[1]

Chapter IX

RETREAT RESOLUTIONS

780 I made my retreat this year at the Escorial, from October 23 to November 1, inclusive. In the course of it I made the following resolutions:

(1) Every year I will make the Spiritual Exercises.
(2) Every month a day of strict recollection.

(3) Every week I will go to confession.

(4) Every week I will fast on three days, namely Wednesday, Friday, and Saturday, and on these days I will abstain from dessert at night.

(5) On Mondays, Wednesdays, and Fridays I will take the discipline or do some equivalent penance. On Tuesdays, Thursdays, and Saturdays I will wear the cilice.

781 (6) At prayer I will consider the rebuke St. Catherine of Siena received.[1] I will also remember how St. Aloysius Gonzaga spent an hour just to say Matins.[2]

782 (7) I will continue making my particular examen on the virtue of meekness. I will remember the meekness of Jesus, my model and master, who said, "Learn of me, for I am meek and humble of heart."[1]

783 I shall remember the meekness of the Blessed Virgin Mary and how she was never moved to anger, even accidentally, nor ever lost her perfect meekness, maintaining an unchanging and inimitable external and internal evenness of behavior. This was so true that one could never discover her inward state from the externals of her voice and gestures.[1]

I will consider how useful meekness is, because humility pleases God, whereas meekness pleases our neighbor.[2]

784 It is better to do less with patience, meekness, and amiability than to do more in haste, anger, annoyance, and unwillingness, for when people see this sort of behavior they are scandalized and withdraw.

785 (8) I will never lose my temper; I will be silent and make an offering to God of all that causes me pain.

(9) I will never complain but resign myself to the will of God, who tries me for my own good.

786 (10) I will always be pleasant with everyone, especially those who annoy me.

787 (11) I will never speak well or ill of myself or my concerns.

788 (12) I will tell the good God, "Lord, if you want to use me, a miserable instrument, to convert sinners, here I am."

789 (13) Before meals I will say, "Lord, I am about to eat so as to have the energy I need to serve you better. Lord of this world's goods, I do not eat out of pleasure, because I want none, but only out of need."

(14) Before retiring I will say, "Lord, I am going to rest to restore the energy I have spent so that I can serve you better. I am doing so because you have ordered me to."

(15) Before studying I will say, "Lord, I am doing this to know, love, and serve you better and to help my neighbor."

Special devotions for each day of the week, in accord with resolutions from other years.[1]

790 (16) In all things I will strive for purity and rectitude of intention, great attention and care, and firmness of will.

791 (17) I will take great care to do every single thing that I am doing as if I had nothing else to do.

With the Lord's help, I have striven to fulfill these resolutions.

792 The thing that has cost me the greatest trouble has been remaining meek in the face of the crowd of people who come to ask for favors at court or for some government post. Despite all the excuses I give them for not being able to help them, they simply will not be convinced, and this has been a source of great torment to me. Before receiving visitors in audience, which I do from 11:00 to noon, I ask God for the grace not to get angry. Between visitors I lift my eyes and heart to a picture of the Blessed Virgin Mary, asking for the grace I need to make it more bearable. I have given people financial aid or a book, and they have gone away less disheartened than when they came.

Chapter X

AN IMPORTANT CHAPTER
FOR THE CONGREGATION

793 On November 14, 1863 I had to preach a sermon on the Blessed Virgin Mary during a retreat I was giving to the sisters, students, and servants at the convent of the Carmelite Tertiaries in Madrid. It was a Saturday, the day on which I do spiritual reading on the Blessed Virgin, and it also happened to be the feast of the Patronage of Our Lady, which had been postponed from the preceding Sunday, the Octave of All Saints. In the course of my reading I ran across this passage:

"The Carthusian Order was in dire straits for vocations because no one wanted to enter such an austere, lonely, and silent way of life. The best remedy they hit upon was to dedicate themselves to the Blessed Virgin by taking a public vow to recite her office (the Little Office) daily. This plan brought them such an excellent stock of vocations that from that year, 1084, to the present, they have never had to mitigate their severe rule. Thus time, which masters all, had to blush; for it has not been able to overcome anyone who places himself under Mary's protection." This advice to say the Little Office was given to them by St. Peter, who appeared to them in the form of a venerable old man.

794 On this day it occurred to me that if the Congregation said the Little Office of the Blessed Virgin as well as the Divine Office, Mary would provide the Congregation with all the vocations it needs in order to grow, spread, and endure.

795 At prayer that very morning, it seemed that the picture of the Blessed Virgin over the altar spoke to me, saying that it would be all right, but with this proviso, that it would be enough if only one member should recite it by obligation, while the rest could say it only out of devotion, if they wished to and had time. Those engaged in the missions should not be allowed to, however, because they would be too busy preaching and hearing confessions. It might also be arranged

that the Little Office be recited by the novices and by those students not yet in major orders.

Chapter XI

ACCOUNT I MADE TO MY SPIRITUAL DIRECTOR OF MY ACTIVITIES DURING THE YEAR 1864

796 I have followed the resolutions I made during my last retreat and fulfilled them, with some imperfections that God has allowed me to commit in order to humble me more and more. Thus I may know in practice that I am nothing but misery and that if there is any good in me, it all comes from God because I am no more than a mere nothing. This year the Lord has made it transparently clear to me how necessary and useful this virtue of humility really is. I have never understood it so clearly.[1]

797 This year I reread the works of St. Teresa of Avila, and the Lord blessed this reading with great gifts of knowledge. How good the Lord is! Since He foreknew the great trials I would have to undergo, He forearmed me with great insights and spiritual help.[1]

798 This year I have been much slandered and persecuted by all sorts of persons. I have been attacked by journalists and lampooned in pamphlets, parodied books, touched-up photographs, and in many other ways—even by the very demons. At times my nature rebelled a little, but I at once calmed myself in resignation and conformity to God's will. I considered the example of Jesus and realized how far I was from suffering what He suffered for me, and so I kept calm. This year, too, I wrote a little book entitled *Comfort for a Slandered Soul.*[1]

799 This year I also wrote a uniform *Catechism* for all Spain; likewise, *The Vocation of Children.* I have reprinted the *Rules for Students* in Latin, as well as *Rules for Clerical*

Communities, Summer Evenings in La Granja, and *Rules for Public Libraries.* This last-mentioned book has aroused great expectations.

800 This year I have given missions to the Servites at San Andrés and the Royal Salesians, during which the Lord and the Blessed Virgin did a great deal of good. I have preached retreats to the Sisters of the Disabled, the Piarists, the Tertiaries of Mt. Carmel and the girls who attend their schools, together with their maids. I have preached a number of sermons at court and at the Escorial, where I also conducted the Spiritual Exercises.

801 My alarm clock goes off every day at 3:00 in the morning, although I am usually already up at that time. I say my devotions and do my spiritual reading until 4:30, when I wake up the servants. Afterward I prepare for Holy Mass. At 5:00 we begin meditation, which lasts until 6:00. At 6:00 I say Mass in my oratory and remain in thanksgiving until 7:00. Then I go to the confessional where I stay until 11:00, when I leave to receive visitors in audience until noon; then I say my prayers, make my particular examen on the love of God,[1] followed by the Way of the Cross, after which I take lunch, etc. Until 8:30, when I and my household pray the rosary together and make our examen of conscience, etc., I busy myself with prayer, study, preaching, visits to the Blessed Sacrament, Forty Hours' Devotion, etc.

Chapter XII

IN THIS CHAPTER I TELL OF SOME CASES I HAVE DEALT WITH THAT ARE INCLUDED FOR THE USE OF PREACHERS AND CONFESSORS.

802 I have dealt with a large number of cases since I have been a priest, however unworthy; but I have never written about them because I have been too busy. But because my spiritual director has indicated that my doing so would contribute to the glory of God and the good of souls, I shall

write down a few of them simply and briefly, just as I witnessed them in my own experience.

803 Today, April 15, 1864, I was told that in the parish of Saint Andrew where I gave the Lenten Mission, 4,000 more souls fulfilled their Easter duty than in previous years. Blessed be God. Glory be to God. Confessions have been made by men who have not confessed for 40 years and by women who have not confessed for 30. "Not to us, O Lord, not to us but to your name give glory."[1]

Evil consequences of the sin of impurity:

804 Today, April 30, 1864, I was called to the bedside of a sick man. I went. He was young, only 19. When I first came to Madrid, he used to come to me for confession and was doing very well; he received the sacraments frequently, prayed to the Blessed Virgin Mary, and followed my advice in everything he did. After a while he fell in with bad companions and stopped coming to confession. On his deathbed he called for me, and when I got there he told me, "I am dying like this because I was led astray by the vice of impurity, by neglecting the sacraments and my prayers to Mary." He died a few hours after bidding me farewell.

805-810[1]

Chapter XIII

MORE EXAMPLES THAT MAY SERVE AS A WARNING

811 Madrid, March 31, 1864. A recently married man told his young and virtuous wife, "I will refuse you nothing, but I want you to avoid just one thing: confession. I don't want a priest running my house, as he surely will if you start going to confession frequently because you will follow his advice."

812 To alienate her even more from the sacraments, he added, "I can't believe that God has entrusted the treasures of

his grace to priests. From my experience, a rich, powerful, wise, and prudent man goes about choosing his treasurer and bursar from the ranks of men who have a reputation for being upright and honorable, well-trained and educated, and he would never choose an immoral, stupid, or gross individual for the job. Clear thinking and common sense dictate that he do no less. How can anyone believe that God chooses priests— such a crass, unscientific, uneducated, and ill-mannered lot— to be the chief stewards of his gifts and graces and the ministers of his Church?" And this irreligious man would go on in this vein, using the age-old language of heretics who have been refuted a thousand times over by the Fathers and Doctors of the Church. Now it's true, of course, that the grace and the effects of the sacraments do not depend on the holiness of the priests that administer them; but still, we can see from this one example how much we need to be men of discipline, education, and holy manners.

813 Madrid, April 1, 1864. A lady who was speaking to me about the administration of a school remarked, "The most stupid boy in the house in always the one who enters the Church's clergy."

814 Madrid, April 15, 1864. A very pious and zealous lady told me, "There is a great deal of ignorance among the clergy. A great number of country parishes would be better off if the people had no priest at all, and just said the rosary together, rather than having to listen to the Mass of a stupid and immoral priest who does nothing but scandalize them."

815 The same day another lady told me that the last time she had gone to Communion, the priest's hands, holding the sacred Host, were so dirty and foul-smelling that it turned her stomach and made her feel like vomiting, so that she couldn't swallow the Host, all on account of that nauseating priest. Woe betide us if, instead of attracting the faithful by our good manners, we drive them away by our gross behavior and unmortified passions. Woe betide us if, instead of being Christ's good odor everywhere, as the Apostle says, we become a plague that drives people off.

816 In 1864, Fathers Carmelo Sala and Athanasius López were on their way to give a mission in the town of Oche, when a woman spotted them and started shouting, "Daughter, lock up the chickens, the missionaries are coming!" The missionaries heard it themselves and told me about it. Later on, during the mission, the woman regretted what she had said and made satisfaction to the missionaries, explaining that she had said it because of the high living to which the last missionaries who passed through town had treated themselves. How very important it is for missionaries to be mortified, virtuous, and exemplary in their conduct!

817 February 1, 1865. On their way from a mission in Pamplona to another in Zaragoza, Fathers Mon and Sáenz, S.J., took the train and sat in first class. Some irreligious men either saw them or heard about it, and they noised it about in conversations and in the press. We should avoid using the train or, if we have to, we should travel second, or better, third class. Best of all, of course, would be to go on foot or on a mule, as Jesus did.

Chapter XIV

WHICH RELATES SOME PUNISHMENTS OCCASIONED BY CURSING

818 On June 18, 1864, in Madrid, a woman from a nearby town approached me with a problem. She was terribly upset and was looking for consolation and some advice as to what she should do. She had a 25-year-old son who was very fond of going out at night with some of his friends from the town. His mother didn't approve of his going out at night, but he paid no attention to her warnings. One night she was very upset about his going out against her wishes and told him, "I can't control you any longer, but the police will!" With that curse on his head, he went out that night as usual and joined his friends—there were eight of them in all. They insulted a woman, the police caught them, and they were thrown in jail.

The woman told me this eight months after it had happened. At that time all the others had been set free, but her son was still in jail. He had been sentenced to 15 years' imprisonment in the penitentiary. His mother said that this was a punishment from God for two reasons: first, for her son's disobedience; second, for her curse on him.

819 On November 25, 1864, in Madrid, a deeply troubled lady from that city came to me and told me that she once had a very lively little daughter, eight-and-a-half years old. One day the little girl played some prank typical of children of her age and vivacity. The mother became so angry that she told the little girl, "I wish you were dead!" The woman told me that her daughter had always been quite healthy, but as soon as she had cursed her, she fell ill and died. The mother saw her curse as the cause of the child's death and was disconsolate over it.

820 Madrid, January 10, 1865. A mother told me that she had two daughters, one 20, the other 11 years old. The elder daughter died and the mother remarked, "It would have been better if the little one had died." The little girl did meet her death, in the following manner: A man seized her and carried her off. He deflowered her, gagged her so that she wouldn't scream, strangled her, threw her body in a ditch, and ran away. This caused quite a furor in Madrid and was detailed in some newspapers, but I learned of it from the mother herself.

821 A spinster told me that she had lived with three men in succession, on a promise of marriage, but had been deserted by all three of them. In her indignation, she cursed them all and wished them evil. All three were stricken exactly according to the evil she had wished on them and according to the terms of the curse she had hurled at them.

822 I could relate many an example from my experience of the effects of cursing, where I have seen curses fulfilled to the letter, according to the terms and circumstances set by the one who uttered them. I have seen them in all walks of life but especially between parents and children, husbands and wives, employers and servants, as well as between faithless lovers.

Chapter XV

823–826[1]

Chapter XVI

WHICH TELLS OF SOME
OF MY EXPERIENCES

827 On December 25 of ..., at 4:00 in the morning, it began to snow and kept on snowing for two whole days. It snowed so much that people born in Madrid had never seen the like of it. Notwithstanding, a woman came through all that snow from a town six leagues away to make her confession.

828 A 64-year-old woman who came to confession to me had been to confession only twice in her life: once when she was ten and again, at the time of her marriage, when she was 20. After three years of marriage, she walked out on her husband. She had been a bad sort ever since she was a child, but after her marriage she went from bad to worse. She had been in various countries and had behaved scandalously wherever she went. Finally she came back to her hometown, Madrid, and began to feel the need to go to confession. It had been 44 years since her last confession, and even the two previous confessions had been bad ones.

When I had listened to the story of her long and very wicked life, and could see how repentant and eager to change her life she was, I asked her whether or not she had kept up some devotion during this time. She answered me that, despite her evil life, she had said seven Our Fathers and Hail Marys to our Lady of Mt. Carmel every day because when she was a little girl she had heard that it was good to say these prayers. In November, 1864, she went to confession and has done well ever since, and I don't doubt that she will eventually reach heaven.

829 Madrid, March 21, 1865. A man who was converted and

came to confession happened to be the one who had made some very wicked and slanderous caricatures and touched-up photographs of me, which have been sold and circulated everywhere.

830 This year a very evil woman, who had committed every sort of sin, was converted. She attributed her conversion to the prayer, "O Virgin and Mother of God," which we say after the sermon. Despite her evil life she said this prayer every day, and finally the Blessed Virgin touched her heart and she made a good general confession, although she had never made a good confession before. When I say that she had committed every sort of sin, I mean it: she had poisoned her husband; she had tried to commit suicide several times but had been nursed back to health although she had been at death's door; she had often tried to summon up the devil and had offered herself to him to carry her off, etc., etc. And just for reciting this little prayer to Mary every day, the Lord preserved her and at length converted her. How merciful the Blessed Virgin Mary is! This conversion took place during the novena to the Immaculate Heart of Mary, in 1865.

Chapter XVII

(Blank in the Manuscript; see *Writings*, p. 160)

Chapter XVIII

**CONTAINING AN ACCOUNT
OF MY RESIGNATION FROM
THE COURT, AND A LETTER
FROM HER MAJESTY TO ME**

831 On May 7, 1865, at 3:30 in the afternoon, the feast of the Patronage of St. Joseph, Jesus told me to be very devout to St. Joseph and to approach him with confidence.

832 On July 17, 1865, at 7:00 in the morning, while I was praying before the image of the Christ of Pardon in the church

of La Granja, Jesus told me, "Anthony, leave." This command came as a result of the queen's recognition of the so-called Kingdom of Italy. There had been some talk hinting of this, and the bishops were beginning to send in written objections and inquiries on the matter, beginning with that of the Archbishop of Burgos.[1] Her Majesty asked me what I thought of these papers by the bishops. I answered that they seemed to be in perfect order and that I would do the same if I were in their place. I said that the others had to write because they were absent, whereas I was present and could talk with her face to face. They wrote for their flocks, but I had no need to because I had but one sheep and she was about to be devoured by the wolf. I meant the queen and she knew it, and so she exclaimed, "God save us!"

833 Since anyone could see that this matter would eventually come to a head, I had been constantly warning her to avoid granting this recognition and to keep clear of the whole question. She had promised me that she would never grant it because it would be an act against both the Holy Father and the King of Naples, a very close relative of hers.[1] She had told me on various occasions that she would rather abdicate than approve such an act, and on other occasions she had assured me that she would rather die. Because I saw that in the final outcome the same thing would happen to her that had happened to the King of Naples, I told her so and exhorted her to die with honor rather than blacken her escutcheon with such a foul deed. To all these arguments I finally added threats and told her twice that if she recognized the Kingdom of Italy, I would leave her service. This was the most painful thing I could tell her because she was madly attached to me.

834 Finally, on July 14, the feast of St. Bonaventure, a black day for the queen and all Catholics, the full Council of State Ministers arrived at La Granja at 9:00 in the evening. The President of the Council, O'Donnell,[1] went alone to the palace and talked with the queen from 9:00 to 11:00, telling her that this matter of the Kingdom of Italy was not so bad as people thought and that its bark was worse than its bite. He told her that it wasn't a matter of recognizing the right in the matter so much as the fact, and that the agreement only af-

fected the holdings of the King of Naples but by no means those of the Pope. To these treacherous arguments he added that the nation's commerce demanded it and that, besides, she could do no less because the army was ready to revolt and descend upon her if she did not recognize the so-called Kingdom of Italy. One could truly say that she was both deceived and threatened into doing what she did.

835 Next day, at the appointed time, all the Ministers of State assembled in the palace and unanimously approved the plan that their president had set forth the night before.

836 This vote of approval was like a death-blow to me. I went to the queen and showed her the evil of what she had done. She could only cry and told me that she had been running a temperature ever since she had given her consent.

837 The whole affair so upset me that it gave me a bad case of diarrhea. Because every year someone in the queen's entourage had died of diarrhea, presumably contracted from drinking the water at La Granja, I seized upon this as an excuse to leave the court and go to Catalonia. I did not want to tell the queen my real intention because she was then four months pregnant and I feared my announcement might cause a miscarriage. She begged and beseeched me with moans, sighs, and tears not to leave. I told her that I had to go to save my life, that I had made more than enough sacrifices for her during the eight years and months I had been at her side, and that she should not ask me to sacrifice my life as well.

838 I left La Granja for Madrid, then on to Zaragoza, Barcelona, and finally, Vich. On leaving the atmosphere of the court I felt somewhat better, but the diarrhea lasted several days, even in Vich.

839 On August 14 of this year, at 9:30 in the morning while I was at prayer in the church of St. Dominic in Vich, during the Forty Hours' Devotion, the Lord spoke to me from the Blessed Sacrament: "You will go to Rome."

840 A Letter Sent to Me by Her Majesty, the Queen:

San Ildefonso,
July 20, 1865

Father Claret, My Dear Father:

My object in writing you these lines is to beg you, for the love you bear me, to be in Valladolid on the second of the coming month, to accompany me to Zarauz. You know very well what would happen and what people would say if they saw me without you. If after you have been at Zarauz you still need more baths, you can leave for a few days and come back. Make this one sacrifice more for your spiritual daughter who owes you so much.

I beseech you, if you agree to my request, to drop me a few lines telling me so, and my joy will be immense.

Pray God and the Virgin to keep us all in good health. The King's health is rather delicate, but you will pray for his improvement. We all trust in your prayers and have every hope in them.

Your loving and respectful daughter,
Isabel.

Chapter XIX

CONTAINING THE LETTER OF HIS HOLINESS

841 As it became evident that the matter of recognizing the Kingdom of Italy was becoming a real issue, Her Majesty the Queen consulted the Holy Father, asking his advice on how to act in the matter. The Pope answered as follows:

"Your Majesty:

The letter that Your Majesty has just sent me, asking my advice as to whether Your Majesty should recognize the present state of Italy, involves grave difficulties, both on the part of the petitioner and on my part, because I cannot answer in the affirmative. The difficulty of Your Majesty's position is not unknown to me, and I am aware that in a parliamentary system the sovereign is often prevented from putting into effect the resolutions he knows must be taken. Nevertheless, such resolutions neither can nor ought to be admitted, if they contravene justice. For this reason alone, Your Majesty will easily understand that my advice will always be opposed to a usurpation that is utterly unfair to those Italian rulers who have been wronged and still more to what affects the Holy See's patrimony, which has been entrusted to me to be handed on to my successors.

842 "It seems impossible that the Spanish nation, so well known for its love of the Catholic faith, a nation which in 1845[1] gave the whole world a shining example of its love for this Holy See and for my own poor person, should presently wish to oblige Your Majesty to set an utterly contrary example. Indeed, I hope not.

843 "It is true that the desire I have manifested to fill the many vacant episcopal sees of Italy has led many to suppose that this Holy See is not averse to continuing its overtures at dealing with King Victor Emmanuel and his government to the point of recognizing the actual state of this Peninsula. But those who think so have committed a colossal error, for it is one thing to satisfy a duty of conscience imposed by Jesus Christ—such as trying by all means possible to provide for the needs of the Church—and quite another to recognize usurpations and thus sanction the false doctrine of the *fait accompli*. I have tried following diplomatic steps to fulfill my duty and even had some hopes of a pleasing outcome during the first stages of dealing with the Piedmontese negotiator; but after returning to Rome I received instructions completely to the contrary, and the hopes I had entertained were dashed, so that now we have returned to the state we were in before the negotiations.

844 "As for the rest, I pray God to sustain Your Majesty and give you the light you may need to make right prevail in your kingdom and save its society, which is exposed to so many dangers and manifest perils.

"I send my heartfelt blessing to you, to His Majesty the

King, to the Prince of Asturias, to the Royal Family, and to all your subjects.

> "Given at the Vatican
> on the fifteenth day of June, 1865
> Pius IX, Pope"

Despite the fact that the queen and her ministers had read this letter, they went ahead with the recognition of the so-called Kingdom of Italy.

Chapter XX

CONTAINING A LETTER WRITTEN TO ME BY THE PAPAL NUNCIO IN MADRID WHILE I WAS IN CATALONIA

845 When I saw the way things were going, I asked the Papal Nuncio to ask Rome what I should do. The Nuncio gave me Rome's response in the following letter:

"To His Excellency, D. Anthony Mary Claret, Archbishop of Trajanopolis.

"My Dear Sir and Beloved Brother: I have presently received a response from Rome concerning your inquiries. It reads as follows:

"'I am not surprised,' writes Cardinal Antonelli, 'that Bishop Claret should be bewildered and in search of authoritative advice on the resolve he should take to bring some calm to his spirit. Certainly, in view of the good he could do for the cause of religion, notwithstanding the recognition of the so-called Kingdom of Italy, he cannot be asked to leave his post at court; but neither can he be asked to stay, if it occasions him any spiritual anguish or if he believes that doing so would be contrary to his conscience. Hence there is no recourse for him but to recollect himself in the Lord and, after imploring divine guidance, to do whatever God inspires him to, for the good of the Church and souls. This is the better part, and this is the advice we would like you to convey to Bishop Claret, in the Holy Father's name.'

846 "I have tried to translate this reply literally, so that you might know the Holy Father's opinion exactly. It can be summarized as follows: You should pray God to enlighten you and then, following the Lord's inspiration, you should either continue or not continue as the queen's confessor. The Holy Father imposes neither of these alternatives, nor will he disapprove of whatever choice you adopt after calling on God's special assistance.

847 "Allow me to make one observation on the Holy Father's reply. It is true that he does not ask you to continue in the post of confessor, but neither does he ask you to abandon it. Hence if you continued in it you would neither be doing something contrary to your duty, nor something displeasing to the Holy Father. If either of these had been the case, the Holy Father would have told you frankly to discontinue your services. The reason he did not tell you that it would be fitting for you to continue is not that he thought doing so was surely reprehensible, but only that he does not wish you to do so if you believe that it would be against your conscience.

848 "This, then, is the heart of the matter; hence you should beg the Lord for his holy lights of wisdom and prudence, to discern whether staying in court any longer is something that goes against your conscience. I know full well that your aspirations, tendencies, and desires would lead you to leave as quickly as possible, and you would have more than enough reasons to be at ease over doing so. But experience has taught me that aspirations, tendencies, and desires are not conscience, and here we are talking exclusively of conscience.

849 "The frank and explicit declaration you have published has removed any possible doubt about your thoughts on the recognition of the Kingdom of Italy. From now on, no one could suspect that you are not in agreement with the bishops and the general outpouring of Catholic sentiment, or that you are hiding or dissimulating your opinion in order to avoid being removed from a palace post. But your removal would make it difficult for you to render the Church some very valuable services, particularly in the election of bishops, and would prejudice the queen's cause in the eyes of the

faithful and the clergy. These last two considerations are of the greatest import and deserve your serious reflection. I need not dwell on the former, but as to the latter, I need only remind you of the revolutionary conspiracy against Her Majesty, especially in view of the fact that, deep in her heart, she is Catholic and devoted to the Holy Father. What would happen if the good, too, became enemies of her cause, as some are imprudently doing? What would the consequences then be, both for the Kingdom and the Church?

850 "The Holy Father has not ceased to hold Her Majesty in affectionate regard. He deeply deplores her recognition of Italy, but because he knows that the queen deplores it too, he sympathizes with her because she neither knew nor could do anything to control the circumstances.

851 "I hope that with God's grace your health has improved and that you will tell me of any new developments, especially any affecting your decision in this matter. In your prayers, do not forget one who is always

> "Your affectionate brother,
> Lawrence, Bishop of Tyana
> Madrid, July 23, 1865"

852 Vich, August 23, 1865. Because I was unable to decide whether to return to court or not, I discussed it with the Superior General of the Congregation of the Immaculate Heart of Mary, who in turn enjoined the four Consultors of the Congregation to pray over the matter until we met again on an assigned day. The day arrived, and of the five votes cast, three were opposed to my returning and two were for it. Following the majority vote, I have resolved not to return. In the meantime I will busy myself by giving retreats and similar services here in this city.

Chapter XXI

CONTAINING A GENTLEMAN'S DEFENSE OF MY INSIGNIFICANT SELF

An article published in a Madrid newspaper, La Esperanza, *January 24, 1865.*

853 "Msgr. Claret, Archbishop of Trajanopolis and Confessor to the queen, had resigned himself to listen silently and indefinitely to the damaging reports, some of them erroneous, some slanderous, that have been spread about him these many years, hoping that God—to whom he prays for his detractors—would enlighten their understanding and abate their ill will.

854 "But yielding to the repeated entreaties of us who, besides respecting and loving him as he deserves, think that it is important for the welfare of the Church to refute or rectify these reports, he has authorized us to publish the following résumé of his life and some of his works. This résumé has been compiled by a person who is as incapable of altering the facts as he is well informed of them. For our part, we take the single liberty of adding one comment, namely, that if any charge could be brought against Bishop Claret, it would be, in our judgment, that of shunning any involvement in politics, even when by becoming involved he might have helped the interests of the Church against political encroachments.

855 "His Excellency, the Most Reverend Archbishop Claret, was born in the town of Sallent, Province of Barcelona, diocese of Vich. He received his elementary schooling in his hometown, after which he was sent by his parents to Barcelona to study design at La Lonja Institute, where he received several rewards. He studied chemistry, general science, and French, and because he felt strongly called to the priesthood, he undertook the study of Latin. His Excellency, Paul of Jesus de Corcuera, then Bishop of Vich, sent him to the seminary at Vich, where he maintained a record of high scholastic achievement throughout his student career.

294

856 "In 1834, having acquired a benefice, he was promoted to major orders, together with Dr. Balmes, the senior member of the diaconate class, Bishop Claret being senior member of the subdiaconate class. At the Solemn High Ordination Mass, Bishop Claret sang the Epistle and Dr. Balmes sang the Gospel. Both were close friends and spent many hours together studying at the same table in the episcopal library.

857 "He was ordained to the priesthood on June 13, 1835 and sang his first Mass in his hometown, where he fulfilled the required residency in the benefice he was ordained for.

858 "Without prejudice to his benefice, his ecclesiastical superior made him acting pastor of the parish for two years and administrator for another two, thus completing a stay of four years, from 1835 to 1839. It must be remembered that the town of Sallent in those days was fortified in favor of Isabel II and, because Father Claret was in charge of the parish and its community of beneficiaries, he was well known and treated by all the civil authorities. In our own court at Madrid, Baron de Meer, then Captain General of Catalonia, and the Marquis of Novaliches, who accompanied him at that time, are eyewitnesses to his conduct. In the course of that four-year period both of them visited the town a number of times, and the Captain General frequently stayed at the Casa Claret, the most prominent house in town. In his official ecclesiastical capacity, Father Claret used to travel from the rectory to visit the Captain General. Hence we have the testimony of these two authorities to give the lie to those who have underhandedly accused the bishop of having been a rebel.

859 "Early in October, 1839, he went to Rome to offer his services for the foreign missions. He remained there until March of the following year, when his doctors advised him to return to Spain because the dampness of Rome was causing him a severe rheumatic condition.

860 "A few days after his return he recovered his health, and his ecclesiastical superior sent him as administrator to the parish of Viladrau, where he began a missionary campaign throughout the principate of Catalonia. At this time he came

to be known as 'Mosén Claret,' 'Mosén' being the common Catalan term for 'priest.' In 1846, however, while he was preaching the Month of May Devotions to Mary in the city of Lérida, people began calling him 'Padre Claret,' perhaps believing that, because he was always preaching missions, he was one of the Franciscans of Escornalbou, a group of apostolic men dedicated to giving missions. This is doubtless why those who do not know his story call him 'Padre.'

861 "At the beginning of 1848 he preached at the court as he was passing through Madrid, in response to an appeal by Bishop Bonaventure Codina of the Canary Islands. He accompanied Bishop Codina to the Islands and gave missions there until the middle of 1849.

862 "On August 4 of that year he was named Archbishop of Cuba, but he resolutely refused the nomination until, at the command of the Bishop of Vich and his spiritual director, he accepted it on October 4. His consecration took place on October 6 of the following year. On his arrival at court Msgr. Brunelli, then Papal Nuncio, conferred the pallium on him, after which he went directly to his diocese.

"In March, 1857 he was summoned to fill the post of Confessor to Her Majesty.

863 "During the last few years Bishop Claret has been slandered on three main counts:

(1) for being a guerrilla leader, a charge that, from what has been said already, is utterly without foundation;

864 (2) for meddling in politics. To this we would only say: ask any of the government ministers from 1857 to the present whether he has ever done anything in speech or in writing to hinder their plans to rise to power or to pursue their particular policies.

865 (3) for distortions attributed to his pious and instructive books. His enemies have gone so far as to rewrite and print scandalous versions of two of the many books Bishop Claret has written. One of them, *The Garland,* is a select anthology of acts of thanksgiving, petition, and love directed to God.

His enemies have issued another book under the same title, illustrated with erotic pictures so obscene that the like of them has never been seen, and they have attributed this work to Bishop Claret.

866 "They have done the same with another work, *The Key of Gold*. While he was in Cuba, Bishop Claret personally directed a series of conferences for newly ordained priests to instruct them in the theory and practice of the sacraments. With this in mind, he wrote *The Key of Gold* for them; the book rapidly caught on in Spain and won the applause of the Spanish hierarchy. And how did his enemies react to this? They wrote a booklet under the same title, with obscene pictures and a revolting text that they attributed again to Bishop Claret. For more than ten years the original book had been praised and circulated among the clergy; now, less than a year has passed since the publication of this diabolic book by the same name, which is nothing but an attempt to discredit, if possible, the original book and its author.

867 "On various occasions, Bishop Claret's friends have asked him to defend himself, but his answer has always been that the best defense was to ignore his detractors and pray for them as Jesus did on the cross: 'Father, forgive them, for they know not what they do,' for people so misguided cannot know what they are doing or saying.

868 "We respect his silence and his prayers; nevertheless, charity and justice demand that we publish these facts, for two reasons: first, to shame the wicked by unmasking them, and second, to warn the unthinking that they should not allow themselves to be deceived by the slanders and inventions Bishop Claret's enemies are always stirring up against him, as the Jews did against Jesus."

Chapter XXII

CONTAINING A REPORT PUBLISHED IN THE PARISIAN DAILY, *LE MONDE*, BY FOREIGNERS WHO HAD VISITED EL ESCORIAL AT THE BEGINNING OF THE YEAR 1865

Le Monde, *Thursday, April 27, 1865.*

869 "The revolution and its soldiers of fortune, trained by the Freemasons, are endeavoring to eradicate all Catholic education and belief in Spain, by subordinating its national policies to the commercial interests of England. The Spanish Church, despoiled of its goods and deprived of the powerful help of its religious orders, has demonstrated, nonetheless, by its fidelity to the Sovereign Pontiff and by its continuing resistance to the irreligious press, that it has been strengthened by trial and prepared for the decisive battles that will establish the freedom of the Church of Jesus Christ. Among the notable works of the Spanish episcopate, one of the most notable is the renovation of the seminary of the Escorial, which has been carried out by His Excellency, the Most Reverend Anthony Claret, Archbishop of Trajanopolis, under the auspices of Her Majesty the Queen.

870 "This heroic prelate, a bulwark of strength to the queen amid a group of vacillating constitutionalist ministers, has managed to form a model institution of clerical learning and, thanks to his own efforts and those of Don Dionisio González Mendoza, vice president, the seminary of the Escorial holds out the promise of bright hopes. The program of studies offered in other seminaries, namely, two years of philosophy, one of physics, and seven of theology, has been adopted.

871 "Dr. González is a man well-versed in the sciences and of an eminently practical bent. Realizing that his young theologians will have to combat a flood of foreign ideas, especially the German philosophers Strauss, Hegel, and Schelling, he has insisted that they make a thorough study of German, and

now 60 of the students can read German works fluently. They also receive a thorough grounding in French and English, not to mention Hebrew and Greek. Some are studying Arabic. One of the learned faculty has compiled Greek, German, and English grammars specifically for the use of the seminary. The theologians will presently be taking courses in church archeology and other sciences related to the study of theology.

872 "The excellent dispositions and remarkable intellectual endowments of the students lead us to expect great things of the restored seminary of the Escorial.

"The notebook entitled 'Notes' contains many more extensive reports on the Escorial."[1]

NOTES TO PART FOUR

Chapter I

703.1 During this tour, the Saint felt especially possessed and moved by God, even in the external works of the apostolate. These facts must be borne in mind in any attempt to assess the theology of his apostolic mystique. His confessor, Fr. Carmelo Sala, wrote to Fr. Xifré: "After this task, enough and more than enough to exhaust the forces of a giant, he told me, 'I know God wants me to preach, because I feel as peaceful, rested, and energetic as if I'd done nothing at all. The Lord has done it all. May He be blessed forever.' It is also noteworthy that, in the midst of all this activity, he has never once diminished the time he spends daily at prayer, spiritual reading, and his other devotions. He eats little and hardly sleeps at all. I simply can't help marveling at this and blessing God for it." (Cf. Fernández, *The Blessed*, vol. 2, p. 427.)

Chapter II

709.1 In the same good-natured vein he told some cloistered nuns in Vich that they would be saved, but only after they had become grandmothers in purgatory for all their faults against silence. (Cf. Puigdesens, *The Spirit...*, p. 153.)

710.1 In the context of religious orders, "common life" refers to a rather uniform mode of living, arising from the vow of poverty and the faithful observance of common rules and constitutions.

714.1 Matt. 25:12.

716.1 Matt. 23:13.

Chapter III

717.1 In 1861 the farm workers of Loja and Iznajar (Granada) revolted, under the leadership of Rafael Pérez del Olmo, a veterinarian of Loja.

717.2 On October 15, the Saint preached in the nuns' convent at Loja and to the clergy. He was unable to preach to the townspeople, because they were not allowed to enter the church before the queen arrived.

718.1 Claret limits himself to a denunciation of these errors, without sociological commentary.

728.1 Cf. *Correspondence,* Letter 1028, to Fr. Xifré.

Chapter V

736.1 He arrived at court on October 19, 1862, at 5 P.M.

741.1 Gisbert, O.P., *Life of St. Catherine,* p. 69.

742.1 The year before, he changed the subject of his particular examen from humility to meekness. (Cf. par. 693.)

742.2 The reference is to the work he published in Madrid in 1859. Meditation 20 is a résumé of the virtues of Christ, especially obedience, humility, meekness, and charity. Meditation 28 marks the passage from the illuminative to the unitive way, i.e., to the imitation of the inward Christ, especially his offering of Himself as a victim.

752.1 2 Tim. 2:10.

Chapter VI

759.1 Paragraphs 759 to 761 are an account of how he forced himself to put into practice the recommendation of Jesus and Mary concerning mortification. (Cf. par. 684.)

761.1 Comparing the resolutions made in Madrid with those made in Cuba, there seems to be a notable advance in his experience of God.

762.1 For Claret, staying in Madrid meant sacrificing his universal missionary vocation: "But since I can't go myself, I'll have others go, my beloved brothers, called the Sons of the Immaculate Heart of Mary" (*Correspondence,* Letter 1018).

763.1 Claret's permanent residence in Madrid made it possible for him to undertake continuous spiritual direction and many took advantage of it, among them St. Micaela of the Blessed Sacrament, the Marquis del Arco, the Bishop of Avila, etc.

766.1 Vocal prayer is no longer considered a degree of prayer; the degree depends on the quality of the prayer. Claret's vocal prayer was really contemplative prayer.

767.1 Claret's mystical life was eminently eucharistic. Most of his mystical graces relate to the Eucharist and took place either during Mass or before the Blessed Sacrament. The Eucharist was the sacrament of his mystical union.

Chapter VII

768.1 A royal residence built by Philip V at the foot of the Guadarrama, 11 kilometers southeast of Segovia, renowned for the beauty of its fountains and gardens.

771.1 He wrote these lines in November, during the Spiritual Exercises that ended the nineteenth, the day when the banquet he refers to took place. The reason that he fails to specify was the queen's name day.

772.1 These two examples break the flow of the text and were added at the insistence of his spiritual director as useful cases for preachers to cite. (Cf. par. 802.)

Chapter VIII

775.1 Royal residence to the south of Madrid, begun by Philip II. They stayed at Aranjuez from April 18 until early June and at La Granja from July 7 to September 9.

776.1 Claret always refers thus to the Carmelites of Charity.

779.1 He also published the following works during this year: *Personnel of the Escorial* (Barcelona); *Respect for Churches* (Barcelona); *The Seminary and College of St. Lawrence of the Escorial* (Madrid); *A True Portrait of the New Philosophers* (Barcelona); *Life of St. Monica* (Barcelona); "The Eclipse of the Sun," a leaflet.

Chapter IX

781.1 L. Gisbert, *Life of St. Catherine,* p. 69. Cf. par. 741.

781.2 Ibid., p. 191.

782.1 Matt. 11:29.

783.1 Mary of Agreda, *Mystical City of God,* 7 vols. (Barcelona, 1860), vol. 2, p. 276. The title of the chapter in question reads, "On the Blessed Virgin Mary's Practice of the Virtue of Temperance." She remarks that "the Lord used this meekness and clemency as his instrument."

783.2 St. Francis de Sales, *Introduction to the Devout Life* (Madrid, 1771), chap. 8, p. 109. The Saint's personal copy.

789.1 "Sunday, in honor of the Blessed Trinity; Monday, the holy angels; Tuesday, my holy patrons; Wednesday, the poor; Thursday, the Blessed Sacrament; Friday, the Passion of Jesus Christ, the poor souls; Saturday, the Blessed Virgin Mary" (*Resolutions,* 1862. Cf. *Writings,* p. 566).

Chapter XI
796.1 In 1864 his retreat lasted from November 13 to 22.

797.1 Cf. par. 242.

798.1 Barcelona, 1864. This little work, autobiographical in character (though veiled in anonymity), is extremely important for an understanding of the Saint's spirit, especially at this stage in his life. (Cf. *Writings,* p. 746.) The campaign of defamation that the press had begun against Claret the year before kept growing until his death. "You can have no idea how hard hell has conspired against me. The vilest slanders, words, actions, threats to my life—every trick has been used to discredit and terrify me. But with God's help, I pay no heed to it" (*Correspondence,* Letter 1079, to Xifré).

801.1 The method he followed in making this particular examen on the love of God is described in his pamphlet, *The Dove.* (Cf. *Writings,* p. 705.)

Chapter XII
803.1 Ps. 115:1.

805–810.1 The Saint remarks, "Here I will relate some of the truly dreadful cases I have had to resolve and remedy. They should be read only by prudent priests, whose discerning judgment has steeled them against temptation." Hence, the compilers of this edition have omitted them, as they think the Saint would have wished them to.

Chapter XV

823–826.1 See preceding note.

Chapter XVIII

832.1 Cardinal Ferdinand de la Puente y Primo de Rivera was removed as tutor to the Prince of Asturias on July 14, 1865.

833.1 Her mother, Cristina de Borbón, was the sister of Ferdinand II; hence Isabel II was his niece.

834.1 General Leopold O'Donnell Jorris (1809–67), Duke of Tetuán and party leader of the Liberal Union, was, with a few interruptions, chief of state from 1856 to 1866.

Chapter XIX

842.1 On May 27, 1845 the Spanish fleet sailed from Barcelona with an army of 8,000 soldiers aboard, under the command of General Fernández Córdoba, headed for Gaeta to bring the Pope back to his throne in Rome.

Chapter XXII

872.1 Notes on the Government of the Diocese, ed. 1865, app. 3, pp. 196–257.

Sallent,
statue of Claret
in the town square

PART FIVE

Supplementary Reading

The compilers of this edition felt that a small selection of additional autobiographical readings was indispensable to clarify certain points in the *Autobiography* and to fill in some of the essential data from 1865, the date at which the text breaks off, until 1870, the year of Claret's death.

I. Supplement to Paragraphs 95–98
A Student Devoted to Our Lady of the Rosary

(*Editor's note:* This text, written no earlier than 1865, corresponds to events that occurred in Claret's life in 1831, when he was 24 years old. Narrated in the third person, it is theologically far richer than the first-person account in the *Autobiography,* partly because it was intended for aspirants to the priesthood at the seminary of the Escorial. Its importance lies in its combined Marian-apostolic interpretation of the vision Claret had during his second year of philosophy at Vich. This interpretation treats the vision not as an end in itself but as the signal for the beginning of a new stage in his life: the apostolate. As a result of this vision, he was confirmed in chastity, which was to be, paradoxically, the source of the fertility of his apostolate. St. Stephen emerges as a symbol of a battle not against flesh and blood, but against spiritual evil. Mary, too, is seen in an apostolic perspective, as the Woman overcoming the seed of the Serpent, precisely through the "tactic" of her fecund virginity. The gift of perfect chastity granted to Claret by the Virgin was to make his zeal more free, more universal, and more fruitful. Of particular interest, too, is the fifth paragraph's stress on Marian sonship, based on the model of St. John the Evangelist, who again traditionally combines the attributes of virgin-apostle. The original is in the Claretian General Archives: Claret, *Manuscripts,* vol. 1. *End of editor's note.*)

In 1831, in the city of Vich in Catalonia, there was a seminarian who was completing his philosophical studies in the local seminary. He was very diligent and always attended classes punctually. He had no friends or companions, so as not to interfere with the plan of life he had written, which contained a list of all his duties and devotions.

He always rose early and on schedule, without giving in to laziness. The first thing he did was to kneel down and offer God and the Blessed Virgin all his thoughts, words, and deeds of the day. Then he immediately began a half-hour's meditation on the life, passion, and death of Jesus Christ. After this he went to hear Mass, and on returning he studied until 8:00, when he took a cup of chocolate. Next, he reviewed his lesson and went to class. When class was over, he jotted down the main points the teacher had touched on and then rested a bit until 11:00, when he began studying for his afternoon classes until noon. At noon he had lunch and rested briefly, did some spiritual reading, reviewed his lesson, and went to class. After class, he went to visit the Blessed Sacrament in the chapel of the Forty Hours' Devotion, and then went straightway to visit the shrine of Our Lady of the Rosary at St. Dominic's church. He never missed these two visits—to the Blessed Sacrament and Our Lady of the Rosary—whether it rained or snowed. On days when he had no classes he lengthened these visits because he had no other friends except Jesus and Mary and visited no other houses except churches.

Every week he went to confession and communion and, because he was a member of the Confraternity of St. Aloysius Gonzaga, he made the yearly Spiritual Exercises in the seminary chapel, conducted by Bishop Paul of Jesus Corcuera, who loved his students dearly and spent a great deal of time with them because he wanted them all to become holy and learned priests.

This student had a great devotion to St. Aloysius Gonzaga and, because he knew that true devotion to a saint meant imitating him and doing everything properly to serve God, the young man aimed at doing so in all things, especially with regard to the virtue of chastity. Moreover, as he loved Mary as his tender and loving Mother, he was always thinking of ways to honor her.

It occurred to him that he should read and study the life of St. John the Evangelist and imitate him. On doing so he found that this Son of Mary, given to her by Jesus on the Cross, was distinguished in all virtues, but especially in humility, purity, and charity, and so our young student strove to practice these virtues.

Despite all his efforts at avoiding all dangers, God permitted him to experience a temptation—the strongest and most violent one he had ever undergone—against the virtue of holy purity, which he loved so much. Around the beginning of 1831 he caught a terrible cold. He was ordered to stay in bed and he obeyed. One day at 10:30 in the morning he had such a strong temptation against chastity that he didn't know what to do to overcome it. He prayed to his guardian angel, St. Aloysius Gonzaga, and all the saints he had a special devotion to, but nothing seemed to help. He made the long sign of the cross, with the three crosses, saying, "By the sign of the holy cross, deliver us from all our enemies, O Lord our God," but all in vain, so that he felt all the more troubled by his passions.

Because he couldn't get out of bed, he made a violent effort and turned over, and at that very moment he saw four things: the Blessed Virgin Mary, himself, the saints he was devoted to, and the demons.

The Blessed Virgin Mary was extremely beautiful, dressed in a rose-red dress and a blue mantle, with a great many rose garlands in her left hand and a crown of beautiful roses in her right hand. She told him, "This crown is yours if you overcome."

She had scarcely finished speaking these words when she placed the crown on his head. Here it should be remarked that the student was in bed, completely enchanted at what he saw happening. The Virgin was floating in the air, without resting on anything, about a yard-and-a-half above his bed. The student could see himself in the form of a lively and pretty child of about 12 years of age, with the crown of roses on his head, kneeling with hands folded in an attitude of fervent prayer. He knew perfectly well by the light he received that this child was a portrait of his own soul. He, too, was floating in mid-air about a yard away from the spectator, to his right. On this same side, about two yards away, but seemingly far up in the air, he saw a group of his patron saints praying for him. The one nearest him was St. Stephen, dressed in a deacon's dalmatic. Because this saint is the patron of his town, he felt that this was why he had helped him in this combat; but years later, when the student was ordained a deacon, the Lord showed him during the ceremony why St. Stephen had been so close to him as the bishop read the Apostle's words: "Our struggle is not against flesh and blood, but against principalities and powers" (Pontifical; Eph. 6:12).

After looking long at the Virgin and his patron saints, the student glanced a little to his left and saw, about three yards away in the air, a great army of demons reforming, like an army regrouping after a retreat.

Thus the vision ended, leaving the student in a state of great joy and encouragement. May all of you be devoted to Mary.

II. Supplement to Part Two (Chapters 23–32)
A. Resolutions for the Spiritual Exercises of 1843

(*Editor's note:* The year 1843 was a very significant one in the life of St. Anthony Mary Claret, the year in which he consecrated himself once and for all to evangelization. The following resolutions are the result either of the retreat he made at St. John's in Olo, before giving up parish life, or of the retreat he preached to the priests gathered at Campdevanol or Gombreny. They represent a basic outline of all the resolutions he drew up during his work as an apostolic missionary and, for that matter, throughout the rest of his life. A characteristic trait that emerges from them is his dedication as son and priest to Mary, as his Mother, Teacher, and Director.

The original is in the Claretian General Archives: Claret, *Manuscripts,* vol. 5. *End of editor's note.*)

(1) Every year I will make the Spiritual Exercises.

(2) Every month I will make a day of recollection and read these resolutions.

(3) Every week I will go to confession at least once. Three times a week, Monday, Wednesday, and Friday, I will take the discipline or do some penance that my confessor advises. On Tuesday, Thursday, and Saturday I will wear a cilice or small chain or do some other penance that my confessor advises. Fridays and Saturdays I will fast.

(4) Every day I will deprive myself of something. Every day I will make at least one hour of mental prayer in the morning, or a half hour in the morning and another half hour in the evening. Every day I will get up on time at a set hour, and I will begin by thinking about God and offering Him my thoughts, words, and actions. Then I will make my meditation and afterward celebrate Mass, with as much seriousness and devotion as I can. Then I will make my thanksgiving and go to the confessional, after which I will recite my breviary devoutly and spend some time studying. Before noon, I will spend a short time in prayer (like St. Peter), and make my particular examen. At noon, I will take lunch and then rest until 2:00. At 2:00 I will recite Vespers and, at the proper time, Matins—devoutly, before some pious image. The rest of the afternoon I will spend studying or engaged in the duties of the ministry. In the evening I will take a walk and afterward make a visit to the Blessed Sacrament and the Virgin Mary. Every day I will do some spiritual reading from Rodríguez, except Saturday, when it will be from either the *Marian Year* or the *Glories of Mary*. At 9:00, the rosary, dinner, retiring. At noon and at night I will make my particular examen on humility. I will strive to stay in God's presence, and do everything through Him. What I find unpleasant I will bear for the love of God and for the forgiveness of my faults and sins, knowing that I have deserved hell, and that what I would have to suffer there is far worse than anything I have to suffer here.

(5) I entrust myself totally to Mary, as her son and her priest. Hence, every day I will say a chaplet of anthems: *Rejoice, O Mary; Permit Me to Praise You,* etc. She will be my Mother, Teacher, and Director, and everything I do or suffer in my ministry will be done for her, for because she has planted the tree, the fruit belongs to her.

(6) I will spend my total working time hearing confessions, catechizing, and preaching publicly or privately, as circumstances permit. (And I neither want nor will accept stipends, for I will bear in mind that it is all a grace that I have received through Mary and "what you have freely received, freely give.")

(7) Jesus is and will always be my Captain. I wish to follow Him, wearing his uniform and colors—the virtues He was clothed in: poverty, acceptance of contempt, and humility.

(8) *Poverty.* If I lack something I need, I will not complain, but rejoice. Insofar as it depends on me I will choose the article most scorned.

My clothing will be decent and clean, but as poor as possible.

(I will never travel on horseback, but on foot, and if I am ever forced to ride, it will be on a donkey, in imitation of Jesus.)

(9) *Contempt.* If I am treated with contempt or am persecuted, I will suffer it, rejoicing at such good fortune and commending my persecutors to God, in imitation of Jesus.

(10) *Humility.* All that I do, I will do for God and Mary alone. Hence, I will neither praise myself nor talk about myself or what I have done, or about my birthplace, relatives, studies, books, or places I have been. If I am praised, I will be silent, saying only, "Not to us, O Lord," etc., and strive to change the subject.

(11) I will firmly resolve never to waste a minute of my time but to spend it all in prayer, study, or charitable work for my neighbors, living or dead. With the help of the Lord and the Virgin Mary, I will accomplish all I have resolved, and whenever I notice, during my particular examen, that I have failed, I will say a Hail Mary, kneeling on my hands.

Anthony Claret, Priest

B. An Apostolic Missionary: A Self-Portrait

(*Editor's note:* The paths of the philosopher, Jaime Balmes, and the missionary, Anthony Claret, crossed again in 1846, when both were at the height of their powers. Balmes had just published his four-volume *Fundamental Philosophy.* In an interview with his former seminary classmate, on July 14, 1846, the philosopher asked the missionary—whose fame he had learned of and whose preaching he had just heard—to give him a brief written summary of the means he employed to achieve such phenomenal results. Thanks to Balmes' interest, we have yet another unintentional self-portrait of Claret, the apostolic missionary. Father Ignacio Casanova, S.J., Balmes' biographer, discovered the following document among the philosopher's papers. It is preserved in the Balmes Archives in Barcelona. *End of editor's note.*)

(1) The object of all my preaching is the glory of God and the good of souls. I preach the Holy Gospel, drawing my comparisons and style from it.

(2) I never take any pay for preaching, other than the food I need to keep alive. Not to be a burden, I always travel on foot.

(3) I have not the slightest self-interest in all the books and pamphlets I have published; hence, I have never copyrighted them. As far as I am concerned, anyone who wants to can reprint and sell them.

(4) God is my witness that no one has given me any secret pay for my works, nor do I have any other object but the one I have mentioned, nor do I seek any recompense but heaven.

(5) The only object of my *Certificate*[1] is to do away with blasphemy and, thank God, much good has come of it.

(6) I have nothing to do with selling pictures, crosses, rosaries, etc. All I do is bless them from the pulpit and grant those indulgences I have faculties to impart.

(7) People have never seen me lose my temper or idly chatting with women. I talk with the same pleasantness, love, and affection to the poor as to the rich, to children as to adults, to the simple as to the well educated. And although in God's eyes I am a great sinner, I can look any man straight in the eyes and say, by the mercy of God, "Which of you can convict me of sin?"

(8) I visit and preach to prisoners in jail. I visit the sick in hospitals and private homes, and a large number of those who come to me or are brought to me say that they have recovered their health; it pains me to see the large group of sufferers that surround me every day. I also put an end to quarrels and enmities and reconcile broken marriages.

III. Supplement to Paragraph 798
Witness to the Truth

(*Editor's note:* As the Saint tells us in par. 798 of the *Autobiography*, during 1864 he was much maligned in the press, in articles, leaflets, caricatures, falsified books, etc. Like Christ, he remained silent. Some of his friends argued with him that he owed it to the Church to defend himself because many were being misled by his silence. Against the huge bibliography of slander that had been written against him, the Saint wrote his apologia on two small pieces of paper, and even these were not published during his lifetime. Father John Postíus, C.M.F., finally published them in 1920 in the Spanish review, *Ilustración del Clero*, vol. 332, p. 306. The original is in the Claretian General Archives: Claret, *Manuscripts*, vol. 5. *End of editor's note.*)

This is His Excellency, the Most Reverend Archbishop Claret's witness to the truth. "There is a time to be silent and a time to speak," says Solomon. Thus far I have kept silent. But seeing that my silence has misled some, I shall speak briefly because the truth needs few words. Like my Divine Master, I will speak not to defend myself, but to bear witness to the truth. The Jews said of Jesus that he was a Samaritan and had a devil. Jesus answered, "I am not possessed by the devil; rather, I

---

1. He refers to the "Certificate of the Society of the Blessed Virgin Mary, against Blasphemy," the charter of a society he organized on April 5, 1845, in Mataró, on the model of the Irish societies against alcoholism. Claret remarked that in many parts of Catalonia, as a result of the efforts of this society, "there is not one-thousandth of the cursing there used to be."

honor my Father, whereas you dishonor me." I say the same. I have had nothing whatever to do, thank God, with the things my opponents accuse me of. This is the truth about me: I was born in the town of Sallent in the province of Barcelona and was baptized at the font of St. Mary's church on December 25, 1807.

I received my primary education in my hometown, after which I was sent to Barcelona, where I studied for four years. In this city during my spare time I studied design, for which I had a special aptitude, one which later stood me in good stead in preparing religious prints.

As St. Mary's parish in Sallent is in the diocese of Vich, the bishop, who at that time was His Excellency, Paul of Jesus Corcuera, sent me to his seminary to continue my studies. I did so and the yearly records show that I passed all my classes.

I was a friend and classmate of Father Jaime Balmes and was ordained with him. At the same ceremony he was first deacon and I was first sub-deacon; he sang the Gospel, I sang the Epistle. I was ordained with a title of benefice in my own parish, St. Mary's. I was ordained a priest on the feast day of my patron, St. Anthony, June 13, 1835. On June 21, the feast of St. Aloysius Gonzaga, patron of the Confraternity I belonged to in the seminary, I sang my First High Mass. I spent two years as substitute pastor and two more years as administrator in Sallent, a town fortified in favor of Isabel II. During these four years I was closely acquainted with Baron de Meer, then Captain General of Catalonia, whom I saw frequently as a lodger at Casa Claret, the most prominent house in town. I lived in the rectory and came to visit him whenever he and his staff arrived in town. He was often accompanied by General Pavía, the Marquis of Novaliches, and as both of them are presently living at court, they can both vouch as eyewitnesses to the fact that I never meddled in politics then or ever in my life but was occupied solely with the sacred ministry.

Because I felt daily more drawn to work for God's glory and the salvation of souls, I went to Rome toward the end of September, 1839, with the intention of offering myself to the Congregation for the Propagation of the Faith, for service in any mission field in the world.

After I had been in Rome for some time, the heavy rains and humidity caused me such severe rheumatic pains that I was advised to return to Spain, which I did toward the end of 1840.

As soon as I arrived in Spain I felt much better, so that a few days later my ecclesiastical superior saw fit to send me to the parish of Viladrau. From there I began giving missions throughout Catalonia until the beginning of 1848, when I went with the Bishop of the Canary Islands and gave missions throughout his diocese until May of the following year.

On August 4, 1849, I was elected Archbishop of Cuba, by royal decree of Her Majesty. I refused it at once and continued to refuse it for two months, but seeing that my refusal was not accepted, I resolved to consult five wise and virtuous priests, on whose judgment I relied implicitly, for their opinion in the matter. Meanwhile I withdrew to make a strict retreat of ten days, during which I begged the Lord to inspire these men with a knowledge of his holy will. At the end of the retreat they informed the bishop of their decision, whereupon the bishop commanded me to accept because it was God's will. I accepted on October 4, 1849, and on October 6 of the following year I was consecrated. I sailed from Barcelona on December 28, 1850 and arrived in Cuba in mid-February, 1851. I returned to Spain toward the end of May, 1857, at the summons of Her Majesty.

As soon as I arrived I presented myself to Her Majesty, and she informed me that she had called me to be her confessor and spiritual director. I realized what a difficult and delicate task this would be, and since then I have asked her a thousand times to set me free and let me retire. Seeing that I was getting nowhere, but that she wanted me to remain at her side more and more as time went by, I resolved to follow the plan of life I have followed faithfully during the seven-and-a-half years I have been in Madrid. I have lived outside the palace and have never come to it except at the summons of Her Majesty.

I have never meddled in politics: I look at and consider the march of events, but I say not a word. I know that one "cannot serve two masters."

In the space of seven-and-a-half years, many government ministers have come and gone and I have met many of them, especially on tour with the royal family. I have treated them all with respect and friendliness, but I have never talked politics with them. On one occasion, one of these gentlemen met me in a station, where I was awaiting Their Majesties. He told me that I should say something or other to Her Majesty in favor of his party. I told him to pardon me if I didn't, and added: "I look upon the nation in its present state as a gambling table, with players seated on either side. An onlooker may observe, but he should be silent and would be very imprudent to make the slightest insinuation in favor of one side or the other. I myself am a spectator and, as such, should not and cannot do or say anything in favor of you or anyone else in this matter. I do what I ought, namely, work as hard as I can with God's help to see to it that Her Majesty should be a good Christian and a good queen; for the rest, it is no concern of mine whether she avails herself of the services of Peter, James, or John in her government."

I believe that all the ministers who have served during this long interval will do me justice in this respect. If some have spoken or written ill of my conduct, they are from the lowest ranks, and don't know what they're talking about. These I can only commend to God, as Jesus did on the cross.

Because people of this sort have somehow gathered the false notion that I have prevented them from climbing to power and satisfying their ambitions, they have taken all sorts of shots at me. They have spared no means or pains but have mobilized everything they could against me. They have slandered my person, vilified my conduct, and falsified my books. I have personally seen and held in my own hands printed works with the same titles as my own, but whose text I would never have written. They have printed such revolting photographs that my pen balks even to begin to describe them.

I have written and published these lines only to bear witness to the truth, as Jesus said before Pilate. For the rest, I will keep a profound silence, only repeating what Jesus said: "This is your hour—the triumph of darkness."

Madrid, December 12, 1864
Anthony Mary, Archbishop of Trajanopolis

IV. The Revolution of 1868. The Path to Exile
A. Resolutions for 1866

(*Editor's note:* Only those parts of these resolutions that are distinctive are included here. The numbering is that of the original.)

(7) I will continue my particular examen on the love of God.

For the love of God, I will take great care to do each and every thing with purity of heart and rectitude of intention.

For the love of God, I will refrain from speaking of myself, my concerns, and occupations, in accord with the Rule (p. 66).[1]

(8) Within myself I will walk constantly in God's presence. I will keep recollected so not to become spiritually scattered. I will keep my imagination busy in the Lord, remembering St. Paul's words, "Are you not aware that you are the temple of God?" (1 Cor. 3:16) and "You are the temple of the living God" (2 Cor. 6:16).

I will think of my heart as the room in which Jesus is seated, of my soul as sitting at his feet like Mary, and my body as busy about the house like Martha, performing the duties of my ministry, to serve them up as a delicious repast for Jesus.

I will think of my soul and body as the two points of a compass: my soul, as one point, is fixed in Jesus, my center; and my body, like the other point, is describing a perfect circle of duties and obligations around Him, for the circle is a symbol of perfection on earth and of eternity in heaven.

1. Claretian Constitutions, ed. Vich, 1865, *On Humility*. Cf. J. M. Lozano, C.M.F., *Constitutions and Texts* (Barcelona, 1972), p. 483.

(9) At the feet of Jesus I will frequently say prayers of aspiration such as, "God is the rock of my heart and my portion forever" (Ps. 73); "May I know myself, may I know thee" (St. Augustine); "My God and my all" (St. Francis).

(10) Jesus Christ taught St. Catherine of Siena to observe this kind of recollection. The Blessed Virgin Mary also taught it to Mary of Agreda (*Mystical City,* vol. 6, p. 41). St. Teresa taught it to her nuns (*Way of Perfection,* chap. 28). Blessed Margaret Mary Alacoque taught it to her novices.

(11) St. Paul taught it when he said, "May Christ dwell in your hearts through faith" (Eph. 3:17), "until Christ is formed in you" (Gal. 4:19). A comparison to a photograph: the image of Jesus will be printed in my heart, to remain there always.

A comparison to a burning-glass: my heart within is like a concave lens, receiving the rays of Jesus, the sun, and focusing them on the soul to make it burn like the seraphim.

(12) Jesus dwells in the house of my heart, cast there as in the cave at Bethlehem. I am like a very poor child begging an alms of the infant Jesus.

(13) I am like a little black slave that waits on the white, shining, and ruddy infant Jesus. I tell Him as the child Samuel did, "Speak, Lord, your servant is listening," and like Saul, "Lord, what would you have me do?"

Lights and Graces (Spiritual Childhood)

"Unless you become as children."

A child in innocence, little in humility, an infant in silence, young in love, detachment, forgetfulness of wrongs, love for my Mother.

What will become of me? Unless I become like the Child Jesus, I will not enter the Kingdom of Heaven!

"He was subject to them." And you? Ah!

"And Jesus grew in wisdom, stature, and grace before God and men." And you? A mule!

I wouldn't give children coins because they would only waste them. I, too, have wasted the gifts of God. From now on I will be like St. Francis of Assisi, who told God that he would take good care of the goods He had given him, so as not to lose them. Like children who give their parents back their gifts for safekeeping, so as not to lose them.

September 20, 1866, at 11:45.

I told Jesus, "O Jesus, don't allow all you have suffered to be lost."

He answered, "It will not be lost; I love you dearly."

"I know," I said, "but I have been most ungrateful."

"Yes, I know. You have been very ungrateful."

This very morning I was thinking that I have been the most ungrateful person living on this earth.

B. *Apostolate during 1866*

I have busied myself giving retreats to the clergy and missions to the laity of the city (San Sebastian), all well attended and fruitful, thank God. I have also preached to the men and women of the St. Vincent de Paul Society and to the Nuns of St. Teresa. God has used me, his unworthy instrument, to set up the Confraternity of St. Aloysius Gonzaga to safeguard our young men, and the Daughters of Mary to safeguard our young women. I have put a fervent priest, fresh from the Spiritual Exercises, in charge of each of these societies. Many have entered and many more plan to do so. I have preached to both of them and given them Holy Communion. I also preached to the Daughters of Charity, to the many boys and girls cared for by the Sisters of Mercy, and to the sick, the elderly, and prisoners in jail. (September 5, 1866, *Correspondence*, Letter 1240.)

Publications for 1866: *The Temple and Palace of the Lord Our God; The Virgin of the Pillar at Zaragoza; Catechism of Christian Doctrine; Practical Method for Making a Good Confession; The Unity of the Catechism.*

C. *Resolutions for 1867*

Resolutions for the Spiritual Exercises made at San Gabriel with the missionaries of Segovia, beginning August 26.

(8) I will strive to have inner peace. Hence, I will not lose my temper, or speak out, or pull a long face, or show any pain or displeasure for whatever is said against me or for whatever blame people may lay on me.

(9) I will think of everything that happens as coming from the hand of God, who tells me, "My son, I want you to do or suffer this just now." (Rodríguez, vol. 1, p. 380.)

(10) I will suffer everything with patience, delight, and joy because it is the will of God, who sees how I suffer, and bear up under work, scorn, sorrow, slander, and persecution.

(15) I will frequently read Rodríguez, Treatise 5, chap. 16, especially the last paragraph where it says, "It is a very slight thing that disturbs and disquiets you and makes you turn back."

St. Michael of the Saints fervently prayed to God for two things: (a) to let him feel all the sufferings of the martyrs; (b) to grant him all the love of the angels and saints. The violence of his sufferings never brought the slightest sigh or moan to his lips.

D. Lights and Graces, 1867

August 27, 1867. I know that I am like an old, unfinished beam set against the wall of Her Majesty's palace, to prevent it from falling. Hence, I will not ask either to stay or to go but will only say, "May God's will be done in me."

I will maintain a holy indifference, always ready to do what God wants of me.

"My son, you know the worth of the Holy Cross and the honor it bestows on trials and tribulations that are embraced."

"Love is as strong as death."

St. Stephen, immovable in the midst of his many enemies, always kept peace in his heart and serenity on his face, which seemed to all who saw him like the face of an angel. God chose to show the beauty and innocence of his soul through this outer splendor. (Croisset, December 26.)

When the Blessed Virgin Mary lost her most holy Son, she did not lose inner or outer peace or have a single thought of anger or indignation. (*Mystical City of God,* vol. 4, p. 249.)

E. Lights and Graces, 1868

Today, June 22, 1868, marks two years since the barricading of Madrid; the fact that we were not killed was a miracle. I spent the day in the vestry of the chapel of the Virgin of Montserrat.

Today, June 22, at 9:30 at night, I went to visit the Blessed Sacrament in the Chapel of the Abandoned. The grating was closed and I saw a great resplendent light near the light from the sanctuary lamp. After a long time it fused with the light of the lamp and disappeared. Now I think I know what it meant.

Afterward, my dreams and desires turned all night on the thought of martyrdom. Beside the light there were also three black shapes in the form of men. These were the three demons or enemies that meant to kill me. I have a great desire to suffer martyrdom.

F. Exile

In San Sebastian we had already boarded the train for Madrid, but after sitting there for a long time, we had to return to our lodgings because of a dispatch that the minister received from Madrid. On the following day we were ordered to head for France. That day I started meditating on the Flight of Jesus, Mary, and Joseph into Egypt and joined the Holy Family in spirit. After a stay of five weeks in Pau, we moved on to Paris, where we have been for a month now. Just think of God's Providence! Let us praise the mercies of the Most High! The Holy

Family had to face privations, suffering, and labors, while this poor sinner has nothing but comforts and conveniences. The only thing that saddens me is the thought of the Holy Family in such suffering and myself in such delight. I can assure you that I have never in my life known so much help and care. This pains me and it is the only suffering I know.

I am lodged in a house belonging to the Sisters of St. Joseph (even this makes me think of the Holy Family). These sisters are dedicated to the education of young girls; they have 103 resident students and still more non-residents. There are 43 sisters. There is a corridor from my room to the church. Every day I say Mass for the Community and give them Communion frequently. After my Mass, Father Lawrence, my chaplain, says his. I and those who have received Communion attend it in thanksgiving. After this, I have breakfast. I have lunch at 12:30 and a light meal at night. The sisters cook and Brother Joseph serves at table.

The royal family is staying presently at the Hotel de Rohan, some distance from my lodgings. Every Sunday morning the queen sends her coach for me, and at 10:30 we all go to Mass at St. Germain. Since it is the principal Mass, services last until about noon. Every Monday and Thursday I teach the prince and the infantas. I spend the rest of my time in the ministry, as I did in Madrid. (*Correspondence,* Letter 1386.)

G. Resolutions Made in France during the Retreat of November 24–December 3, 1868

(11) While dressing in the morning I will think of the Incarnation, in which our Lord put on our nature, and I will thank God for it.

(12) While undressing at night I will think of death, and my bed will remind me of my burial.

(13) While in bed I will turn my heart toward the nearest church, to think about our Lord in the Blessed Sacrament, asking the angels to watch for me so that, while I do God's will in sleeping, my heart may keep vigil.

(14) God wants me to eat and sleep not as a luxury, but as a necessity and for my humiliation, so that I can see how poor I am to still be needing such worldly things, whereas in heaven there will be no need to eat or sleep. And so I say, "Lord, I do these things because it is your will."

(16) For each day's spiritual reading, a chapter from Rodríguez. Meditation on the Passion of our Lord Jesus Christ, from La Puente. Particular examen on the love of God. Ejaculatory prayers. Do and suffer all for the love of God.

To persevere and advance in perfection:
1. Well made mental prayer.
2. Turning to God frequently to ask his help and thank Him for it.
3. Mortification of the senses, faculties, and passions.

318

4. Frequent reception of the sacraments.

5. Mass both celebrated and attended.

6. Well recited rosary.

7. Deep humility, like that of the publican and sinner.

8. Fervor, like that of the vinedressers.

Virtues. Love of God and Jesus Christ.

Grace. Devotion to the Blessed Virgin Mary. *Ave, gratia plena.*

I should weed out the roots of faults, flee from the occasions of faults, and remove obstacles to the occasions of virtue.

"Charity is a virtue that is essentially aimed at action" (St. Thomas IIa–IIae, qu. 24, art. 4, ad 3).

Make frequent acts of love.

My God, you are all-powerful; make me holy. I love you with all my heart.

Publications for 1868: *Appreciating Time; Doctrinal Talks.*

H. Confessor to the Queen

(*Editor's note:* Eight small folded pages, of which Father Clotet writes: "Father Puig thinks that he [Claret] wrote them in Paris, before leaving for Rome in 1869, both because of the handwriting and because they had talked about it.")

(1) Sacrifices I have made to please Her Majesty.

After a stay of six years and three months in Santiago, Cuba, I had to resign from my diocese and was made titular Bishop of Trajanopolis, although to this day the government has not given me the Bull of my appointment.

Formerly my yearly salary and rights came to 25,000 duros in all. After my resignation I was assigned 6,000, which I have always had trouble collecting and with a loss of 10 percent in the transaction.

At the outbreak of the September, 1868 revolution, the provisional government canceled my salary and I have received none since.

As soon as the banker heard that we were in France, he wrote my last monthly allotments off as a loss.

Before I was ordained I received my first benefice from the community of Sallent, which provided me with sufficient canonical support to be ordained. When I was consecrated Archbishop, I had to renounce my benefice, so that I am now without diocese, without benefice, and without support.

When Father Dionisio grew ill, I asked Her Majesty to let me go live at the Escorial or resign from its presidency. I resigned. True, I didn't make anything as president, but at least it offered me the possibility of room and board. Now I have nothing—not even a stone on which to lay my head.

I was also Guardian of the hospital and church of Montserrat in Madrid. When I was put in charge of that establishment, I spent 6,000 duros of my savings from Cuba. Since the revolution I am no longer Guardian, as I have been informed in the following lines: "You have been relieved, by your voluntary abandonment, of the post of Guardian of the hospital and church of Montserrat." So now I have neither house to live in, church to say Mass in, or confessional in which to hear the confessions of the faithful who call on me.

When Her Majesty appointed me her confessor, she assigned me a yearly allotment of 3,000 duros, which was always paid; but now, because of the present difficulties, I receive only half of this.

(2) Duties I have performed.

The only title and duty I have is that of confessor and director to Her Majesty, Queen Isabel II.

I believe that with God's help I have fulfilled this single obligation to the best of my knowledge and ability. For this service alone I have been retained. I have prayed constantly for the well-being of the queen, the king, and the whole royal family.

Not out of obligation, but only out of good will, and without once asking for or wanting the least remuneration, I have also been professor of religion and morality, confessor and director of the Infanta Isabel from the time she was five years old until she was married, and even after her marriage. I am pleased in the Lord that she has turned out to be a lady of such learning, religion, and virtue that she is a credit to her parents and the Spanish people and the admiration of all foreigners.

The prince received his first lessons in religion and morality from me and even now I am his instructor in these important matters.

The three infantas, Pilar, Paz, and Eulalia, have received their instruction in religion and morality from me and will continue to do so if that is the will of God and Their Majesties.

(3) Tasks and trials I have suffered.

The tasks and trials that I have had to suffer during these years are such that only God and I know them, for I have borne them and continue bearing them.

My character and lively disposition have always drawn me away from the palace; my leaning was always toward the missions. Nevertheless, to please Her Majesty I have submitted and done violence to myself.

I have had to put up with all sorts of dishonor, slander, mockery, and persecution, which often went as far as threats against my life. I have been the target of lampoons, caricatures, and ridiculous and debasing photographs.

Formerly I was admired, appreciated, and even praised by all; today, with very few exceptions, everyone hates me and says that Father

Claret is the worst man there has ever been and that he is the cause of all Spain's ills.

V. The First Vatican Council
A. *Impressions from Claret's Correspondence*

On April 24 [1869], I saw the Supreme Pontiff, the immortal Pius IX. We had arrived in Rome on April 2, and on April 3 I petitioned for an audience. On April 11 I attended Mass with the other bishops and, because many outsiders had come to see the Pope, I was in hopes that I could talk with him again at greater length. Well, in fact I have spoken with him at length and he was most kind and consoling. He told me, "*Caro mio,* I know the slanders and evil things that have been said against you. I have read them." Then he began to quote the Scriptures and give me reasons for consolation; but, thank God, I was and am at peace. (Letter 1409, to Xifré, May 2, 1869.)

They want me by all means to be present and to take an active part in the Council. (Letter 1414.)

When my turn came to speak I told him, "Holy Father, the disciple should not be more respected than his teacher, nor the servant than his master." On hearing me say this, and seeing my tranquility, the Pope manifested the joy he felt in his heart and we went on to talk of other matters.

This climate simply doesn't suit me. I have been here three times: the first time, I got sick; the second, I didn't feel well all three weeks I was here; the third, which has already been four months, I have suffered a great deal.

My occupations have been and are the sacred ministry. Today I am very busy with preparations for the Council. As I have been to and seen so many places, I am asked a lot of questions on different details, and this keeps me very busy. I hope for some great results from this Council; you will doubtless remember what I wrote in my book, *Notes for a Plan to Preserve the Beauty of the Church.*

It can be said that the Lord's designs for me have been accomplished. Blessed be God. I hope that what I have done will have been pleasing to God. (Letter 1419, to Mother Antonia Paris, Rome, July 21, 1869.)

I have been very busy preparing material for the Council. I have also written a Life of St. Peter of Nolasco, at the request of Father Reix, and he has had it translated into Italian.

I have also written a work on the divinity of Jesus Christ and another on the rosary.

There are many who are looking for material goods to come out of the Council, as the Jews had worldly expectations of the Messiah. I am looking for spiritual goods: to know what we can rely on. I am hoping that the Council and its teaching will be a searchlight to show us a safe haven amid the storm and tempest that is still mounting and spreading. Alas for the earth!

I have suffered more than usual and have felt a deep desire to die. It seems to me that I have fulfilled my mission. In Paris and in Rome I have preached God's Law: Paris, the capital of the world and Rome, the capital of Catholicism. I have done this both by word of mouth and by writing. I have observed holy poverty in what concerns me and today, thank God, I receive nothing from the diocese of Cuba or the queen. (Letter 1425, to Curríus, October 2, 1869.)

The Council has begun and is going well, thank God. The sessions are being held in one of the side chapels of the Vatican that has been prepared for them. The benches are placed in a semicircle, and during the sessions the doors connecting the chapel with the body of the church are closed. On Sundays we meet in the Vatican Choir for High Mass and a sermon in Latin. We also meet in the synodal hall of the palace, in the Pope's presence. Moreover, all the Spanish bishops meet in the house of the Cardinal Archbishop of Valladolid to discuss those matters that affect our country.

At the Council we are seated according to the date of our consecration. I am number 40—one of the old timers. (Letter 1431.)

I have been very busy. Almost every day we have a session either in the Council chamber or in the Pope's chapel. I leave the house before 8:00 and don't get home until 2:00 in the afternoon and, at times, my head feels like a bomb. On the twenty-ninth of this past May, I had something like a stroke. (Letter 1446.)

There are two main causes for this latest trouble I've been feeling: first, the extraordinary heat at the beginning of this summer; second, the business of the Council itself, especially the matter of the Church and the Pope. Because I can't bear that anyone or anything should trespass in this matter—I'd gladly shed my blood for it, as I said in open session—when I heard the errors and even heresies and blasphemies that were being spoken on it, I was so overcome by indignation and zeal that the blood rushed to my head and affected my brain. My mouth wouldn't hold back the saliva and it ran down my face, especially on the side where I have the scar from the wound I received in Cuba. Besides this, my speech is greatly slurred. I have undergone all the treatments ordered by the doctor and they have brought me considerable relief. (Letter 1451.)

The labors and fatigues of the Council have kept me very busy upholding and defending the rights of the Church and the Holy Father. In the presence of all the patriarchs, archbishops, and bishops, in full session, I stated from the pulpit that I was ready to give my life's blood for this cause. My words made a deep impression, as did those of all the Spanish bishops, all of whom have behaved admirably. An English archbishop [Cardinal Manning] came to see me and told me, "It may be said that the Spanish bishops are the Pope's Imperial Guard." May it all be for the greater glory of God. My health has been somewhat affected by it all. (Letter 1447, to Mother Paris.)

With the Lord's help I am disposed and resigned to God's will, whether He gives me good health or this indisposition (not to mention that of the hernia, which often causes me a great deal of suffering); even if He should choose to send me death, I put myself entirely in his holy hands. (Letter 1451, July 1870, to Xifré.)

B. Resolutions for 1869 and 1870

Resolutions of the retreat made in Rome, October 5–14, 1869
1. Every year I will make the Spiritual Exercises.
2. Every month I will make a day of recollection on the twenty-fifth.
3. Every week I will go to confession.
4. Every week I will fast and deprive myself of something on Wednesday, Friday, and Saturday.
5. I will practice mortification by using the discipline, cilice, or their equivalent, on the six weekdays.
6. I will mortify my senses, faculties, and passions.
7. I will strive to keep inward peace without growing angry or being displeased with anything.
8. I will consider that God is always in my heart. "The God of my heart and my portion forever" (Ps. 13:26). "Not my will, but thine be done." "Teach me to do your will, for you are my God."
9. I will strive to walk always in the presence of God, doing and suffering everything for love of Him.
10. At prayer I will meditate on the mysteries of the rosary. The same at Little Hours, Vespers, etc.
11. Every day I will say the three parts of the rosary.
12. I will constantly remember "two years and ten months."[1]
13. I will never say a word of self-praise.
14. I will strive to do ordinary things as perfectly as possible through God and the B.V.M.
15. Every Sunday I will read these resolutions in order to fulfill them better.
16. I will say frequently, "Long live Jesus; death to sin; death to self-love, the enemy of the love of God."
Self-love and egoism are but pride and sensuality.

---

1. This laconic expression appears first in his retreat resolutions for 1868 and would seem to indicate that he had received a knowledge of the exact time of his death.

Things I will impress upon people "in season and out of season":
1. To recite the rosary well
2. To attend Mass well on holy days of obligation and on other days as well, out of devotion
3. To visit the Blessed Sacrament
4. To receive the Blessed Sacrament not only at Easter but frequently throughout the year and to make even more frequent spiritual communions
5. How to walk in the presence of God
6. How to do ordinary things well
7. How to make a good spiritual examen
8. How to practice spiritual reading
9. How to practice mental and vocal prayer
10. How to offer all things to God
11. To confess frequently.

My particular examen will be on:
1. The love of God. The virtue I will always practice and ask for will be the love of God and neighbor, remembering what St. Teresa says.
2. The grace I will ask for will be devotion to the Blessed Virgin Mary.
3. Familiar conversations with the sick in hospitals for the poor and in military hospitals.

In the street or wherever the occasion presents itself, my subject will be religion, the sacraments, the holy rosary, etc. I will speak to all as the opportunity presents itself, but especially to boys and girls, giving them a medal, a holy card, etc.

Resolutions for 1870

For the glory of God, the good of souls, and my own mortification, I resolve:
1. Always to speak in Italian or else be silent, except when speaking with Brother Joseph, in sermons, or with any Spaniard who comes to see me.
2. To visit the Blessed Sacrament every day.
3. To visit hospitals for the poor and the military every Wednesday.
4. "In whatever you do, remember your last days, and you will never sin.
   "In every work and at every hour, examine your conscience and, once you have discovered some fault, strive to correct it with God's help, and in this manner you will reach perfection" (St. Teresa, *Counsels,* p. 591).
5. "What you meditate on in the morning, keep in mind all day long" (Ibid., p. 31).

6. "Never stop humbling and mortifying yourself until you die" (Ibid., p. 50).
7. "Always make many acts of love, because they inflame and touch the soul" (Ibid., p. 51).
8. "Train yourself in the fear of God, for it makes for a contrite and humbled soul" (Ibid., p. 63).

Homage

As a homage to the Blessed Trinity and the Blessed Virgin Mary, during the month of May, I offer each and every thing I may do. The impelling cause will be the love of God.

The intentional cause will be God's greater glory. The end cause will be the will of God. I will be very intent and most careful, doing everything in fully conscious imitation of Mary. I will do each particular thing well, even the commonest and most ordinary.

Not only will I remember what Jesus suffered every hour of his life, but in everything I do I will recall what Jesus did and how He did it, so that I may imitate Him both as to the intention He had in acting and the perfection with which He carried it out.

On waking in the morning, I will remember how Jesus awoke and offered Himself to the eternal Father. I will get up promptly and offer myself and all my works to God. At prayer I will think of how Jesus used to pray.

May 26, 1870, feast of the Lord's Ascension.
1. The earth will be an exile to me. My thoughts, feelings, and sighs will be directed toward heaven.
2. "Our conversation is in heaven." I will neither speak of or listen to anything except what concerns God or leads to heaven.
3. My desire is to die, in order to go to heaven and be united to God. "I desire to be dissolved and to be with Christ." Like the Blessed Virgin Mary, my sweet Mother.
4. I have to be like a candle that burns and spends its wax and light until it goes out. The members of the body seek to be united to their head, iron filings are drawn to the magnet, and I want to be united with Jesus in the Eucharist and in heaven.

"One beholder loves God more," says St. Bonaventure, "than a thousand wayfarers."

VI. Concerning the Congregation of Missionaries
A. *In Connection with the Revolution of 1868*

Selections from the *Correspondence* of Claret

Let us give thanks to God. The Lord and the Blessed Virgin Mary have graciously accepted the first fruits of our martyrs. I had desired to be the first martyr for the Congregation, but I have not been worthy of it and another has gained the upper hand on me. I congratulate our martyr and saint, Crusats, and send best wishes to Father Reixach for his good fortune in being wounded, and to all the members of the Congregation for their honor in being persecuted. Courage and trust in the Sacred Hearts of Jesus and Mary. Storms and hurricanes can't last forever; after them comes a calm. Let everyone pray a great deal; that is what we need most at present. Let everyone trust in Jesus and Mary; they are our parents. (Letter 1376, October 7, 1868, to Father Xifré.)

As far as possible see to it that the priests live together in groups of two, with one or two brothers to cook for them. Let them live as if they were in a mission house, keeping the Rule and recollection. In the various towns they are staying in, let them busy themselves hearing confessions, encouraging and counseling the faithful, and exhorting them to pray and frequent the sacraments.

All that I have, I leave to the Congregation—it is all at your disposal to pay for travel, rent, and food. Have faith and trust in Jesus and Mary. I, thank God, am quite content and in good spirits, even happy. I reflect on the fact that God is so wise, good, and powerful that out of these trials He can bring great good to the Congregation. As you know, St. Luke, whose feast it is today, talks of the sower who plants his field. The wheat springs up beautifully and grows so well that the whole field looks like one great carpet of green. But a strong wind has blown out of the north, bringing with it such a cruel frost that the wheat leaves have been scorched by it. And, as if this were not enough, a great blanket of snow has covered the field completely. The hireling will be frightened, but the sower trusts that the snow will melt and that the cold will give way to fair weather. Then it will be perfectly clear that all these adversities have only made the wheat strike deeper roots and the stalks bear fuller ears of grain. (Letter 1378, October 18, 1868, to Father Xifré.)

Jesus Christ told his beloved disciples, "Watch and pray, lest you enter into temptation." I tell all of you to do the same. Watch and pray, lest you falter in your vocation. If any of you fail, it will be your own fault, for not praying. God keeps his promise, says St. Paul, and He will not allow the temptation to exceed his grace, which He gives us so that we may resist and be all the better off because of that very temptation. But we must ask this grace of the Lord through the intercession of the Blessed Virgin Mary. (Letter 1391, January 2, 1869.)

B. The Apostolate of Christian Education

The Lord has permitted us to suffer this persecution, not to exterminate the Congregation, but to make it grow and expand. Just as the snow I wrote you about last year falls on the field but does not kill the wheat, but only makes it strike deeper roots, so the revolution will not kill the Congregation, but will only make it better rooted and more productive.

All members must keep the Rules and Constitutions as perfectly as they can. "This is the will of God, your sanctification."

They should bear in mind what paragraph 63 (chap. 16) says and reflect on the words, "to catechize children, the poor and the ignorant." To accomplish this they should have schools for boys like those of the Christian Brothers, who have so many of them in France and Italy, and are doing a great deal of good. I believe that at the present time they are doing the most good for the Church and offer it the best expectations.

God and the Blessed Virgin have reserved this as a special mission for the Congregation in Spain. I by no means intend to imply that everybody be employed in such schools. I only mean that a few—a very few—be appointed to do this work, in view of their zeal or at their request.

These schools will grow to the degree that they correspond with grace. God and the Blessed Virgin will attract the proper workers so that, without losing sight of their primary object, they will dedicate themselves to this new branch: "You should practice these, without neglecting the others."

A very zealous person worked very hard to bring some members of the Congregation of Doctrine from France, but he failed to do so because the Lord and the Virgin have set this work aside for our Congregation, and I trust in Our Lord and Our Lady that the members will not turn a deaf ear to this call.

Don't be alarmed, now, and start thinking that everyone must be set to teaching. I have already told you how to go about it.

God and the Blessed Virgin will inspire you to know what to do. But if someone does not like this sort of work, I beg you not to make him do it. Leave him in peace; otherwise he will be overcome by sadness, he'll be like an apple with a worm in its core: a blast of wind hits it and it falls from the tree. So if someone like this were to fall from the tree of the Congregation, it wouldn't be surprising. But don't let that stop you. Take heart; God and the Virgin will not abandon their work.

P.S. With these schools our members will find favor in God's eyes and men's; without them they will always be slandered and persecuted by the vicious, who want to sin and don't like anyone reprehending them for it. As Gerson says, working with adults involves two very hard and sometimes fruitless tasks; but working with children involves just one task and one that ordinarily is of great profit and importance. Nevertheless, let them bear in mind the words of chapter 7, paragraph 18, on chastity. They need not admit all the children in town, but only those who.... (Letter to Xifré, July 16, 1869.)

C. *Expansion of the Congregation*

I am pleased that you have agreed to let some members of our Congregation go to Africa. Perhaps in time they will be able to found another house there.

Concerning Mexico, I will speak with the archbishop, who is a friend of mine and is presently here [in Rome]. However, according to the last reports I heard, no cleric or friar is allowed to wear the cassock in public there, and no more than three are allowed to a house.

There is more freedom in other republics. Chile is the best in this respect. In Guatemala I have a very good and zealous Capuchin friend. As regards expanding in the Americas, I have been giving it a good deal of thought and commending it to God. (Letter 1416, July 4, 1869.)

I am delighted to hear that you have undertaken a foundation in Chile; the Holy Father will be pleased, too.... America is a great and fertile field, and in time more souls will enter heaven from America than from Europe. This part of the world is like an old vine that bears little fruit, whereas America is a young vine. I have been pleased with my visits and dealings with the bishops who have come from over there. They are well educated and virtuous and have inspired great hopes in me. I've already grown old—I'll be celebrating my sixty-second birthday, Christmas. Even more than old age, the rupture has discouraged me. All we need now is for the weather to change and I'll be at death's door. If it weren't for this, I'd fly there myself. But since I can't go myself, I visit the American College here in Rome. (Letter 1428, November 16, 1869.)

D. *Mary and the Claretian Apostolate*

(*Editor's note:* This note was found among Claret's sermons on Mary. He had probably written it to preach to his missionaries in Prades, before seeking refuge at Fontfroide. Given his usual neatness and correctness, the handwriting is very careless. The "soul" he refers to is doubtless himself. He had always felt that he was Mary's instrument in the apostolate and often referred to himself as her arrow. The symbolism in this note is much more daring, and the identification with Mary is much closer. Mary's maternal activity in the Church must be made visible in the activity of the missionaries. *End of editor's note.*)

On Ascension Day, 1870, a devout soul was kneeling before the altar of the Blessed Virgin Mary, from 11:00 to noon, meditating on the mystery of the day, when it came to him that the Sons of the Congregation are like Mary's arms and that they must, by their zeal, draw everyone to Mary: the good, so that they may persevere in grace; sinners, so that they may be converted.

Jesus is the head of the Church; Mary is its neck, and what is most immediate about her is her heart.

The arms of Mary are the Missionaries of her Congregation who will work zealously, hold everyone in their embrace, and pray to Jesus and Mary. The Blessed Virgin Mary will use them as her arms and maternal breasts, to feed her little ones, as a mother would seek out the services of a wet nurse. Yes, the Missionaries are wet nurses, who must feed the poor at the breasts of wisdom and love, and provide for them equally from these two breasts. Thus, like good and healthy mothers, they must see to it that they, too, eat frequently—both for themselves and for the sake of those they have to feed, just as all good nurses do. The food they must take is prayer—mental, vocal, and ejaculatory—and spiritual reading, moral theology, dogma, and sermons.

E. Parting Words to the Congregation

(*Editor's note:* Claret, persecuted in France by agents of the Spanish revolution, was forced to take refuge in the Cistercian monastery of Fontfroide, but he felt that even there his presence might endanger his missionaries and the monks, and so he had decided to return to Rome. Neither Father Xifré nor the monks would hear of it, both because they were aware of his ill health and because the climate of Rome had never agreed with him. The broken, mysterious quality of his phrases reveals something of the agony of his utterly generous spirit. *End of editor's note.*)

I am still of the opinion I spoke to you about on the night we left Prades, namely, that I should go to Rome. I can't be of any help to you, nor you to me. On the contrary, I believe that we will be prejudicial to one another, without wanting or intending to do so. I am a mysterious being...like a refugee...like a fugitive from justice, and what's worse, I don't know how long this can go on.

Hence, I have resolved to depart....

If you wish to bid me a final farewell, I will wait for you; if not, let this be my farewell to you and all the members of the Congregation. (Letter 1452, August 15, 1870, to Father Xifré.)

VII. Death

The following are excerpts from *The Admirable Life of Archbishop Claret* by Father Jaime Clotet, C.M.F., paragraphs 333–350, inclusive.

333 Let us return to the Spanish Missionaries' house in Prades, in the Eastern Pyrenees of France, where Archbishop Claret stayed shortly before his death. One day he called in one of the fathers of the Communi-

ty to give him an assignment and remarked to him that the end of his life was approaching.

334 When the father in question asked him what he thought about the events in Spain, he answered that the Spanish people would keep the faith through the intercession of the Blessed Virgin Mary, their Patroness.

335 Because it was well known that Father Claret never meddled in politics, one might have thought that he would be left in peace among his little band of followers. But this was not to be; rather, there was a movement afoot to imprison him. When the Bishop of Perpignan and other friends learned of this, they arranged to spirit him out of Prades into refuge at the monastery of Fontfroide. When the archbishop received the sad news of his forced departure, he said with great resignation, "May God be blessed and praised!" On leaving for his solitary retreat, the only things he packed were two pairs of socks, a shirt, and some handkerchiefs, as he used to do when he was going out to preach a mission.

336 This happened on August 6, 1870. The police arrived at the mission house just a few hours after the archbishop's departure.

337 After his arrival at the monastery of Fontfroide, despite his weakness he attended the conventual Mass every morning, and Vespers and Compline every evening. He also went down to the church frequently to visit Jesus in the Blessed Sacrament, to make the Stations of the Cross, or some other devotion. His main preoccupation was with the trials the Church was undergoing and the number of souls that were being led astray. He never bothered about his own misfortunes; he was completely forgetful of himself. No one ever heard him utter a complaint about anyone or express any resentment. He said that his glory and joy were in the Cross of Jesus Christ. He never ceased praying for his persecutors.

338 On September 4 a prediction he had made five years earlier was fulfilled, namely, that Napoleon III would suffer a humiliating downfall. When the French army was defeated in the war with Prussia, the French emperor was taken prisoner, losing both his liberty and his empire, and died in a foreign land. On the twentieth of this same month, another of Claret's predictions was fulfilled when the Italian army entered Rome.

339 Because his health had improved somewhat, he started work again on some of his projects but without lessening his devotional practices.

Even here, though, persecution sought him out. Having learned of his retirement to Fontfroide, the irreligious press began publishing furious articles against him, accusing him of plotting a conspiracy and of gathering firearms for the partisans of Don Carlos.

340 While the servant of God held his peace in his beloved solitude, preparing for the final struggle, he was struck by the illness that was to bring him to the grave. Toward the beginning of October, 1870, he had an attack of neuralgia. During the night of October 4 it grew so bad that neither he nor the chaplain attending him got any sleep. He got up the morning of the fifth, but he was so weak that he hardly had enough energy to move or enough appetite to eat anything. His condition was much worse on the eighth, and because he was aware of the gravity of his illness, he repeatedly asked to receive the sacraments. When he was told that two specialists from Narbonne had come to examine him, he answered that before he saw them he wanted to see to the needs of his soul, and he insisted on receiving the sacraments. After making his confession, he received Viaticum, with admirable faith, piety, and fervor, from the hands of Father Xifré, the Superior General of the Congregation.

341 The illness ran on with many ups and downs, and some of his crises were so severe that the prayers for the dying were said over him five different times.

342 Even in the midst of these sad events, a band of republicans from Narbonne were planning to tear him away from his bed of pain and search the monastery for Carlist weapons; but God frustrated their ignoble designs.

343 The peace, joy, and fervor that he displayed during his last illness were admirable. He never tired of kissing the crucifix and uttering fervent prayers of aspiration.

344 Just before he began his last agony, aware that this crisis would be his last, he asked one of the fathers who was watching over him to give him absolution. Making the sign of the cross, striking his breast, kissing the crucifix devoutly, and repeating some prayers of aspiration, he entered his last, long, and sorrowful struggle. At last, holding the crucifix in his hands, in a state of imperturbable peace, he gently gave up his spirit to the Lord. It was 8:45 on the morning of October 24. His last moments were those of a saint.

345 His sickroom became an oratory as a constant file of monks came to pray beside his body. On the following day his body was moved to

the church, where it lay in state until the twenty-seventh, the day of his burial. On the day of his death and on the day following the sky was lit by the aurora borealis.

346 During these days it was noted that his body kept its flexibility. All the monks and their guests kept kissing his ring and his feet.

347 On Thursday the twenty-seventh, at the beginning of the fourth day after his death, his funeral service began. During the Solemn Mass, a bird appeared to join the choir and seemed to provide the accompaniment used at solemn funerals. While the celebrant sang, the bird stopped singing. He flew down from the gothic arches of the church, came to rest upon the earthly remains of the saintly archbishop, and disappeared at the end of Mass.

348 Before the body was placed in the coffin in which it was to be carried to the grave, it was noticed that the body had still not lost its flexibility.

349 His body was buried in the monks' cemetery because civil authorities would not grant a permit for interment in the church.

350 Because bishops and archbishops are princes of the Church, their funerals are usually solemnized with a cortege of illustrious personages, military bands, and a sermon preached by an eloquent orator. The burial of Father Claret, once Archbishop of Cuba and confessor to the queen, had a cortege of three humble Spanish missionaries and three French priests; the music was that of a bird's song; the silent funeral oration was that of the profound reverence of the bystanders. The following epitaph, the last words of Pope St. Gregory VII, was inscribed on his tombstone: "I have loved justice and hated iniquity; therefore I die in exile."

INDEX

Numbers refer to paragraphs
in the *Autobiography*.
For Supplementary Readings,
consult *Contents.*

Abandonment: of Christ on the cross, 653; to the will of God, 885; Cf. Resignation.

Abstinence: Cf. Fasting, Mortification.

Academy of St. Michael: original idea for, 581; approval, organization, members, 332; king and queen charter members, 582; distributes books, 640; Claret designs emblem of A., 581, 701.

Account of conscience, 757-767, 768-774, 775-779, 796-801.

Adoain, Stephen, O.F.M.Cap. (co-worker), 514, 516, 595, 598, 599.

Adversities: for our good, 125; providential, 138, 166, 167; Cf. Sufferings, Troubles, Sickness, Humiliations.

"Advice to" series: why he wrote series, 475; to various classes of people, 313-314.

Agriculture: efforts on its behalf in Cuba, 566-567; he himself plants trees, 567; writes book, *Delights of the Country,* 568.

Alms: generosity in giving, 133-134; to prisoners, 570; to the sick, 571; books as the greatest alms, 328.

Aloysius Gonzaga, St., 91, 102, 781.

Alphonsus Liguori, St., 294, 300, 654.

America, 596, 605.

Amigó, Anthony, Oratorian, 69, 85.

——, **Joseph,** pastor of Sallent, 23.

Angels: guardian a. in temptations, 95; in Marseilles, 127; aid and protection of a., 269; during missions, 464; a. of kingdoms, cities, etc., 268; aspiration to the a., 269; devotion to St. Michael, patron of Academy of St. M. and Religious Library, 329, 332; nine choirs of a., 654.

Animals, domestic: symbolic examples of virtue, 664-673, 380.

Anthony of Padua, St., 102, 226.

Antonelli, Cardinal, 845.

Apostle: Claret as a. aboard ship, 130; studies ills of society, 357; yearning for apostolate, 113, 638, 728; commitment to apostolic life, 153, 156, 161; a. of Mary, 159, 160, 163; a. of the rosary, 677; a. of the pen, 705 (Cf. Writer, Books); Cf. Apostolate, Zeal, Missionary, Preacher.

Apostles: inspiration for his apostolate, 223; great zeal of, 223-224; prayer to, 654.

Apostolate: —*Qualities of:* continual, 111; combines work and total trust in God, 274; manifold a.: preaching, hearing confessions, distributing Communion, 589; a. "in season and out of season," on all occasions, 335-336, 461, 509; Cf. Conversations. —*End and motives of a.:* directed to sinners, the just, souls in purgatory, 264-265; four motives, 202-213; salvation from eternal punishment, 1-17, 751; compassion for sinners,

333

Index

Barjau, Anthony (co-worker), 502, 514, 526-527, 556, 588, 599, 600.

Bertríu, Ignacio (co-worker), 502, 575, 605.

Bible: love of, 113-120, 132, 151; daily reading of, 637, 645; well-spring of his apostolate, 113-120; heard God's call through B., 114, 120; the Lord explains verse from Isaiah, "The Spirit of the Lord is upon me...," 118; harm of not knowing the B. (St. Teresa), 254; would rather read B. than current events, 399; distributes B., 799, 113.1.

Bishops: Claret's role in election of Spanish B., 630.

Bonet, Gregory (co-worker), 502, 603.

Books: publishes his first b., 313; his b. written on basis of needs in ministry, 315; only God knows how he could write so many, 324; the most productive b. he wrote, 323; should be small and manageable, 312; he distributed b. everywhere, 333, 544-545; b., the best alms, 328; his aim in publishing b., 42, 312, 325, 328, 475; b. are food for the souls, 311; usefulness and need of b., 311; advantages of b. over preaching, 310.

Bres, Fortián (protector), 34.

Brunelli, Msgr., papal nuncio to Madrid, 495, 500, 862.

Bruno, St., 88, 499.

Caixal, Joseph (friend and co-worker), 329, 476.

Calumnies: Cf. Slander.

Canary Islands: voyage to C., 701, 861; his going there providential, 477; missions in public square, 481; preaches in all parishes, 480; plan for hearing mass confessions, 482; escort and reception, 483; example of not traveling on foot, 484-485; coat torn five times by crowds, 486; return to Spain, 486; praise to God for journey, 487; Cf. Missions.

Capuchins, 595, 598, 601.

Cards, holy: means of apostolate to children, 275; distributed during pastoral visitation of Cuba, 545; conversion through, 707.

Carmel, Our Lady of: member of Confraternity of O.L.M.C., 94; devotion to, 765; Congregation of Missionaries founded on feast of O.L.M.C., 490.

Carthusians: his desire to become one, 77-82, 88-89, 499; means to detach him from the world, 113; how they obtained vocations, 793.

Casadevall, Luciano, Bishop of Vich, 489, 499, 104.2.

Catechism: his attendance at and love for, 23-26; never missed, 39; taught c., 106, 109, 284; explication of c., 170, 284; taught c. in Cuba, 562; orders pastors to teach c., 559; memorized c. as a child, 23, 26-27; CCD, 560; Claret's method of catechizing, 286; had Cuban seminarians teach c., 560; catechism books for all ages, 285; *The Catechism Explained,* first book issued by Religious Library, 476, 799; usefulness of c. and need to know it, 26-27; tool against irreligion, 735; basis of all religious instruction, 275; most useful tool in adult instruction because most needed, 287; useful at all times and in preaching, 288; teaches c. to prisoners in Cuba, 570; Claret's lifelong dedication to catechizing children, 284; first thing he did during a mission, 275; children learn easily, are preserved from error, grow in virtue, and influence adults, 275; Christ's example, 276; the Apostles' example, 277; Blessed John of Avila and his disciples, 280; example of Saints and Doctors of the Church, 277-283; Brothers of Christian Doctrine, 282; Claret teaches c. to Infanta Isabel, 614; drawings for catechism, 56.

Catherine of Siena, St., 212, 235-236, 741, 781.

Chant, Ecclesiastical: why he wrote book on, 327.

smithy, 342; distraction and a swiftly turning wheel, 67; the sorrow of Jesus, 425; intense spirituality, 665; humility: the wheel without water, jumping into a pit but not being able to get out, the capstone of a building, 344, 346, 350; humility the root, meekness the fruit, 372; prayer as hunger and thirst, 444; meekness and catching fish, 373; preaching to sinners like cooking snails, 471; sinners like walnut-trees, need to be beaten, 536; religious truths like rosebuds, 26; an old servant in Mary's employ, 43; sadness like ballast against the winds of vanity, 353; vanity like a hen's cackling, 354, 401; poverty, the shortest string on the harp of virtue, 370; various virtues compared, 336.

Compassion: natural inclination to c., 9-10; c. for others, 129, 150; c. for sinners, 205-212; for those who weep, 173; for workers scolded, 32; Cf. Character, Souls, Zeal.

Conception, Immaculate: mentions the mystery, 154, 157, 273; celebration of I.C. in the Jesuit Novitiate, 142, 144; pastoral letters on, 549, 674.

Confession: weekly, 107; general c. to Fr. Bach, 85; twice a week, 86; resolution to confess at least once a week, 644, 740, 780; hears first confessions, 103; loves to hear confessions in spare time, 304; hears every day, 763, 777; not wasting time while hearing c., 263; method used in Canary Islands, 482; a woman converted, 828; confession of one of his slanderers, 829; repugnance to speak or hear about c., 402; various attacks against c., 811-812.

Confessor: assiduous: time he spent in confessional, 637, 646; bad effects of c. without meekness, 377; c. to ladies of court, 616; to palace servants, 778; to Infanta Isabel, 614, 616; to queen: election, 587-588; receives news of nomination, 614;

leaves Cuba to accept, 588; woman comes through heavy snow to confess to him, 827.

Congregation of Missionaries (Claretians): title, 1, 492, 686, 852; foundation of C., 488, 701; first Spiritual Exercises, 490; place of foundation, seminary of Vich, 488; advisers, Soler, Passarell, Bishop Casadevall, 488-489; cofounders, 489; all cofounders have persevered, 490; first days, 491; thanksgiving to God for, 492; thanksgiving to Heart of Mary, 493; advice on how to increase vocations, 793, 795.

Consolations: amid work in Canary Islands, 486; spiritual c. from the Lord, 675; Jesus is his consolation, 755; Cf. Mysticism.

Contempt: he seeks c., 666; asks the Lord to make him feel c. (maxim), 748; asks Blessed Virgin for a desire for c., 749; tolerates c. for the conversion of souls, 752; resignation when he is treated with c., 785; things that deserve c., 651; Cf. Humility, Slander.

Conversation: idle c. avoided, 399; c. against charity, about food, news, etc., 399; spiritual c., 153; everyday c. can do much good, 334; uses every occasion for c. about last things, 335-336; fireside chat converts a pastor, 335; using symbolism of flowers, etc., in c., 336; edifying c. while traveling, 336; evil c. avoided, 53.

Corcuera, Paul of Jesus, Bishop of Vich, 84, 855.

Court: moral reform at c., 769, 772; desire to leave c., 621, 623, 625, 632, 762; reason for wanting to leave c., 662; God wants him to stay, 623; edifying conduct of c., 616; a calvary for Claret, 620-621; the Lord orders him to leave, 832; Claret leaves, 837; nuncio counsels him, 845-851; resolves not to return, 852; Cf. Queen.

Sacrament, 39; aspirations to, 269; Eucharistic grace of conservation of species, 694; Blessed Virgin confirms reality of this grace, 700; Jesus speaks to him from Blessed Sacrament, 839; Cf. Communion, Jesus Christ, Mysticism.

Evangelists, 654.

Evangelization: Cf. Apostolate, Gospel.

Examen, Particular: practices it, 742; while in Madrid, 637, 646; time for p.e., 801; on the love of God, 801; on humility, for 15 years, 351; on meekness, 746, 782.

Example: of the saints, an incentive, 214-263; power of e., 23, 45, 53, 144, 146; apostolate of e. at banquets, 408-409; e. as warnings, 802-830; animals as e. of virtue, 664-763; Cf. Apostolate, Comparisons.

Exercises, Spiritual: before Holy Orders, 102; Ignatian, 306 ff.; first time he made them, 139; learned how to make them with Jesuits, 152; his novitiate copy reprinted in Vich, 307; begins them fervently, 165; edifying retreat in Cuba, 611; makes them with his household, 513; not aimed at sensible consolations, 102, 142; more solid, lasting effects than missions, 309; initiated and fostered humility in him, 342; good effects of, 737-738; books and pamphlets reinforce results of, 475; powerful means for the conversion of priests, 308; Claret makes them every year since he was a student, 92, 107, 138, 306, 611, 644, 740, 780, 787; Claret gives them, 800; in various shifts, 776, 852; to all walks of life, 305; to the clergy, 308, 474, 491, 497; commands Cuban clergy to make ten days of, 553; gives them to Cuban clergy annually, 512; in Puerto Príncipe, 525; in Bayamo, 528; in Madrid, 638; to priests and seminarians in Canary Islands, 480; priests and seminarians at Escorial, 737; to the queen, annually, 615, 768, 778; to

the Infanta Isabel, 614; queen's example in making S.E., 616; ladies of court make them annually, 778; Claret preaches S.E. to members of St. Vincent de Paul Society, 638; to separate groups of men and women, 309; to nuns, 263; to the nuns of Madrid, 638; to the Sisters of Perpetual Adoration, Piarists, Tertiaries, 776.

Exorcism: said before each mission, 273; prudence in using e., 183-191; many priests deceived in using e., 190; Cf. Possession.

Ezekiel, 119, 217, 662.

Fábregas, Dominic, C.M.F. (cofounder), 489, 489.2.

Faith: Claret prays for firmer f., 655; the Lord grants it, 681; Claret would give his lifeblood to defend the f., 467; bodily effects of f., 181; foundation in f., Cf. Upbringing; f. as motive for the apostolate, 11; fear of losing f., 157; f. and the Eucharist, 767.

Fasting: twice a week, 145; on vigils of our Lord and our Lady, 644; three times a week, 740, 759, 780; Cf. Mortification, Food.

Fervor: in his actions, 653; how he grew cold in f., 82.

Fidelity: in the service and love of God, 670.

Food: time and number of meals, 646; in Cuba, 610; reason for mortification in f. and drink, 403, 759; proper intention in eating, 744, 789; Claret eats little, 137, 745; eats what is set before him, 405; abstains from meat, wine, and liquor, 405; eats poor food, 132; in the palace, eats little to edify others, 408-409; eating on knees, 146; recommendation of Jesus and Mary that missionaries be mortified in f. and drink, 406; example that confirmed this teaching, 407; Cf. Fasting, Mortification.

sermons, 181, 231, 241; cases he dealt with, 802-822.
−*enemies* of the m.: the very knowledge of their existence, 116; slandered, as Jesus was, 201 (Cf. Slander); burdens he had to bear, 161; Cf. Apostolate, Zeal, Work.

Missionaries, Claretian: foundation of, 488-494; their prophetic mission in the world, 686; recommendation of Jesus and Mary for C.M., 406 f., 684; Cf. Congregation.

Missions: love and zeal for the m., 259-260; starts preaching m., 172, 291; names he had to give m., 292, 468.
−*obstacles* to m.: the irreligious and the government, 457, 459; evil environment, 459; diabolic persecution, 462-463; did not rashly expose himself to danger, 465; courage in the face of danger, 465-466; protected by Mary, angels, saints, 464; toilsome journeys on foot, 460.
−*methods* he used in m.: résumé of previous day's sermon, 293; gentle beginnings, 469-471; order of sermon topics, 456; method of hearing large numbers of confessions, 482.
−*burdens* during m.: both good and bad moments, 465; start of m. always accompanied by persecutions, 352-353.
−*results* of m.: conversion of M. Ribas, 472-473; means to achieve results, 475; cases he dealt with in ministry, 802-822.
−*to all classes* of people: priests, seminarians, nuns, 474 (Cf. Priest, Clergy, etc.); in Segovia, 407; in the Canary Islands, 481, 483, 486; in Cuba, 511, 522, 526, 587 (Cf. Archbishop); in Gerona, 497; en route to Cuba, 509; desires to go to foreign m., 111, 112; Cf. Missionary, Preacher, Apostolate, Zeal.

Model Ranch, in Puerto Príncipe, 563, 598.

Modesty: nature of, 387; involves words, deeds, manners, 384; m., a missionary virtue, 384-389; m. impossible without mortification, 390; how he strove to practice m., 385; resolves to practice m., 389; Jesus, model of m., 387; imitation of saints' m., 389, 393; sorrow for faults against m., 389; Cf. Mortification, Humility.

Montserrat (Monastery and Shrine of the Virgin), 329, 476, 500.

Montserrat (Hospital and Church in Madrid), 598, 635, 776.

Mortification: −*excellence* of m.: he glories in the Cross of Christ, 658; in one act of m., he can practice ten virtues, 414-415; value of suffering, 421; m. a property of strong and courageous souls, 417; a missionary virtue, 390-427; the greater the m., the brighter the virtue, 416; how worth of m. is to be measured, 418.
−*necessity* of m.: maxim, "Give me blood...," 413; impossible to be modest without m., 390; or to be perfect, 412; m. necessary if we are to help souls, 392; we must suffer m. that come to us from without, 680; m. convinces people, 135; Jesus insists that the missionaries practice m., 684.
−*exterior m.:* scorned by worldlings, 412, 413; practices of ext. m., 740, 757-761, 780; the discipline and cilice, 87, 107, 411, 644; things we should abstain from, 653; m. at table, 132, 367, 408-409, 759-760; object and motives of ext. m., 403-405, 407, 761; never revealed his preferences, 29, 410; Jesus and Mary recommend m. to missionaries, 406; m. necessary for missionaries, 407, 816; fasting twice a week, 107; m. of the senses, 393-398, 399-410 (Cf. Conversations).
−*interior m.:* immense value of suffering, 421; m. of the will, 149-151; continual and total m., 391.
−*goal* of m.: conversion of souls, 262; examples of m., 228, 229, 393.

Moses, 263, 374, 663, 682.

Index

divine help amid p., 464, 477; Cf. Slander, Assassination.

Perseverance: hopes for it through Mary, 154; means of achieving, 264 f.

Peter, St., 94, 196, 223, 439, 654, 664, 679, 697, 793.

Pius IX, 332, 581, 844.

Pladebella, John (co-worker), 502, 514, 597, 598.

Plan of Life: as a seminarian, 86 f.; Cf. Schedule.

Politics: political motivation, 629; never meddled in, 625, 629, 854; prudence in avoiding subject while preaching, 291, 458; slandered for meddling in p., 864; Cf. Archbishop.

Poor: love for the p., 10; apostolate to them, 562-569; aid to, 665; sermons to, 704.

Pope: love for, 836; defends his temporal rights, 841-844 (Cf. Italy); Pope's letter to queen, 841-844.

Possession, diabolical: cases presented to him, 183; cases of true p. rare, 183, 187; feigned p. to get attention, 188; Cf. Exorcism.

Poverty: fear of consequences of p. (St. Teresa), 245; resignation amid p., 785; excellence of, 370; necessity of, 359; examples of, 353, 370; how Christ practiced p., 359; desire for, 467; voluntary, 130; Claret seeks the poorest, 649; asks the Lord to inspire priests to practice it, 371; Claret's personal p., 132, 359, 486, 634; detachment from money, 133, 360 f.; results of p. in society, 133-135, 362; Cf. Detachment, Mortification.

Prayer: necessity of, 191; power of, 191; qualities of, 392, 663, 741; care with which Claret prayed, 781; p. as a means of the apostolate (St. Teresa), 255, 258; (St. M. de Pazzi) 260-262, 263-273; p. as preparation for preaching, 665; effects of p., 691, 761; the Lord asks him to pray more, 678; the more p., the better, 745; apostolate of p., 242, 265; enjoins p.

on Cuban clergy, 554; p. to angels and saints for souls, 264, 267, 268. *−mental* p.: daily, 86, 108, 610, 645. *−vocal* p.: method of, 766; two prayers composed by Claret, 154, 157; devotions, 646, 765; accompanied by meditation on mysteries of rosary and Passion òf Christ, 741; Claret prefers vocal to purely mental prayer, 766; p. to Mary before every mission, 270-272.

Preacher: desire to preach, 764; p. is God's instrument, 704; Claret a tireless p., 504, 639, 703; Marian p., 668; faults of preachers, 287.

Preaching: excellence of, 238-240; effects of, 117; object of, 697; rectitude of intention in p., 241, 439; preparation for, 288, 665; sources of Claret's p., 300; sermon topics, 468; missionary methods and approaches, 289 f., 469, 670 f.; vocation to p., 681 f., 697 f.; places Claret preached in, 454 f., 587; makes Sunday p. obligatory in his diocese, 559; p. to different classes of people, 263, 474, 637, 705, 776; p. and politics, 291; Cf. Missionary, Apostolate, Preacher.

Presence of God: awareness of, 764; prevents sinning, 673; resolves always to remain in, 648, 748; Cf. God.

Press: powerful weapon for good or evil, 310; Cf. Religious Library, Writer.

Pride: origin of evil, 92; things that lead to p., 188; Claret is proud by nature, 666; Cf. Humility, Vanity.

Priest: spiritual and bodily physician, 172-182; should stand between the world and its ruin, 662; vocation to priesthood, 40; follows it, 64; ordination day, 701; assistant at Sallent, 104-106; administrator, 106-112; regent of Viladrau, 167-174, 193; felt tied down in parish, 112, 120, 174; better a missionary than a canon, 631; preached separately to priests, 304, 474; clergy conferences,

sities, Slander, Persecution, Will of God.

Resolutions: at court, 642-650; retreat r., 740-756, 780.

Rest: takes only a little r. (maxim), 745; rises at 3:00 a.m., 637, 645, 801; retires at 10:00 p.m., 646; siesta, 646; mortification in taking rest, 757; rectitude of intention while resting, 744, 789.

Rodríguez, Alphonsus, S.J., 43, 413, 746.

Rosary: excellence of r., 45; a means of the apostolate, 266; his shield in the apostolate, 271; remedy for the evils of Spain, 695 f.
—*Claret's devotion to:* as a child, 44 ff., 48 f.; in the factory, 46; in Barcelona, 66; confrere of r., 94; r. schedule, 94; consecrated Bishop on feast of r., 499; recites it aboard ship, 130; leads r. during missions, 266; recites r. in Cuba, 610; says whole rosary every day, 66, 108, 610, 646, 765, 801; manner of reciting r., 741; aspiration in honor of r., 269; visits to Our Lady of the R., 86; receives grace of conserving Euch. species in Church of R., at La Granja, 694.
—*Apostle of devotion to r.:* Mary tells him he should be the Dominic of modern times, 677; propagates devotion to r., 55; preaching and teaching how to recite r., 266; sermon topic, 296; substitute name for a mission, 468; distributes rosaries, 337, 545, 779; making rosaries (J. of Avila), 229; the queen and her court recite r. every day, 616, 768; Cf. Mary.

Rose of Lima, St., 239.

Rovira, Philip (co-worker), 502, 514, 596, 598.

Sadness: strives never to allow himself to be overcome by s., 650.

Saints: need for s. (St. Teresa), 244; their glory and joy, 244; intercession of the s., 97, 267; aspiration to the s.,

269; Fathers of the Church an incentive to his apostolate, 225-227; effects of reading the Lives of the S., 214-226; daily reads life of the s. of the day, 87, 616; s., models he proposes to imitate, 642, 650; women s., as missionaries whose zeal should embarrass men, 234-263.

Sala, Carmelo (Claret's confessor), 816

Sala, Stephen, C.M.F. (Cofounder and Claret's successor as director of the Congregation), 489, 496.

San Martí, Lorenzo (co-worker), 502, 514, 526, 595, 599, 600.

Santiago, Cuba: Cf. Archbishop.

Schedule: plan of life, 642, 643, 644-650; s. of day in Cuba, 610; in Madrid, 637, 644-650, 801; each day, 645, 646.

Self-Will: denial of, 149-151, 649; to do all things with a will, 790; Cf. Humility, Character, Mortification.

Sermons: different from doctrinal instructions, 294; essential vs. optional, 294; distribution of essential s. on various days of mission, 295; introduced by résumé of previous day's s., 293; based on congregation's needs, 294; style of s., 297-299 (Cf. Comparisons); sources, 300; themes, 295 f.; preached as many as 12 in a day, 704; preached everywhere, 304; never discussed his s., 400; grateful for criticisms of s., 400; Cf. Preacher, Missionary.

Sick: visits the s., 110; daily, 170, 173; in the evening at Madrid, 637; in Viladrau, the s. only die in Claret's absence, 173; s. drawn to him as they were to Jesus, 180, 181; preaches special sermons to s., 474; in the General Hospital at Madrid, 479; Cf. Charity, Social Work.

Sickness: providential, 166, 167, 182; bearing s., 653; returns from Rome because of s., 859; s. because of queen's recognition of Kingdom of Italy, 837-838; Cf. Adversities.

Silence: love of s., 50; importance of s., 709; recommends s. to nuns, 709; s. and fortitude, 651; keeps s. to save reputation of sinner, 72; s. during retreats, 611, 740.

Sin: hatred of s., 17; ease with which some commit s., 11, 206; punishment for his own past s., 621; exemplary punishments of s., 802-822; malice of s., 16 f.; Blessed Virgin tells him to repent and be vigilant, 676; fleeing the occasions of s., 72.

Sinners: sad state of s., 160, 205-212, 239; compassion for s., 251; conversion of s., 231; prayer as means of converting s., 264 f., 236; confesses that he is a s., 664; Cf. Zeal, Apostolate, Missionary.

Sisters: Cf. Religious Women.

Slander: to be borne patiently, 653, 667; joy amid s., 628, 745; silence amid s., 745, 853, 867; resignation amid s., 798; love of s. infused by God, 679; reason he is slandered in Madrid, 628; kinds of s., 798, 863-866; effects of s., 729; borne as an apostolic means of converting sinners, 759; pardons and loves his detractors, 628; suffers much from s. at beginning of missions, 352; s. of the "early risers," 477; Cf. Persecutions, Assassination.

Socialism: its principles and effects, 719-727.

Socialists: their teachings against the family, 719; errors they spread, 719-727; harm they cause and media they use in making propaganda, 717-728; slanders against priests, 729.

Social Work: Claret studies ills of society, 571; President of League of Friends of the Country, 571; founds model ranch at Puerto Príncipe, 563, 598; work among the poor, 562-568; education, 561, 568 ff.; establishes credit union, 569; economic uplift of poor brings moral uplift, 569; work among the sick in hospital, 571; among cholera victims, 537; among prisoners, 570 f., 637; alms, 113 f.; Cf. Apostolate, Archbishop, Charity, etc.

Soler, Canon Jaime (co-worker, bishop), 365, 488, 496, 499.

Sorrow: acts of s., 655; for past vanity, 341; s. over ills of Church in Andalucia, 728; Claret asks for deep s. for sin, 655; granted it by the Lord, 681; Blessed Virgin tells him to repent, 676; Cf. Pardon.

Sorrows, Our Lady of: devotion to, 675; her image left on his arm after incident at Holguín, 580; he thanks her for freeing him from the attempted assassination at Altagracia, 586; Confraternity of O.L.S., 94; Septenary of O.L.S., 298; substitute name for a mission, 468; Cf. Mary.

Souls: love for s., 155-156; defends those s. the Lord entrusted to him, 664-665; his books written for their salvation, 325; his labors for their salvation, 752; the converted s. is God's banquet, 753; novena for All Souls, another term for mission, 468; Cf. Zeal, Apostolate, Missionary.

Spiritual Exercises: Cf. Exercises.

Spiritual Life: Claret resolved to lead both an interior and exterior spiritual life, in his work, etc., 419; his life is that of Jesus, 754; Cf. Fervor, Jesus Christ.

Straight Path, The: Claret's best-seller and the book that brought about most conversions, 323; 39 printings in Claret's time, 476; everyone at court has copy, 616.

Study: application to s., 87; s. to the point of illness, 89; s. during evening at Madrid, 633; occupied in s., 764, 801; importance of s. for preaching, 665; rectitude of intention at s., 744, 789; plan of s. for Escorial, 870-871; Cf. Knowledge, Work.

Suffering: value of, 651; mission of s., 624, 650; advantages of s., 624, 636; desire and love of s., 679, 761; offers to work and suffer even death, 698;

asks God for s., 748; thanks God for s., 752; how to bear with s., 667, 752, 785; he glories in s., 748; chooses the most painful, 649; reasons for not complaining amid s., 650; reward of s. (St. Teresa), 244; Cf. Troubles, Adversities, Slander, Persecution, Humiliation.

Sunday: day of greatest devotion, 39, 40, 47, 48.

Temper, Evenness of: resolves to keep e.t., 650; in imitation of Jesus, Mary, and Joseph, 650; Cf. Character, Meekness.

Temptations: against Mary, 51; against his mother, 52; against chastity, 95 ff.; Mary defends him from t., 701; how to overcome t., 51 f., 95-97; Cf. Mary, Sin.

Teresa of Avila, St., 242, 263, 654, 688, 797.

Thanksgiving: Cf. Gratitude.

Time: appreciating t., 180, 184; the use of t., 263; Cf. Worker, Weaver, Schedule, and Retreat Resolutions for 1843.

Tobacco: Claret did not smoke, 410; abuse of t. displeases people, 815; Cf. Mortification.

Tongue: mortification of t., 384-385, 400-402, 653.

Trajanopolis: Cf. Archbishop of T.

Travels: Claret, like Jesus, traveled mostly on foot, 121, 123, 126, 367, 432; stopped by brigands while t., 123-125; discomfort while t., 460; used road-map of Catalonia, 460; God's Providence during his t., 461; talks religion with mule-drivers while he t., 461; t. on foot edifies people, 484; incident of the camel on Lanzarote, 485; voyage to Cuba, 504; rule aboard ship, 506-508; arrival in Cuba, 509; difficulties of Cuban t., especially heroic trip to Baracoa, 539-543; apostolic t. in Andalucia, 702-708.

Trisagion: recites T. every morning,

637, 765; remedy for ills of Spain, 695 f.

Troubles: immense value of t., 421; love of t., 465; accepting t. is best homage to God, 423; the t. of Jesus as an incentive, 425-427; t. borne for the salvation of souls, 752; Cf. Adversities, Suffering.

Union with God: asks it of the Blessed Virgin, 449; Cf. God, Mysticism.

U.S.A., 601, 608. Cf. Supplementary Readings ("The Tender Vine").

Upbringing: Cf. Manners.

Vanity: Claret's v. in dress as a young man, 72; v. of the world and its riches, 77; v. of things, 244, 254; v., the source of many conversations, 68, 77; his past feelings of v., 341; v. of some preachers, 401; v. of some false cases of possession, 188; Cf. World, Humility.

Vilaró, Manuel, C.M.F. (cofounder, co-worker), 489, 502, 511, 526, 592, 596.

Vincent de Paul, St., 226, 304, 503, 704.

Virtue: power of v. against evil, 53; v. is convincing and persuasive, 135; undertakes practice of certain v., 144-146; courageous in v., 123 f.; tests of v., 149, 151; Jesus, model of all v., 428-437; acts of v. in Jesuit novitiate, 143 f., 147; v. essential for a missionary, 340-453; missionary must be virtuous before he preaches v., 388; most necessary v. is love, 438 ff.; all v. can be practiced in one act of mortification, 415; beauty of v. and mortification, 416; Cf. Priest, Missionary.

Visitation, Pastoral: how he went about it, 538; made p. v. despite difficulties, 544; gave missions and made p. v. throughout Cuba, 500; Cf. Archbishop.

Vocation: at 12 years of age, 701; free gift of God, 14; consults his spiritual

227, 475, 735; barking out against God's enemies, 671, 672; yearning for the apostolate, 675, 762; Claret offers himself to Mary to save souls, 156; offers himself to Jesus to bring Him into souls, 669; to work for Him, 675, 788; z. demands purity of soul, 379; the hen: an example of true z., 380; Claret asks God for a prudent z., 383; fatal consequences of bitter z., 376; Joab as example of false z., 382; difference between true and false z., 378; prayer, a means to obtain z., 264, 265; motives for z. (St. Teresa), 243, 251; z., an apostolic virtue, 686; Cf. Apostolate, Missionary, Souls.